LIFE BEFORE STRATFORD

The Memoirs of Amelia Hall

edited by

Diane Mew

DUNDURN PRESS
Toronto & Oxford
1989

Editor: John Parry
Copyeditor: Leslie Derbecker
Design and Production: Andy Tong
Printing and Binding: Gagné Printing Ltd., Louiseville, Quebec, Canada

The writing of this manuscript and the publication of this book were made possible by support from several sources. The editor and publisher are particularly grateful to the **Ontario Heritage Foundation**, an agency of the **Ontario Ministry of Culture and Communcations** for a grant in aid of publication.

The publisher wishes to acknowledge the generous assistance and ongoing support of **The Canada Council, The Book Publishing Industry Development Programme** of the **Department of Communications,** and **The Ontario Arts Council.**

Care has been taken to trace the ownership of copyright material used in the text (including the illustrations). The author and publisher welcome any information enabling them to rectify any reference or credit in subsequent editions.

J. Kirk Howard, Publisher

Canadian Cataloguing in Publication Data

Hall, Amelia Wells.
  Life before Stratford

ISBN 1-55002-061-7 (bound). — ISBN 1-55002-062-5 (pbk.)

1. Hall, Amelia Wells. 2. Canadian Repertory Theatre of Ottawa — Biography. 3. Theater — Canada — History —20th century. 4. Actresses — Canada — Biography. I. Mew, Diane. II. Title

PN2308.H34A3 1989   792'.092'4   C89-095246-9.   65484

Dundurn Press Limited
2181 Queen Street East, Suite 301
Toronto, Ontario
M4E 1E5
Canada

Dundurn Distribution Limited
73 Lime Walk
Headington, Oxford
OX3 7AD
England

LIFE BEFORE STRATFORD

The Memoirs of Amelia Hall

edited by
Diane Mew

CONTENTS

PART THREE: THE CANADIAN REPERTORY THEATRE 1949-1953

PREFACE

I first met Amelia Hall in December of 1975. A mutual friend had suggested me as someone who might be able to help with her memoirs, which she was then in the process of setting down on paper. So one wintry afternoon Millie arrived at the door of my apartment carrying a manuscript almost as big as her diminutive self.

I had no connection with the Canadian theatrical community, although of course I had seen Millie on stage. But we established an immediate rapport. I had been an avid theatregoer in England and a regular supporter of two of Britain's leading repertory theatres. Millie and I soon found we shared a knowledge of the plays that had long been the staple of repertory theatres all over the English-speaking world.

We became friends, and over the years we were to have many animated discussions on the manuscript and what was needed to shape it into a publishable book. I used to drive Millie down to Stratford in the spring, my small Toyota loaded with her costumes, props, painting equipment — and the manuscript. The return trip in the fall was something of a ritual. We would load the car up again and stop for a leisurely lunch in Stratford before braving the highway home to Toronto. Millie would regale me with all the theatre gossip, the triumphs of the season, the exciting crop of young actors that year, the inadequacies of her digs. Over the dessert would come the casual comment: "I'm afraid I didn't do much on the manuscript, dear."

She always intended to get down to work on her memoirs, but somehow her life was so full; it would have to wait until her retirement. That time, of course, never came. When she died suddenly in December 1984, the manuscript was still unrevised.

In fact, Millie was attempting to write two books in one: the story of her own life and times as a professional actress in Canada in the 1930s and 1940s, and the history of the Canadian Repertory Theatre of Ottawa — the first year-round professional theatre company in Canada. Gradually over the years, she became convinced that the story of the CRT, which she ran almost single-handedly from 1949 to 1953, was the more important element. Paradoxically, as the professional theatre in Canada developed and flourished, especially at Stratford and Niagara-on-the-Lake, she was determined that the early struggles and the pioneer role played by the CRT should not be forgotten. She looked upon it as a nursery for Canadian actors, and a glance at the photographs on pages 113 to 128 shows how many of Canada's finest actors gained their early stage experiences at the CRT.

These memoirs end in 1953 with Millie's appearance as the first Canadian actor to speak on the Stratford stage when she played Lady Anne opposite Alec Guinness's Richard III. It had always been her intention to end there: she considered that the subsequent story of Canadian theatre — and her role in it — had been sufficiently documented elsewhere. But she was acutely aware that only she could write the history of the Canadian Repertory Theatre and its forerunners. It was that history, and her own struggles to earn a living as a professional actress in Canada, that she wanted more than anything else to put on record. The scrapbooks, playbills, and other archival material which she kept over the years, and on which this book is based, were voluminous. Fortunately for future students of Canadian theatrical history, she donated them all to the National Archives of Canada.

Had Millie lived to revise her book, undoubtedly she would have changed many things. That enormous boxful of manuscript she presented to me that afternoon in 1975 had to be trimmed, cut, and reorganized, and some descriptions of productions at the CRT that were dear to her heart have been reduced. But it is my belief that this book preserves her picture of some of Canada's early theatrical history. I hope her friends will hear her distinctive voice coming through these pages, and that a wider audience will come to know a much-loved lady of the Canadian theatre.

Diane Mew
Toronto
August, 1989

A publicity photograph taken in 1953 just before Amelia left the CRT to take part in the first Stratford Festival season. *Photo: Bill Newton*

PROLOGUE

WHAT DO YOU DO IN THE DAY-TIME?

It is 9:30 on a spring morning, and I am hurrying through Confederation Square in the heart of Canada's capital. My sights are set on Sussex Street near the Chateau Laurier Hotel, then along Sussex to Guigues Street, by the Roman Catholic basilica. Facing the basilica is LaSalle Academy, a Roman Catholic school for boys, and the brothers of this establishment are landlords of, believe it or not, the Canadian Repertory Theatre. It is 1950, and Rideau Hall (Government House) is occupied by Viscount Alexander of Tunis, who sometimes frequents the Guigues Street theatre, informally, without fanfare.

This morning I have been hailed by an acquaintance and questioned about my dalliance in this venture. I detect in his attitude suspicion, incredulity, a touch of pity. He knows that every Tuesday we open a new play and present it for the remainder of the week. Doesn't the Little Theatre on King Edward Street do the same, about six times during the season? But we who are involved in the Guigues Street venture *never stop*! Week after week we grind out plays. Don't we *work* at anything? We actors are being asked, persistently, "What do you do *in the day-time?*"

Here then is what we do to fill in the daylight hours.

Wednesday morning at around 9:45 we arrive at the auditorium of the school on Guigues Street. Rehearsal begins at 10, and there has to be time to go down to the Green Room below the stage and divest oneself, in season (and all the world knows, it's a long winter in Ottawa), of overshoes, overcoat, earmuffs, and winter woollies.

9

Everyone has to be there at 10 today because we are starting the new play — for next week. Let us say the play is Eugene O'Neill's *Ah, Wilderness*. We don't take time to read it through. Presumably everyone has had the new script at least overnight.

We start right in, working as best we can on the set of this week's play, and we usually block the entire play, which is in the traditional three acts. Blocking the play means telling the actors where all the furnishings are going to be and where the doors and windows are, and then moving the actors about so that they don't bump into one another. The director may choose to block only one act today and spend the whole day on that act. We stop at 12:30 for a half-hour lunch break. At the beginning of the season the company has been consulted as to whether they wish to take half an hour or a full hour for lunch; we have no union rules!

After rehearsal the actors have time to shop, or go home and rest, or study their roles, then have dinner at a restaurant, and return to the theatre anywhere from 7 on for the evening performance of the current play, which, let us say, is *Life with Father*. When the curtain comes down on the last act around 11 o'clock, we will take off our make-up in the two dressing rooms below the stage, meet any backstage visitors, and then walk home to study our lines for tomorrow. If I am directing the play in rehearsal I will study the script. Sometimes I am acting in the play as well as directing it, and then there are lines to be learned.

Thursday morning at 10 we work on act I. Everyone is supposed to know act I, having learned it the night before. Of course there will be a good deal of prompting. No one is supposed to hold a book, but we *do* make exceptions when we know people. Lynne Gorman will always be word perfect by Sunday, and so will Christopher Plummer. Betty Leighton is already word perfect, and George McCowan has total recall. Sam Payne may be prompted on every line for four pages and then say, "I'm afraid from here on I don't know it." Roars of laughter!

On Thursday night, after the performance of *Life with Father*, off we all go home to learn act II of *Ah, Wilderness*. On Friday morning at 10 we work on act II without our books, and after lunch we may take time to review act III.

Friday evening, after *Life with Father*, we go home to learn act III of *Ah, Wilderness*.

On Saturday we can rehearse only from 10 till noon, because we have a two o'clock matinee of *Life with Father*. Act III is therefore always short-changed.

During Thursday, Friday, and Saturday, many changes will have been made in the original blocking. Much of the director's original plan, if he or she had one, will have been discarded as the director and the actors work together.

On Saturday night crew members will take a number of hours after the performance to take down the set and move the furniture and props to ready the stage for the new play. They will bring the flats for the new set up from the basement paint room, and they will move the old set flats down into the basement. This involves taking each piece outside in the Ottawa winter night and then down into the basement. Since Saturday is the one night when the actors let their hair down and accept invitations to parties, the crew will always arrive at parties late.

Sunday everyone can sleep in. But there is little sleeping in for the small crew, which will spend Sunday fixing the new set and having it in readiness by 7 o'clock for the first run-through of the whole play. Sunday afternoon the actors will do their laundry, work on their lines, and gather together any costume pieces that they are providing from their own wardrobes.

Monday at 10 we start run-throughs again, and now, as the furniture starts arriving in various loads, we keep adding it to the set. We probably will not have all the sets and props till Tuesday.

The actors have Monday evening off! But the property mistress and the stage manager, and other people who constitute the crew, work all Monday evening and into the small hours. Sometimes they do not get home. The director and the stage manager spend much of this evening setting the lights — a long process. The designer ought to be there too, and sometimes he is. We are not as orthodox as we would like to be.

Tuesday is full dress rehearsal, starting at 10 in the morning. This means costumes and make-up. It is panic time if any important prop has not appeared, or doesn't do. We stop at 3:30 if we can and open that night at 8:30. Somewhere along the line the actors have been handed the scripts for the next play, and the property mistress, costume mistress, set designer, and production manager have been handed their notes for what is needed next week. The property mistress on Wednesday will start her rounds of the Ottawa shops to charm the proprietors into lending, lending, lending.

On Wednesday the round begins again.

And that, ladies and gentlemen, is what we do in the day-time. What on earth would have possessed me to get into that sort of life?

PART ONE
CLARA BAKER'S PUPIL
1916–1939

CHAPTER 1

TRANSATLANTIC CHILDHOOD

My father, Arthur Hall, was a Yorkshireman who had emigrated to Canada as a young man. His sweetheart, Elizabeth Metcalfe, followed him to the new world in 1912, and they were married in Toronto in April, the day after she arrived in Canada. Two years later, in 1914, they returned to England for a visit, just as the First World War broke out. There was no thought now of returning to Canada, and my father enlisted in the 16th West Yorkshire Regiment. Not long after I was born, in 1916, and just six weeks after he landed in France, he was reported missing, presumed killed. His name is on a memorial in that part of France, at Thiepuel, among those of eighty thousand men who were missing in that bloody section in February 1917. My father was just twenty-seven. Of these events I have no actual memory, yet they are ever-present in my childhood.

I have heard people say that they do not remember their childhood. I remember mine as if I were already an octogenarian. I always have. I remember a child who walked head down over the moors of Yorkshire, who was mesmerized by the green of grass, who thought that tiny English daisies grew especially for her, who first noticed the sky while lying under an apple tree in blossom in a public park, and who saw in the sky the embodiment of freedom and space. Nothing was so personal and mysterious as the bluebell woods then, multitudes of bluebells that, once picked, lost heart and died. Never could they be persuaded to live in a jam jar.

Joy of woods and skies and field! Joy of singing when the sun returned in the morning! Joy of singing before a journey, be it by train, or by charabanc, or on one's feet! The people I observed from a perambulator: ladies side-saddle on their mounts; a lorry parked, and shelves lifted out ... and the sudden hush ... a soldier on each shelf.

Night and the call downstairs, "Goodnight, mamma!" "Goodnight: go to sleep." Close my eyes and think my Big Thought, "Where does the sky end?" But I cannot think this thought. I cannot think *end*. I feel dizzy in the attempt. I seek safety under the sheet.

Morning always new. Blue-ringed cups at breakfast, and maybe a visitor. Hospitality! Wriggling while fitted for clothes. A canary sits on my head.

Shock of the silent house when we return home after Christmas, from a house where there were men. We stand about and do not speak. The fire to build. Woman and child alone.

We crossed the Atlantic on the S.S. *Minnesota* in April 1921, when I was five. I hailed the voyage with joy, thinking it would be a day-long sailing venture from a seaside town. I sat on a piece of luggage and sang what I thought appropriate Songs for a Journey. When in mid-Atlantic I realized what an enormous event was taking place in our lives, the solemnity of this occasion made tumult within me, and I wept. "What if my dada comes back from France, and we aren't there to meet him?"

I did not speak of this again.

In Canada we had taken a frame cottage in the east end of Hamilton, Ontario, and this cottage had an outside toilet, at the bottom of the garden, with two holes. This toilet I considered the house's outstanding feature. But we were not in this house very long. We began to travel and eventually returned to England. We had been in North America about a year.

Back in England there was a housing shortage. We stayed for a while with relatives, and one young couple who harboured us had a little row house temporarily, on one of the streets from which no speck of green could be seen, unless it was a blade of grass struggling to appear between the cobblestones. In this brick-and-cobblestone district, in the industrial North, the toilets were down the street, a sort of Ladies and Gents shared by a number of these "town houses," as we might call them today in the inflationary seventies in Toronto. I did not question this arrangement any more than a child questions an outside toilet on the farm or at an old summer cottage. The house was clean, the furnishings were comfortable, and there was an atmosphere of good humour and love there.

The truly happy part of my childhood was spent in England. Everything that has mattered to me started there. It was in this shabby district, in the local school, that I learned to read. I was seven years old then, and because I could neither read nor write, I had begged to be sent to school. I had seen Toronto and Hamilton in Ontario, and Palmira in New York, and Chicago, and Fargo in North Dakota, but I could not spell any word that had more than three letters. In the crowded classroom of that council school in Leeds, the teacher taught me painlessly in six weeks to read. Then we moved away. She came one Saturday to pick me up at my new home, to take me to her home to tea. After we arrived at her rooms, she left me in the sitting-room, before the pleasant fire, while she went upstairs to change. When she reappeared, this dark-haired lady was in a red velvet gown, and there was a fine tortoise-shell comb in her hair. I was honoured. After tea we played paper and pencil games, sitting in a huge chair. Lovely lady whose name I cannot remember, who gave me the reading skill, and a social occasion!

In my second school I was placed with five-year-olds because I had been in my first school only six weeks. A visit from my mother, demanding of the headmistress that I be allowed to display my reading skill, resulted in a promotion. That brief session is the only time in my life I have ever felt physically a giant. I was an object of great curiosity there because of my enormous size!

The third school was an Anglican church school, on Green Lane, as good as in the country, and it was bliss. The teacher was a lively mother of three called Mrs Norman, with a robust sense of humour. If the classroom became dull, which was seldom, one's imagination could take to the ancient road outside, where Roundheads and Royalists came riding. I was skeptical of the reality of fairies even in those days, but I *knew* that the Past existed, still.

There was a lad in class who on occasion would be asked to entertain with a monologue, and these monologues, simple and amusing, I would go home and recite, fully memorized, to my mother. But these joyous days did not last. I was promoted to a higher grade mid-term, where I was terrified of the male teacher ever asking me a question, since I understood nothing of the work they were doing.

The fourth of my English council schools was a fine institution in Roundhay, a district of Leeds, and here the boys and girls were in separate schools. One day I came from class with the news that our teacher, Miss Mather, had asked the girls which of us was the best actress in the play we had done, and after various performers had been nominated she had said, "I think Millie was the best." What role had I been playing, mother wanted to know, and would I recite it for *her*? I explained that I couldn't recite the role, since I had had nothing to say. The play was *The Pied Piper of Hamlin Town,* and I was part of the crowd. A wise woman, Miss Mather, whether Millie was best or not!

We seemed to spend a great deal of time on literature in that class, and I learned many poems, long and short. I used to go home and recite them, and mother applauded, because she would have found it agony herself to have stood up in class to be heard. Her delight was contagious, and it was good to know that she was pleased.

My mother was devoted to the theatre. The first live performers I ever saw and admired were amateurs. These were a group of Pierrots who performed at our church, in a little side room. It was a mission church in Leeds, for though mother was raised in the Anglican church, I had been christened Methodist. Some of the Pierrots were my relatives. The costume was of white satin, with black pompoms down the blouse and on the conical hat. The Pierrots sang, had ridiculous conversations, and were outrageously comic. I loved them. At the English seaside, where we often holidayed both in and out of season during my seventh to ninth years, we saw professional Pierrots on the piers, and Punch and Judy on the sands, and better still, we attended the music hall. Here there were comics in spectacularly mismatched jackets and trousers, with their broad music hall technique; and there were ladies in splendid gay-nineties gowns, ostrich feathers in their hair, singing popular songs and walking grandly the length and breadth of the proscenium, embracing the house with big gestures and brassy warmth. This, I felt, was something that would be most satisfying to do when one grew up.

But when I was eight there was a greater delight still: a play. This was a thriller called, I think, *Interference.* Someone has committed a murder, and the leading character, a doctor, has discovered the ody; thinking the crime to have been committed by someone he ves, he has determined to cover up for the culprit by destroying ny incriminating evidence. He proceeds to rearrange the props in the room. This pantomimic scene lasts about ten minutes. We begin observing the doctor with relaxed interest, anticipating his every move. We know how his mind is working. Suddenly his next move is not what we had expected. All right, he is not going about the business in the order that *we* would have taken, but what of that? But just a minute, can it be that he doesn't realize that on the table is that bit of evidence that just *has* to be removed? Alas, can it possibly be that it is not the doctor who is careless but the *actor* who has forgotten? Oh, if we only knew!

He is checking the whole room; now he will surely notice. No! He has turned to leave the room! Ought we to call out to him, and warn him? If it is the *actor* who has forgotten, then it is our duty to help. But if it is the *doctor* who has forgotten, then will we spoil the plot if we tell him? Such an agonizing dilemma! He is at the door! Oh, he has paused. He looks back once more. He "cases" the room, sees the incriminating little article on the table, swoops down upon it, and is gone. The house sighs and laughs in relief. And I have had my first lesson in theatrical suspense.

When I was nine we left for Canada once more for a second try, and all these delights were left behind us. Again we went to Hamilton, and I was not happy at school.

My mother began her twelve-year stint at Allan's, where they made men's shirts amid an insane clatter of sewing machines that I preferred not to remember between my rare visits there, where Miss Webber was the forewoman. Often mother worked from 8 a.m. to 8 p.m., and I think she was glad of the overtime money. Sometimes she brought work home with her, because it was piece-work, and you got paid for how much work you did. A sensible arrangement. My aunt looked after me, until a couple of years later, when she returned to England with her husband. Often when mother got home it was 8 o'clock and I was off to bed. We seemed to be growing apart. I did not read books, and I was constantly nagging to escape to the movies.

My mother started to take me to the Grand Theatre to see any companies that came to Hamilton. Matheson Lang, Sir John Martin Harvey and his wife, and one or two others came on occasion; mother went to everything and took me most of the time. Sometimes I was bored, as I was with Matheson Lang in *The Chinese Bungalow*. But at any rate I was *there*. We always sat in the gods at the Grand. Les Enfants du Paradis. The seats were not chairs but narrow wooden benches, with high wooden backs, torture to sit on for long. One learned to turn this way and that, favouring now this cheek and now the other.

It was about this time that my mother decided to encourage the talent I had shown in England, and my lessons in elocution commenced with Vere Blandford Rigby. I was ten years old. I don't know how mother afforded lessons for me, but I was never told on any occasion that there was any necessity we could not afford. I practised my elocution for an hour every day, though I often had to drive myself to do it. Because of my joy in singing and because of my strong diaphragm, Mrs Rigby thought I might eventually become a

16

singer. Very shortly I had my first engagement, to recite at a church in nearby Ancaster. When we arrived at the church hall, mother was fraught with tension; she sat herself on the side steps leading to the stage and held her hand over her mouth while I walked onto the stage. But nothing went amiss. I remembered my words, and the first enormous hurdle had been jumped.

Later I played Cinderella in Mrs Rigby's "Recital." In my early days of studying elocution I was never able to attend a party or a social gathering without eventually being asked to recite. This made social life somewhat agonizing. I would withdraw into my shell in the early part of an evening, feeling rather ill. Once I had been "requested," and had started on my first number, all butterflies in the stomach would disappear, and I was quite prepared to give encores! For such entertainments I preferred humour. This "home entertainment" links me with the heroines of the past, who were always asked to sing or to play in the drawing-room. Last Christmas day I went to a party of this type, and it was the jolliest evening I had spent in a long time.

We moved into a four-roomed apartment over the movie house on Main Street East, a providential location that I accepted as a reasonable substitute for the Promised Land. The theatre manager would be certain to make the gracious gesture of inviting me to enter his portals free of charge whenever the mood might take me, which would be every evening, if only mother would allow! But no gesture or words of magic incantation were ever offered. If there was a "free list," we were not on it.

So I read movie magazines, played Ludo with my best friend, Molly Waitt, and pushed under her door down the street innocent messages written in a secret code of shameful simplicity or raced on roller skates with my terrier Trixie down the steeply inclined streets running from the base of Hamilton Mountain to Main Street, Trixie leaping and barking ahead of me on a taut leash.

Trixie was about two years old and woefully undisciplined when mother announced that an apartment was no place for a dog if it had to mope and pine alone all day scratching at the doors and that a new master was willing to take her from us. The day that Trixie pranced outside with me for the last time, so full of hope, only to be left behind at a stranger's house, straining after me with woeful eyes, was the most awful day of my life up to that time, and one of the worst days of all my life. I have never "owned" an animal since, though I still give a piece of my heart to an animal on occasion. No one, no creature, ought ever to be made to feel, even for a brief time, abandoned.

This was a period of mindless pursuits and adolescent boredom. In spite of all the frustrations of this unsettled time, when I was aware that my mother seemed burdened and troubled in her mind, I managed to push ahead in school and did my last two grades, seven and eight, in one year. I was ready to enter high school when I was twelve.

The summer after I turned twelve we went back to England again, I don't know why. Once again we sold all our furniture. Boarding the train in Hamilton, and embraced by friends who expected us never to return, I burst into a flood of tears. Aware that I had probably bade an eternal farewell to Molly, I promptly locked myself in "Passengers will please refrain from flushing toilets while the train is standing in the station," and all the way to Toronto I alternately wept, or washed my swollen lids, until we arrived at the station. Rattlings of the doorknob and demands to know if I was all right could not divert me from this lonely, agonizing vigil.

At the Hamilton railway station Molly had handed me an envelope which contained the following poem:

To Millie

Friend of mine, when you are lonely,
Longing for your distant home,
And the images of loved ones
Warmly to your heart shall come;
Then, mid tender thoughts and fancies,
Let one fond voice say to thee,
'Dear Millie, when your heart is heavy —
Think, dear friend, of me.'

Think how we two have together
Journeyed onward day by day,
Joys and sorrows ever sharing,
While the swift years rolled away.
Then may all the sunny hours
Of our youth rise up to thee,
And, when your heart is gay and happy —
Millie, dear, then think of me.

I was twelve then. Molly and I had met when I was ten. So those swift years that had rolled away were exactly two. The funny thing is, in all the swift years that have rolled away since then, we have been friends, and no one has shared my joys and my sorrows more completely than this friend, Molly Waitt (Mrs Roy Gow), over whose lines I sorrowed in the washroom that awful day.

Once aboard ship I entered a new life and a new world. The ship was the *Duchess of Bedford*, one of the "drunken Duchesses," because they lurched about going up the St Lawrence. Some of the male passengers were paying me attention and compliments, and I discovered that nothing in the world is sweeter than flattery. My head turned. At meals I flirted discreetly with the waiters, and at "children's tea" I held court, now warm, now cool. But dignified, I thought. Once ashore I grew a little bit bolder. At Blackpool (for we never got to the moors I loved, or to the bluebell woods, or to the abbeys), I made solitary, secret morning trips to the bustling market-place, just to stand not too near to, and yet not too far from, the young Eastern carpet merchant, for the pleasure of seeing his white teeth glisten in his dark face and his eyes sparkle as he acknowledged my stare. Then off nonchalantly, devil that I was! Safe behind the windows of buses and trams I caught the eye of passing schoolboys and bestowed a tiny, enigmatic smile.

It was a remarkable summer for me in England because at last I read the whole of a long novel, *A Tale of Two Cities*. I had learned to read easily, but this had not turned me into a great reader. It took me the entire summer to read this novel, with occasional side excursions into true confession magazines or the *News of the World*. I do not recall whether or not I had yet read *Streets of Sin* (the story of the "Brothels of the East," as it explained on the cover), which I devoured huddled on the backstairs of a house on Toronto's then sedate Huron Street, while I was spending a weekend there. I had also read *Grand Hotel* in secret, but that novel had shocked me. Strumpets and whores were *one* thing, but these Grand Hotel characters were people like *us*, clever and artistic (which I wasn't yet, but meant to become), and they were acting like whores. It made me feel quite faint!

One afternoon at Blackpool, bored with the crowds and the synthetic amusements, I walked a long way by myself and finally sat down on a bench under a wooden awning and stared gloomily at the grey sea. It was a dull day. Hordes of people walked the promenade behind me, at a short distance. Suddenly a keening, whimpering noise reached me from behind, and I turned around. Sitting on the bench that backed on to mine, and facing away from the sea, toward the promenade, a young woman was crying. A man was whispering sharply in her ear, and he was twisting her arm.

I stared, horrified. I stood up. My impulse on rising was to approach the promenading throng and shout, "Look! He's hurting

19

her! Make him stop!" But I didn't do that. I couldn't do it, and I couldn't understand *why* I couldn't do it. I knew that if it had been a *dog* that he was hurting I could have spoken. Why did one feel it was necessary to mind one's own business if it were a woman who was being hurt? I walked away. I felt that people were tawdry, and so was I.

In two months we were back in Canada — in Hamilton. There followed a strange interlude in two boarding-houses. It is extraordinary how many questions we never ask. I never asked my mother for what reason she had suddenly sold up and gone back to England. Years later I asked her why we had so quickly returned to Canada. (The English still go back home and change their minds and hurry back to the dominion.) The interlude of the boarding-houses we did not discuss, but she must have endured them in order to rally her finances. It was a situation utterly alien to the mainstream of our lives, and so I could put these vignettes out of mind as soon as they were out of sight. But I have not forgotten them.

The first was not really a boarding-house. We knew the people beforehand, though I remember no relations with them afterward. I learned there to elude with dexterity the sly, reaching hands of the husband, who must have been fifty, since he seemed to me an old man. I was too embarrassed for his wife's sake to make complaint. It was while we were in this wee house that I found a book in mother's drawer on the facts of life for girls, and I read it. I wondered when she intended to give it to me. When she never did, I presumed that she had realized that all she had to do was leave it in her drawer and it would be read.

The second boarding establishment provided that special kind of nastiness that I associate with wax works and chambers of horror. That taut boarding-house keeper had been born in England, a country she despised; so I despised her in return. She had two daughters in their late teens or twenties, and the younger was plump, pretty, and foolish. There were two boarders besides ourselves. One was a phlegmatic, heavy-set spinster of twenty-seven, who could have been ideally cast as the lugubrious retarded sister in *Ladies in Retirement*. This grown woman muttered her adolescent confidences to me as we passed some sluggish hours on the small porch. She was in love with Rudolph Valentino, who was dead. The sole man in this morbid household was a young English nondescript emerged from the most bottom drawer — wet-lipped, probably damp-handed, eyes slithering behind thick glasses in search of easy prey.

Such was the younger daughter, and that something was afoot between them was soon obvious to me. Daily, from my world apart,

I watched the ripe virgin grow more foolish. As we sat around the supper table each dreary evening, there was, as I recall, no talk, let alone conversation; but there were undercurrents, and sly looks, or giggles, and a terrible boredom, a vacuity whose surface, like a mudhole in Yellowstone National Park, was forever about to erupt and bubble with elemental force. What a suitable subject that supper table would have been for a Daumier: the vinegary housekeeper, my young mother just home from work (for, no time to be lost, she was back at Allan's), myself the new penny, and those frustrated young women, each wanting to receive from this Paris his gift of the rotten apple.

After our departure I think the plump giggler married the grey wet slug. I saw her once walking down the street, weight on heels, heavy with child — heavier with misery.

It was after that brief encounter that I grasped the life-line of poetry and soon fell in love myself, with one Rupert Brooke, who, alas, like Valentino, had been suddenly sprung "Into the shade and loneliness and mire/Of the last land."

We next went to live in Niagara Falls for six months, looking after Mrs Rigby's house and husband while she studied theatre in England at the Royal Academy of Dramatic Art (RADA). It was a bleak winter in many ways, especially because of the weather, but it changed the course of my thinking. At the high school the student body was somewhat unmanageable, and some teachers could barely cope. One literature teacher knew not what to do to keep the horde quiet, except assign to us for memory all the longer speeches in Shakespeare's *Julius Caesar*, and we copied them out either on the blackboard or in our notebooks. At home I would recite these speeches in front of a bedroom mirror (as Tyrone Guthrie would say years later to all of us, "Practise in the bedroom and amaze us in the morning!") and I discovered that this was the greatest fun in the world. Uncritically I decided that Brutus was the noblest of men and that I loved him.

At this time I was plagued with my first Canadian suitor, but I declared that at twelve *I* was too young, that at sixteen *he* was too old, that he frightened me with his ardour, and that I was much too busy anyway. I refused to join the class clique, although emissaries arrived from the leaders. I said I did not like dirty stories, either. Dear me. I was for a brief while the wonder of our small student world, the short girl with long curls who was nuts.

Every Saturday morning I went for my voice lesson with my new elocution teacher, who came every weekend from Hamilton. She was Mrs Clara Salisbury Baker. The Salisburys were of United Empire Loyalist stock, and Clara was one of a remarkable family. She had married an Englishman and had studied at RADA. She had the most beautiful speaking voice I had ever heard.

Clara Baker always treated me as if I were grown up. It must have been at my second lesson that she read to me my first *real* poem, distinct from a poem written for children. It was "The West Wind" by John Drinkwater. It begins:

> It's a warm wind, the west wind, full of birds' cries,
> And I never hear the west wind but tears are in my eyes,
> For it comes from the West Land, the old brown hills,
> And there's April in the west wind, and daffodils.

She could not have chosen better. By the end of her reading there were tears in *my* eyes. All my pent-up everlasting longing for home and England and the moors and the woods came to the surface, and I was caught in the spell of poetry once and for all. She then introduced me to the Queen Mab speech from *Romeo and Juliet,* and I made my first difficult effort to read a Shakespearean play on my own.

I started to practise voice exercises and to read poetry out loud for two hours every day, while on occasion my spurned suitor lingered outside listening to my peculiar vocal exercises — much to my chagrin, to Mr Rigby's guffaws, and to my mother's merriment. We were like a small conservatory, Mr Rigby practising his singing and me declaiming my poetry. He arranged for me to appear at a Lions' Club luncheon at the Fox Head Inn, where I gave a stirring rendition of Alfred Noyes's "The Highwayman." All the Lions were most gentle!

As for my suitor, I read some years later that he had been awarded the DFC and bar. Lloyd Swartz was a tenacious lad.

Between 1929 and 1933 Clara Baker's pupils gave recitals both in Hamilton and in Niagara Falls. Choral speaking, individual readings of poetry, and scenes from *Twelfth Night, Romeo and Juliet* and *The Merchant of Venice* were performed. All costumes for the Shakespearean scenes were designed and executed by Mrs Baker, from whose nimble fingers and fertile imagination flowed a constant stream of clothing, curtains and upholstering. She could never resist a sale of fabrics at Stitsky's or Eaton's, from which emporia it was her passion to return home laden with whole bolts of fabrics and yards of superior lace or trimmings.

As I look back at the critiques that those recitals drew from the local newspapers, I am impressed by the high quality of criticism. Ella Reynolds was the music and drama critic for the *Hamilton Spectator*, and though I recall only on the very periphery of my memory ever meeting her, she took a great interest in me and often reviewed my recital work. I have a three-page letter in which she outlined a course of reading for me in 1933, and some of her recommendations I regret that I have not read even now, including "Tennyson's 'Princess,' as this poem embodies the idea of modern woman and her place in the world." In the final paragraph of her letter, Miss Reynolds advises: "Good luck, and in studying all poetry, all literature, put your own interpretation upon it ... no one else's. Your interpretation will change as you change, but see through your own eyes."

In 1930, when I had won both first prizes at the Hamilton Welsh Eisteddfod in the under-fifteen and also in the open class, she had written to me, speaking of Clara Baker:

> I think, quite honestly, you are with the best teacher you could have anywhere around these parts, and if you stay with her you will get the "real thing", and advance in your art in a fine way. Seek books, Millie. Read ... read ... read! Saturate yourself in poetry — all kinds of it — lyric and dramatic; read Shakespeare, and don't forget to read — or at least make acquaintance with — Milton's *Paradise Lost*, and read it aloud so that you may hear the beautiful sonorous roll of our English mother tongue. Read Dickens to get the feeling of emotional prose — read our own Bliss Carman for lovely lyric delicacy. But never forget, that along with imagination, emotion, beauty, insight and all other things must go spirituality — that inner quality of loveliness which is of the soul. That may sound strange to you, my dear, because you are young, but gifted as you are you will have understanding beyond your years, and it is, of all, the most precious gift — the one that gives all art an eternal value.

By this time we had returned once again to Hamilton, and I entered high school.

CHAPTER 2

TEENAGED LADY MACBETH

It was the Depression all the time I was in high school and university. I used to spend a lot of time in Hamilton's central public library, on Main Street West, looking up Shakespearean authorities such as Bradley, and the place was always full of men, sitting at the tables, turning over magazines and newspapers. It was warm there, and they could not trudge the streets all day. I wanted to look at their faces and show sympathy yet was afraid to intrude. I used to stand on the library steps and talk with a young-old man who had long hair and a beard. He beseeched me once that I would always appreciate the sweet unfouled air and that I would never smoke. One day I went to answer a knock at the back door of our apartment in an old house on Victoria Avenue, and he was there. He was terribly embarrassed when he saw me and excused himself right away. He had come to beg. I think it was not the Depression that had made him a tramp. He looked like Walt Whitman, whom I loved to read, and later on, when I read Saroyan, I recognized him there.

Because I was an only child is perhaps the reason why I enjoyed seeking out adventures by myself. A murky adventure came my way during the weeks when I was collecting cigarette packages, empty, to enter a contest in which my perseverance won me twenty-five dollars. Walking along Main Street East toward town one twilight, I decided to drop into an old house whose front door opened on to the sidewalk, a house where there were stage costumes to rent. It was because of this function that I was acquainted with the place and knew that the proprietress smoked. She was a bloated Cissie Loftus strumpet type, good-hearted. Rather nervous she seemed that evening, and I was not long in her parlour before she guided me back into the hall. No sooner were we there than the front door opened, admitting two short men. The door quickly closed. The silence was pregnant. The men stared at me, my lady stared at them, flattening herself against one wall as if to ward off a blow, breathing heavily, her eyes wide with fright. Then I broke the frozen stage picture, gave a most polite good evening to the two gents, glided past them with all immediate speed, and was out on the sidewalk in a jiffy, breathing God's good air with a new appreciation. Of course I never told a soul. For what purpose was that costume business a front? Years later when I played the Bawd in *Pericles* I breathed the same nauseous air.

Life made quick impressions. You needed only to be tickled by a feather, not prodded with a pitchfork.

During these early years of my teens I was forever reciting at churches and at banquets, or at clubs like the Eastern Star. I had to turn down offers, they came so thick and fast. Very few organizations paid the artists, and most of the time we went for the experience. There are people who still can't get it into their heads that performers expect to be paid, and paid well. Besides the many offers to the professional actor to give a lecture or to read from plays or poetry, or to direct plays, for very little money, there are also requests to perform what will demand a considerable amount of work, with no fee at all!

As if the riches presented by occasional touring companies were not enough for a growing girl, a company of actors came to the Grand for at least two seasons, headed by Maurice Colbourne and Barry Jones. I went with mother almost every week, rushing up those steep stairs to the topmost balcony. We saw a lot of Shaw, much of it boring for me, yet I wouldn't have missed it even then. Then there was a day that Ethel Barrymore came to the Savoy with *Whiteoaks of Jalna*. I was older then, maybe fifteen, and I found the play disturbing. Of course I identified with Finch, and when Gran (Ethel Barrymore) advised him, "Don't be afraid of life. Take it by the horns! Take it by the tail! Make it afraid of you," I squirmed back into my seat, appalled at the realization that I would never dare do *that*. I told mother I wanted to go backstage and see Miss Barrymore and tell her that I was going to be an actress and had been preparing for this since I was eleven, and please, what would Miss Barrymore advise? Mother acquiesced, for it never occurred to her that I might be afraid of taking anything by the horns — even Miss Barrymore. So off we went. And there was the closed door. And I stood and stood and could not bring myself to knock. Were there not tales that Miss

Barrymore *drank*? That did not seem to make sense; yet I persuaded myself that the wonderful actress I had just seen cold sober on stage would now open to my knock, reeling and roaring, and bid me be off with my impertinence and never dare darken a stage door again! I fled.

Consciously and unconsciously now, I was beginning to learn my craft. The Birmingham Rep came to Hamilton with *The Barretts of Wimpole Street*. I turned away from the stage to sob against the high wooden back of the bench I was sitting on in the gods, overcome by Elizabeth Barrett's confession to Robert Browning that she could never really satisfy the passionate love he wanted. At the same moment I was fully aware of the choreography of the action on the stage, of the groupings and stage pictures, and when I read the play some time afterward I found that I had a "prompt book" copy of all that production's business in my head.

I was browsing one day as usual in the public library when I came across a little poem that expressed so well my own attitude to my burgeoning concert work:

> If I do prove the pleasure but of one,
> If he judicious be,
> He shall be alone a theatre unto me.

With this philosophy I went forth and recited Shakespeare and Keats and Shelley, and even the Greeks on occasion. The audiences did not walk out. I think that the public has better taste than it is given credit for. There wasn't any need for television to cater, as it has, to the lowest common denominator. One ought not to underestimate an audience. The one time I am able to love people in the mass is when they are the audience and I have for a while a responsibility toward them, while at the same time they have a responsibility toward me.

In my second year as a high school student I entered Delta Collegiate, in Hamilton's east end. I had visited the school when I was eleven, to entertain at the Lampadion Society, which was a student organization that put on concerts after 4 o'clock on Fridays. When I first attended the collegiate, our home room teacher, W.S. Mallory, went home and said to his wife, "You ought to see what I've got in class! Sits on the front row, her feet just touching, and she has long curls." When Wilf Mallory learned that my father had been killed in the war, he befriended me and took me home to meet his wife and babies. He had been through the war himself.

That child-like appearance of mine that had so tickled Mr Mallory kept me out of the school plays. I think they must have chosen the plays from those catalogues of dramatic works for which the royalty for a three-act play was something like five dollars a night. These plays were about sophisticated university kids.

In my fourth year when I was fifteen, two of the teachers, Mr MacDiairmid and Mr Watson, decided to do the trial scene from *The Merchant of Venice*, and here as Portia I came into my own. When on the day of performance someone jumped a cue and we cut two pages, Portia was able to twist the play back into line, because of her impeccable memory and stage know-how.

I had learned from Mrs Baker how to memorize. Since I was twelve I had been learning new poems every week, some as long as Shelley's "Ode to the West Wind." The trick was to read the poem *right through*, aloud, maybe four times each day, in succession, and by the end of about five days I would know it. The poems I learned then, in this manner, when my brain was quick, I have for the large part not forgotten since. But if I tried to memorize in the way they had taught us in school, laboriously reading over and over one stanza at a time, then I never knew that poem, ever.

My last year at Delta, when I was sixteen, Mr MacDiairmid and Mr Watson, encouraged by what we had accomplished with the trial scene, decided to do the whole of *Macbeth*. I read for the role of Lady Macbeth and got it. Our Macbeth was David Ongley, who had been out of school for a while but had resumed his studies because he was going into law.

I recall a big row with David over the interpretation of one scene, and behind his back I wept, "Just because he is *engaged* he thinks he knows everything!" This must have been for the ears of Margaret Hubbard, who had become my very good friend in our final year. Her best friend, June Strickland, the cleverest student in the school, was our prompter, and she did not need to hold the book, because she knew the whole play by heart. I am sure she still knows it, for when she and her husband, Professor William Ruddock of the University of Toronto and Margaret Hubbard (Mrs Hugo Ewart), and I get together, we still say, when we don't know the answer to any literary question, "June will know!"

My mother made my robe for the sleep-walking scene. "Gee, what a swell nightgown!" somebody said very loudly when I walked out on stage. I have a photo of the cast, at curtain call, and at my feet are boxes of chocolates and bouquets of flowers. I am standing stiff and "tall," to no avail, and look as if I am in torment. Perhaps I was thinking, "Please take me very seriously! I mean to go on doing this sort of thing for the rest of my life."

Mr Watson used to send me around the fifth forms to read poetry. I used to read for them a poem that said:

Kiss me and say goodbye.
There is no other word to say but this,
Nor any lips left for my lips to kiss,
Nor any tears to shed when these tears dry.
Kiss me and say goodbye.

We love that sort of thing when we are young. I would not find it so easy to read this poem aloud now, not if I was thinking about what I was saying.

During all this high school period I was having my weekly private lesson with Clara Baker, who now lived on the second floor of a most beautiful house on James Street South. I was attending at least one evening class at her apartment, and a Sunday afternoon class, after which we always took our tea, usually in the big kitchen. "All good parties end up in the kitchen." I used to bake and ice a cake for these occasions. It was over our boiled eggs there one afternoon that I expanded my knowledge of the facts of life. A young man called John Bell told a story about a famous actress and nobody laughed. There was a deadly hush at the table. Then somebody changed the subject.

A few days later Mrs Baker, at the beginning of my lesson, said to me, "John told a story on Sunday. Did you understand it?" "Well, I didn't understand it *before* he told it, if you know what I mean, but after he had told it, and all of you were embarrassed for me, then I put two and two together and thought I understood it. Did it mean that some people fall in love with members of their own sex?" So a year later, when I was seventeen, and a young man asked me, "Are you a lesbian?", I was knowledgeable enough to answer truthfully, "No."

I had learned about VD when I was fourteen and had been working my way through that large drama section at the Hamilton public library. The play was called *The Green Hat*.

"Mother, what is the worst disease a man can have?"

"Why do you ask?"

"Well, in this play, at the end you learn that the man who committed suicide did so because on his wedding night he told his wife that he had *the worst disease a man can have*, and when he saw the look on her face he turned and jumped out of the window! So I am wondering why she looked at him like that. If he had TB she surely would look sorry and sympathetic."

28

So mother told me about venereal disease and how you got it.

A while after this incident, a film came to town on this subject, and mother took me to a performance of *For Ladies Only*. Unfortunately it was an old film, and it "flickered" like a Charlie Chaplin. This made some of the dramatic bits very funny indeed; a lot of the "ladies" laughed, and I hated them for it. In fact, the women in the audience revolted me as much as the swollen joints and ulcerating sores that we saw on the screen.

Whenever I was at an evening class at Mrs Baker's, some gentleman would walk me home afterward. Later when we were at McMaster University, and we would rehearse in the evening, always at the end the boys would arrange who would walk home with whom — even if it meant only to a residence next door. I was amazed when in Ottawa in 1940 I seldom found anyone walking me home after a rehearsal at the Ottawa Drama League. I think I was born just in time to enjoy the last, fading light of gallantry. It was very pleasant, I think. I have lived a very free and independent life, and, I repeat, gallantry was very pleasant.

I was studying all this time for my associateship of the Toronto Conservatory of Music (ATCM) in speech and drama. Under Mrs Baker's direction I took exams every year. I had from the age of eleven entered poetry-speaking contests such as the Eisteddfod in Hamilton and had won the medal each time. When I was sixteen I entered a poetry-speaking contest at the Canadian National Exhibition (CNE), held each year in Toronto during late August and September. I think I had to recite two pieces, and one of them was the scene in *Julius Caesar* between Brutus and Portia. At the special concert that we gold-medal winners gave on the final night, a man rushed up to the footlights at the end and hailed me. He wore a brown suit and a brown bowler and was small and round like a vaudeville comedian. He said, "Honey, you are very good, but you shouldn't be doing this stuff. You are a born comedienne." A funny thing to say to a coming Shakespearean actress, but I liked it. How did he know?

During my last year in high school, we left our little cottage in the east end and moved into two rooms on the second floor of yet another large boarding-house. Because of the Depression, the family from Wales who lived there had decided to rent all its bedrooms, and we were five boarders in all. Mother saw this "boarding in" as a chance to save more money for my university education.

None of the men in this Welsh family was working, and a terrible thing it is to see a man hanging about the house, helping with the chores, or doing the baseball scores, while all the women in the house go out to work. These men could become themselves again only on

Friday nights, when they went off to the Anglican Church of the Ascension to choir practice, and again on Sundays, when, well-dressed in carefully preserved best clothes, they attended church. Sometimes there would be an evening out as someone's guest at a community concert, and then the unemployed would sally forth in their evening clothes.

Everybody dressed formally in Hamilton. In spite of the Depression, all the girls at Delta had been well dressed. When I first started to go out to dinner parties at the age of seventeen, I had evening clothes, some of the dresses bought at sales, but most of them made for me by the wondrous Mrs Baker, who loved to sew as much as she loved to speak poetry.

When I was sixteen I was taken to a graduation dance at Hart House, at the University of Toronto. I told none of the girls about this. Mrs Baker made me my first evening dress for this occasion. It was pale blue "eyelet," trimmed with orchid and pink organdie, and it had a wide satin sash. My hair was held back by a black velvet ribbon — hardly up to the minute, but it suited me. "For God's sake, get excited!" said Mrs Baker, as I stood on the kitchen table while she turned up the hem.

Mother took me to Toronto for this affair. At 554 Huron Street, just north of the University, where we stayed with old friends, I could not eat any of my dinner that night. I felt like one of the Greek maidens about to be sacrificed to the Cretan Minotaur. What *did* one talk about? What if a boy made passes? Why wasn't I as capable as other girls of knowing what to do on these supposedly light-hearted occasions? The event proved quite painless. One of my dances was with a Japanese student, who was obviously as tongue-tied as I was. Another partner kept up a jolly flow. He was a charming Older Man, whom everyone called "H.H."

On our frequent weekends in Toronto I would spend Saturday afternoons at the Royal Ontario Museum, mostly with the furniture and with the period dresses which were often so tiny that even I could not have worn them. Most of all I went to visit a friend there, called Lohan. He is of porcelain, about life-size, and his gown is a splendid green. He used to be placed in a position where you could see him before you actually entered his gallery, and as you walked toward him he would smile a greeting of great good humour. As one came nearer he looked into one's very mind and heart, still smiling. But when you got right up to his feet, he looked right through you, into something that you were as yet unable to see. He was my dearest friend in Toronto. I had earlier gone through a period when my dearest friends were Keats and Hamlet. It was while having a delightful mental conversation with Keats, on a walk along King Street in Hamilton to a lesson, that a drunk tried to pick me up. Down to earth with an angry thud!

In Toronto our other haven was always the Royal Alexandra Theatre. An Aldwych farce there, *Cuckoo in the Nest*, was the funniest play I had ever seen. It was Christmas Eve, and after the play we walked home to Huron Street above Bloor, all the way up a deserted Yonge Street, a light dusting of snow on the sidewalks. In the thirties they rolled up the sidewalks in Toronto at night. The quiet of Toronto at night and on Sundays during the thirties may seem hilariously funny now, but in some respects the laugh is on us today. The Bloor streetcar stopped at the corner of the street. When ladies went out, they wore a hat and gloves. I think there were trees on Bloor Street then, and lots of large houses, and some of these were tea rooms, where we could sit and relax after shopping. In those innocent times meat and groceries were delivered to the Huron Street house after a phone call to the grocer; a man would come up the street with horse and cart, selling fresh fruit in season; bread and milk were delivered, and the postman always came twice.

Nobody had ever heard of a TV dinner, and in the pantry at 554 Huron Street there were always fresh fruit pies in season and the homemade crust was flaky pastry. There were a lot of books in the house, old or up-to-the-minute, and when any were to be given away, I was often on hand. Thus it was I claimed a set of twenty-five hard-covered *Punch* anthologies, and in studying the cartoons of Phil May and George du Maurier I became a small authority on the costumes of the nineteenth century, and on the jokes. Of the thirties I can say that, like the curate's egg in the cartoon, parts of it were excellent!

At the CNE one late summer there were screen tests. I took one, passed, and was asked to report for duty that midnight, to be in a film. That my mother allowed me to go all by myself, at that time of night, at the age of sixteen or so, fills me with wonder now! I arrived on the set and discovered that my role was that of a girl standing in a long line to get into an exhibit! I stood there for about an hour, acting my head off. One of the crew, the cameraman I think, grumbled to me about the whole lousy set-up, and after a while he and his buddies went on strike and we were all told to go home. Thus it was that I travelled all the way by myself back to Huron Street, arriving at No. 554 at about four in the morning. Not liking to rouse the household at such an hour, I sat on the porch and watched the milkman arrive, and then the sun. I realized that I "had been had."

CHAPTER 3

MCMASTER AND THE
PLAYERS' GUILD

In my final year at Delta Collegiate the principal, Mr Michael McGarvin, was eager for me to get a scholarship to university, but I did not fulfil his hopes. It was a summer of stifling heat in Hamilton when we tried our examinations, and as fast as I learned a subject, lying at home on the bare cool floor in my slip, I forgot it. The knowledge seemed to pour out of my mind like the sweat out of my body. I passed the examinations, but I did not distinguish myself. That fifth year of high school was far harder than university.

I waited a year before entering McMaster University, in order to get my ATCM in Speech and Drama. There was lots of time because I was only seventeen. It was not easy, I discovered, to discipline oneself at home, and there was time in which to remember that mother was still working at Allan's, making men's shirts. We had moved to Victoria Avenue, to a second-floor apartment in a large old house. It was haunted. At any rate, weird things went on in our apartment all the time I lived there, footsteps in the dining-room when it was empty, tappings on our second-floor windows, streaks of light when visitors got up from chairs, and things that went "Ping!" across the room. There was a Tinkerbell that danced all round the living room and fearsome bangings on the under-side of the solid footstool on which my feet rested while I studied. Usually all this nonsense stopped whenever mother was around, but one day she came home and scoffed at what I had to tell her, and behold! — there was an angry rattling above her head that even *she* heard. Fortunately I did not attach too much importance to such phenomena. There *are* more things in Heaven and Earth than are dreamed of, but there are some things between Heaven and Earth that ought not to detain us from graver matters.

Sir Ernest MacMillan was one of the examiners when I took my ATCM examinations. He was kindly and respectful, making me feel that the occasion truly gave him pleasure. The examinations were of two kinds — written theory and practical work, in the form of spoken poetry and scenes from plays classical and modern.

During this period I started to direct plays for the Hamilton Dickens Fellowship. Usually the members expected one to make one's own play out of scenes from the novels. This was not easy for me, because I am not a widely read student of Dickens. At a rehearsal in my apartment when I was sixteen, I sat in silence for about two hours while the grown-up cast argued about whether or not children are conceived in sin. There was a strong-minded woman in the group who insisted they were. It was all beyond me then and still is.

It was at this time also that I joined the Hamilton Players' Guild and the Attic Club. My mother approved of the former but deplored the latter, because it met in what she declared was a fire-trap. I have recently been informed by Hunter MacBain, one of the founders, that she was absolutely right.

In 1933 I was invited by the Hamilton Players' Guild to give my first of three solo performances there, during evenings of one-act plays. Shortly after my debut at the Players' Guild (an association that convinced me I had "arrived"), I directed my first one-act play for it. It was *X Equals 0*, by John Drinkwater, and I had a clever and distinguished cast of six handsome men. Such was my excitement and so pleased was I with myself the one night that this was performed that I jumped up and down in the wings for almost a full half-hour, silently clapping my hands.

My career then took a strange turn. I went to a play reading of *The Lilies of the Field*, a Guild major production, and to my surprise came away with the role of the forty-eight-year-old mother! So it was off with Juliet's cap and on with the talcum powder to whiten my hair. When I had finished being made up, I looked like the familiar Hamilton bakery cart picture, which advertised "The Loaf That Stopped Mother Baking." Ever since I left Hamilton I have done my own make-up.

Miss Caroline Crerar, a sister of General Crerar, was the president and grande dame of the Hamilton Players' Guild. A slight lady of forceful character and awesome energy, her commands and exhortations to me over the telephone, especially about the procuring of sandwiches for the after-play parties, could probably be heard through all four high-ceilinged rooms of our Victoria Street apartment. Miss Crerar wore a black velvet ribbon across her forehead, in a style not in vogue in the thirties. I always thought of it as a Bloomsbury touch. It became popular again in the seventies and has been affected even by young men, but they get their inspiration from the Navajo Indians rather than from Virginia Woolf. I look back with joy on the zest of Miss Crerar, who would talk to me nineteen-to-the-dozen, her eyes darting meanwhile all over the room, not wanting to miss a thing.

My last play at the Guild was translated from the French, and at last I got to play a sophisticated young thing, wearing fine clothes. I didn't enjoy it much, because it was not very well produced in comparison with the other plays I had done at the Guild. Yet there was satisfaction in being told, "You've grown up, Millie!"

Shortly after becoming a member of the Guild I joined the Attic Club, which met on the top floor of an old building on King Street East facing Gore Park, in the heart of downtown Hamilton. Here I made lifelong friends. The club had originated in 1932 with a few young enthusiasts, and when I joined it the membership was around twenty-four. Unlike other little theatres of the period, the Attic Club was experimental, being chiefly concerned with playwriting and improvisation. I recently came across a description of our activities written by Jack Galilee and Hunter MacBain, which gives some idea of the Heath Robinson nature of our enterprise.

> At first glance it does not look like a theatre. There are no orderly rows of comfortable seats: instead there is a most extraordinary miscellany of chairs, benches, forms and stools. Over against one wall is an old-fashioned stove, and even as we take our seats a youth in nondescript costume and hideously smeared with grease paint shovels in some coal and then slinks out of sight ...
>
> We compose ourselves in an effort to enjoy the atmosphere. This, to be true, does need some effort, because if the atmosphere is any indication, the building is in the process of burning down! But no, we are reassured, it is only the overheated stove spouting smoke, and that sharp odour of burning rubber and hot tin is merely the stage electrician coaxing the last

watts of power for his overloaded lighting arrangement ...

But now the seating accommodation has become exhausted and several of the audience are seated on the floor almost in touching distance of the stage curtain ... There is some diminuendo in the conversation ... The senior female member of the Attic Club is standing in front of the curtain.

She (Freda Waldon) explains that it has become almost a tradition for her to set forth the aims, methods and procedure of the Attic Theatre Club ... Back in 1932 seven young men in Hamilton banded together to form a little theatre that would be more or less experimental. For some time they met in each other's rooms, to read plays and to talk theatre. They even assayed to produce them in such confined quarters that sometimes the audience consisting of one or two became inextricably involved in the action of a cast of five or six. But this condition did not last long. A clubroom was found, a stage built, curtains hung, lighting equipment and switchboard built ...

It is impossible to list the work done by the Club in the last eight years. One-act plays by the principal playwrights of America and Europe have been presented, from Shakespeare, Shaw and Ibsen, to Noel Coward and Molière. Our own prolific Hunter MacBain pours forth a constant succession of historical burlesques, Greek comedies and O'Henry-cum-Shaw impromptu. At Christmas time the Club has given one of The Chester Mysteries, which with Shaw's *Village Wooing* and Vernon Sylvain's *Road of Poplars*, may be pointed to as some of the highlights of the Club's productions.

A highly original feature of both public and private Attic Club performances is *impromptu acting*. The usual procedure in the presentation of an impromptu play is as follows: the director assembles a cast on the stage, generally in full view of the audience, where he or she outlines a plot as briefly as possible and assigns the characters. As soon as this is done the stage is set, the costume cupboard raided for appropriate apparel, and the play begins. The players make up their own lines as they go along and act according to the inspiration of the moment. In the history of the Attic Club hundreds of such plays have been presented, including several *three* act ones with playing time of an hour or so. Of course, all impromptus are not successful. It would be phenomenal if they were. Much depends on the plot, much more on the teamwork of the cast ...

Productions are arranged with no regard to box office appeal. Attendance at performances is by invitation only and expenses are borne largely by the members themselves.

However, the chief activity of the Club is not the production of plays for public performance. The chief activity is centred about the regular weekly meetings where the many branches of dramatic art are studied and discussed, where plays are presented before the members only and where the most violent experiments in theatre are undertaken. Because of the training made available in these weekly meetings the Attic Club has never excluded from its membership rank amateurs. The only qualification for membership is eager interest in the drama and willingness to work at it.

The Attic Club ceased to exist in 1942, because most of the men had enlisted. But I have fond memories of those times. It was altogether a do-it-yourself organization, and that was why it was so much fun. I have a mental picture of Hunter MacBain at club meetings, sitting silent, with an old battered hat over his face, lost in contemplation for a time, and then whisking the hat away, his eyes gleaming with inspiration for an impromptu! He would cull members from various parts of the room, hold a whispering session with them as if he were a rugby coach, and then furnishings would quickly be assembled on the stage (which was level with the rest of the ancient floor) and the impromptu would begin.

Many of the impromptus and the written plays were satires on the politics of the decade, especially on fascism. Sometimes an impromptu could become a battle of wits, and the main theme could be lost in clever repartee and hilarious jokes. I was not good at these impromptus, being lost for words. It was not just theatre that held me to the Attic Club; it was the cleverness of its members. Just to be there and listen to them was a delight to me.

When I arrived at McMaster University, the "big play" of each season was directed by Bill Atkinson, who came from Toronto every Saturday afternoon to put us through our paces. Bill, much loved by all of us, was a fine actor and director, a pillar of the Dickens Fellowship in Toronto, and one of that band of Canadians doomed forever to work in office or factory when they ought to have been in the theatrical profession. In my fourth year at "Mac" I played Grazia, the young girl with whom Death falls in love in *Death Takes a Holiday*. One Saturday afternoon I had been trying at rehearsal to play a scene of hysteria, and I couldn't do it. I went home disgruntled. At home my mother had laid out on my bed some white material she had bought for Mrs Baker to make my dress for the play. "I hate it!" I howled, and I flung the stuff across the bedroom; then, leaning against the bedroom wall, I sobbed hysterically. Mother was amazed, even more so I. This was what I ought to have done at rehearsal! This was how you did it! I carefully made note of all that was going on inside my body, so that I could reproduce it next time on stage. The white material I had hated was not used. Instead Mrs Baker made me an evening dress of white cheesecloth. It looked wonderful on-stage.

In another play at "Mac" I did not get the leading role I wanted, and when I heard the news I had a half-hour of blazing rage! I have never forgotten that moment, and I have never repeated it. I have had disappointments, but I would not want to let ambition sear my insides. I would not mind, though, excavating out of my innards what I felt then, when I had that half-hour of murderous rage. The actress who *did* secure this leading role was Dorothy Foster, who has since served the Players' Guild with distinction, especially on-stage. She is an actor who could have graced the profession.

At McMaster many of the boys had part-time jobs. Bob MacGregor used to turn up at rehearsals for *Berkeley Square*, fresh from the furnace room and covered with soot, to do his role as the Duke of Cumberland. I once asked Bob to play for me in a play for the Dickens Fellowship (the amateur theatre is always desperate for men), promising that he would have no lines and would have only to stand at a table and serve punch. Bob promised to turn up on the night. He did, and made such a Dickensian jollification of serving the punch that the rest of the play became background!

Discipline was evident in the rehearsing of the prestigious big play at Mac, but I learned in my first year that for lesser productions the attitude of the actors was deplorable. Promptness at rehearsals and in the learning (the *correct* learning) of lines did not go hand-in-hand with university "dramatics." The night before I presented my first one-act directorial assignment to an astonished student body, a delegation came to me and insisted that I take over the leading role because I knew the lines better than did the girl who had the role. I took over, with three prompters on hand. The leading man made an entrance too early, excused himself, and lumbered off; someone else cut two pages, and we had to wind ourselves back; the curtain descended before the final line and had to be pulled back part-way by eager hands while voices whispered hoarsely, "Keep going!" There was much spirit, little discipline.

I mention this because a long time later, when the universities were first giving a serious look at "dramatics" as a study, Professor Emrys Jones told me that students looked on it as a "pipe" course and that it was not easy to make them take seriously attendance at rehearsal, attendance *on time*, and prompt learning of the words. People who have no desire for discipline ought never to "get up" a play. So-called dramatics ought never to be touched by the fuzzy-headed or by the social-minded, and if such people do, they should keep the resultant mess to themselves.

Of course, sometimes the best laid plans ... We worked hard on scenes from *The Taming of the Shrew* in our sophomore year, in modern dress, but that did not keep the set from falling down during the presentation. I couldn't have liked it more. Many an amateur effort I have watched while seated on the floor because I had slipped off my seat in convulsions of laughter and was glad to hide behind the seats in front while I stuffed a handkerchief into my mouth to deaden my guffaws. Some of these efforts I had directed myself. When I said that messes ought not to be thrown open to the public, I was not including these little acts of God, such as scenery collapsing, revolvers not going off, and pianos that play apparently all by themselves when no one is seated at the instrument. These catastrophes are hard to endure when one is *on-stage*, but they are a delight when one is in the audience.

In my freshman year I started writing poetry and had a little sonnet published in the *McMaster Monthly*.

Prologue to Spring

I fear the advent of this teeming April's
Familiar rain and warm caressing breath
More than all springtimes past. Once more in travail

Rapt earth has ceased to mourn last summer's death
And all time's aching beauty she has hurled
Into one golden day, one night
That sighs with the sorrow of its own loveliness.
This world of spring, compelling, amorous,
Will cry to me with voice more poignant than before.
Prologue the past's uncomprehending years:
The morning flush of beauty and its sore
Inexplicable loneliness was theirs;
But I must feel that power which creates Earth —
The complete, bitter ecstasy of birth.

I composed it sitting in the living-room of our apartment in that fine old house on Victoria Avenue, where for four years I would occasionally walk the perimeter of the carpet in the throes of essay composition, where tea would flow, high talk would flourish, and I would spirit-walk this little stage where I would experience so much of intellectual pleasure and suffer my first and most desperate agonies.

One afternoon of my senior year, in the McMaster Library, I pushed across the table three new poems of mine to Charles W. Dunn, most highly respected of literary scholars in our year and later to be on the faculty at Harvard. Charles read my tragic lines and nearly laughed his head off; so after such honest literary criticism I kept my sorrows, and my poetry, to myself. The culmination of these verses was a line in which I had described "A knife that's in my heart and shall be till I die." It was this "knife" bit that set Charles to making the library rafters ring. I suppose he had a mental picture of me walking around for evermore with this knife sticking out of my left breast, a sort of companion piece to Anne Boleyn with 'er 'ead tucked underneath 'er arm.

Cornered by Mrs Baker at my lesson during this time, after a feeble attempt to explain my tears, I confessed that I had discovered that life is awful. "How do you older people manage to go on?" Clara Baker read me Wordsworth's *Tintern Abbey*, and so began the struggle to carry on, if, escaping my own miseries, I might eventually begin to hear "the still, sad music of humanity." I knew what he meant when he wrote "often do I seem/ Two consciousnesses, conscious of myself/ And of some other Being."

The pain that I wrote of did not, as I had insisted it would, stay in my heart for ever. Other pains, new delights, unforeseen considerations and conundrums of life eventually put this pain quite out of heart and countenance. Yet while it lasted, and it lasted a long time, it was heavy enough, and no pain since has so eaten at my vitals and consumed my energies. Sometimes I remember this when I find myself bristling at the lack of vitality in some of the young.

I wrote a good deal of poetry while I was at McMaster, and some erudite essays, all of which would be beyond my reach now. This made me a friend of that great old gentleman, A.E.S. Smythe, an Irishman who was an editor at the *Hamilton Spectator*. He had known Yeats. I used to drop in for tea, where the cups were always ready on a tray in the living-room. The library in his large apartment was like the stacks in the public library, each section up to the ceiling with narrow aisles between. Mr Smythe was president of the Hamilton Theosophical Society, where my mother and I sometimes went to lectures.

During my university days I used to spend the summers at Lake Simcoe, in Stephen Leacock country, and there I looked after the four daughters of the Reverend Reggy Thomas, of St Thomas's Church on Huron Street in Toronto, and his wife, Mickie. We used to go to the church-yard, and "Granddad" Thomas would show us the tree under which he was to be buried. Stephen Leacock and Mazo de la Roche are buried there. Every night I read Shakespeare to the little girls. It is quite easy to read him to youngsters: when you get to a long speech, you read the whole of it through and then tell them briefly what it means. In the afternoons we used to perform scenes. I was able to say "my cup runneth over" when the seven-year-old declared one evening that "Granddad goes on and on like Mercutio!"

Toward the end of one summer I got a call to go to the CNE and adjudicate the poetry-speaking contest, having been a former winner myself. When I arrived, fresh from months in the country, bronzed and with flowing locks, they despaired! "You look so young! Nobody will believe you know *anything*!" So I got a hat and pushed all my hair under it and made myself look like the spinster out of an English farce. Any woman *that* plain has to be clever. It is only fair. Thus, I passed muster.

The summer job at Lake Simcoe was the only one I had during university, and it was pleasure rather than work, because the Thomases were dear friends. In my final year I did a little weekend work on occasion in a florist shop in Hamilton. I soon learned how hard florists work. My friends "Boggs" Hubbard and June Strickland popped into the shop, as Gracie Fields says in the song, to see Millie working. They did not see how I could possibly be efficient. "Your head is in the clouds."

I passed out of university with much better marks than I had entered into it. Perhaps this was because I was unhappy, and when I am unhappy I have to work. I was unhappy then, the way my friend Hamlet had been unhappy, and I knew now what he meant when he said:

> this goodly frame, the earth, seems to me a sterile promontory; this most excellent canopy the air, look you, this brave o'erhanging firmament, this majestical roof fretted with golden fire — why, it appeareth no other thing to me than a foul and pestilent congregation of vapours. What a piece of work is a man! How noble in reason! how infinite in faculties! in form and moving, how express and admirable! in action, how like an angel! in apprehension, how like a god! the beauty of the world! the paragon of animals! And yet, to me, what is this quintessence of dust?

I made a new friend at this time. On a trip to the Royal Alex in Toronto to see Maurice Evans, I discovered that Richard II and I saw eye to eye on so many things! I went home and learned all his words.

> I live with bread like you, feel want, need friends! ...
> For God's sake let us sit upon the ground,
> And tell sad stories of the death of kings.

Youth is a terrifying time. Then it is that you decide if you are going to live or going to die; and if you are going to live, you have to decide what it is that is going to live on inside you, and what it is that you are going to kill off.

It was at this most mirthless time that I had to decide what to do after I was presented with my BA. Many PHDS were unemployed. I might have to follow in the footsteps of many of my friends and go to the dreaded OCE — the Ontario College of Education, on Bloor Street in Toronto. How often in my childhood had my innocent little feet walked past that institution and knew not what was within! To escape OCE I now turned up at the *Toronto Star* offices one morning and besought an enormous man with a large cigar to give me a job as a reporter. That interview lasted about three minutes. I was more kindly received at a publishing house. Then the inevitable interview at OCE, with Professor Diltz, who wrote books on English literature for the schools. He painted, in very dark colours, a picture of life in the publishing business and in the newspaper business. My strong practical bent turned me toward OCE.

All I want to remember of that year at OCE is the evening I cried my eyes out and decided to leave, and Boggs Hubbard and another friend walked me up and down Madison Avenue while Boggs did acrobatic feats on lawns to try to make me laugh. But she said something I could not forget; "Do you think you have some great talent?" I could not answer that.

There were awful occasions, such as the morning we were eating breakfast before the sun had risen, hastening to get out to the distant schools where we did practice teaching. I remarked to the world, "This is it! I'm going to get married!" and from the landlady who was about to depart for the kitchen there issued a snort that spoke with terrible eloquence her thoughts on the institution of Marriage.

I applied for a $150 scholarship offered by the Imperial Order of the Daughters of the Empire (IODE) to children of soldiers, and I received it, but that year the IODE decided to cut it to $75. This was the one gift I received toward my education, and it was very welcome. Dr Bell, of the Bell Singers, did me the kindness of saying that he hoped I would stay in teaching: "You have a certain delicate refinement rare in the profession." I blessed him for his words, but from every side I heard the word "efficiency." I made up my mind that I would show them how very efficient a dreamer could become if she set her mind to it. To be efficient is not difficult if you are intelligent. I'd show them efficiency! With a vengeance.

I left OCE with a plum of a job, to teach for the Ottawa Collegiate Institute Board at the High School of Commerce. My mother could now leave Allan's.

The day we moved into our Ottawa apartment, on Cooper Street, eight minutes' walk from the Peace Tower, the street was loud with the blaring of radios. "What a noisy street this is!" I remarked, surprised. A few minutes later, "That sounds like the King's voice!" said my mother.

It was. The Second World War had started.

PART TWO
A DOUBLE LIFE
1939–1949

CHAPTER 4

THE OTTAWA DRAMA LEAGUE

I developed into a Canadian around 1940. It was Ottawa that did that for me, Ottawa and all the beautiful countryside in Ontario and Quebec that surrounds it. There were rivers, and a lot of sky, and the countryside was never far away. There was French-Canadian architecture, and French Canadians (a people who had existed for me before this time only in the history books). I could not make contact with the French-Canadian students in the school, unless they were artistic, and then they opened to me, but the French Canadians who were actors or painters became my friends. Around Ottawa I saw nature as it had been revealed to me by Canadian painters.

But though it might lift my spirits, love of nature and my joy in painting were not enough. I knew this was not the way life was meant to be for me. At first, of course, I got quite a kick out of landing such a good teaching job. I was chosen by the Ottawa Collegiate Institute Board in the summer of 1939 on the strength of my having an ATCM in Speech and Drama. My BA in English and philosophy from McMaster was essential of course, but the ATCM clinched it. I got pleasure out of this: when I had applied to the IODE, as the child of a soldier killed in action — asking for a scholarship to study speech and theatre abroad, to bring my skills back to Canada for the edification of Canadian youth — I had received a polite letter explaining that my plans were idealistic but hardly practical.

I felt no call to teach; maybe that was why I was good at my job. I couldn't imagine a life without poetry and Shakespeare, but I didn't care to dissect it as if it were a corpse. So I always taught Shakespeare as a play for the stage and not as a book for study. Yet I had no fault to find with the teaching that I had received at Delta Collegiate in Hamilton. Those teachers, along with my dear Clara Baker, had created my love of literature.

You learn a lot about yourself when you work at a job that you feel can never make use of all your juices. You learn the worst. I soon learned that frustration brought out in me a terrifying efficiency.

The trouble with OCE was that it had told us only about how to teach. I had left there knowing nothing about methods, except that one of them was called the Dalton method, and I did not have a clue as to what it was. I did know that I knew my subjects inside out. What I soon realized I lacked totally was knowledge of human nature and life, in spite of all my knowledge of Shakespeare, who is the authority on human nature. Nothing had been said at OCE about *people*, their varying intelligences and their turbulent hearts. I entered teaching thinking that my task was to fill their heads with knowledge, in such a way that they would love what they learned. Right away I discovered that this was to be a labour of Hercules.

The years rolled on and on, and I glimpsed the importance of looking into their hearts and their environment instead of expecting too much from their heads. It was a struggle with myself. They seemed always content to be *ordinary*, and I had expected all young ones to long to be *extraordinary*. But I had been warned at the beginning not to expect too much ambition in a civil service city.

I decided I couldn't leave until I felt more love. Good discipline I had always kept, because I was clothed in authority whenever I faced an audience. Love, however, could not stop the interruptions — the telephone ringing, the knock on the door, the paperwork, the forms to be filled in, the special auditoriums with films too poorly projected and sound that grated and did not edify. Classes were huge at the time, fifty often, and groups moved from one classroom to another every thirty or thirty-five minutes. There was seldom time just to *talk*, except in the "repeater" class, where only about twenty of the thirty enrolled turned up on any given day, and since these had invariably neglected to do their assignment there was nothing for me to do but rage ... or let them talk to me.

"Miss Hall, do you believe in God?"

Since those days I have met, whenever I have been on tour, many former students of mine, always radiant young women, happily married. I had worried too much about their becoming mere cogs in the great machine.

All the years that I was teaching at the High School of Commerce in the day-time, I was living a second life at night at the Ottawa Drama

League (ODL). This "home away from home" was the first discovery I had made in Ottawa. I think it was Captain Chance who took me there one Sunday afternoon in 1939, as I walked in at the basement entrance of the ODL's quarters, the Little Theatre on King Edward Street, through the workshop, and up the stairs to the wings. I couldn't believe my eyes when I saw that huge stage. Bill Adkins was there, and we were introduced. Next I met Dorothy White in the foyer and was offered the ingénue role in Dodie Smith's *Dear Octopus*, because I had more or less an English accent!

Later I was given the plum role of the girl in Saroyan's *The Time of Your Life* and was warned by Bill Smith of the workshop that I was very foolish to play a prostitute in Ottawa, that one just couldn't get away with that sort of thing. But I played it, and no one ostracized me. (Maybe I wasn't very convincing!)

I later embroidered my delineation of a prostitute by playing one for Crawley Films, in a series on VD. I was sparingly made up as a teen-age pick-up, accosting a young man played by a fellow ODL actor, Bill Ruddock, later a professor at the University of Toronto. As we were filming this scene in front of a drugstore, on a very cold, wintry night, someone in the crowd that had gathered shouted out, "Geez, I knew her when she was a school teacher!" Soon this film was completed and shown to the boys of Glebe Collegiate, and one of these boys, who belonged to the ODL, was able to boast that he knew every prostitute in the film! My school principal, Harry Pullen, chuckled and said that I couldn't have played it if I didn't have a feeling for the part! Everybody got a kick out of it.

Harry thought it was a wonderful thing that I had this stimulating hobby (acting, not prostitution!) that gave me a life away from my job. Whatever I did at the school in the way of theatre — directing plays, or entering a choral-speaking group in the Kiwanis Festival, or asking for a week off to attend the Dominion Drama Festival — the board and Harry gave me every encouragement, and no people have ever made me feel more appreciated.

Early in the war our ODL Workshop organized a troop show. It was in this group that I met a young man of twenty-three called Charles Olmsted. The impressive thing about Charles, besides his good looks, was his serious intent about getting into theatre. Had it not been for the war he would have been pursuing this objective, probably in England. He had already studied in the United States and was engaged to an American actress. He was sitting on top of the world.

Charles was mad about the work of Noel Coward. He and I learned to sing Coward's songs, and we "got up," as Guthrie would have put it, scenes from his plays. Our favourite was *Red Peppers*, from *Tonight at 8:30*. Once or twice we performed bits of this at parties, and word of it reached the ears of Mr Evelyn Shuckborough, of the British high commissioner's office. Evelyn was going to do a program at the ODL of three of the *Tonight at 8:30* scenes, and he sent for us to hear our *Red Peppers*. We were ready to burst with delight when we were hired!

Young Olmsted was not only a most personable actor with a lovely sense of humour, but he was a good director as well, as I had found out when he directed a few sketches for the troop show. He had given me lessons on how to act like a femme fatale, and he made a good job of it, considering the material he had to work with! The night before we were to start our rehearsals of *Red Peppers* at the Little Theatre, I had a phone call from Charles. It was all at an end for us. His call-up to the RCAF had come through, but I was to go ahead, because Evelyn would find me another George Pepper. I was inconsolable.

The next evening I met Saul Rae of the Department of External Affairs. He was to be my George Pepper. I harboured a lot of resentment against the Fates, but nevertheless Saul and I were to work very well together. He was far better than I in the song-and-dance bits, though these were my favourites, and I was perhaps ahead of him in the "straight" bits. Saul was himself a brilliant composer of very amusing songs, writing both music and lyrics. Charles had had that talent, too.

All went well at rehearsals, and then one night, while we were on-stage, someone in the orchestra announced that Charles Olmsted was in London, Ontario, with spinal meningitis. This had always been one of the most dreaded diseases, and I was sick with fear for Charles. I wanted to drop *Red Peppers* there and then.

We didn't drop it, of course, and it was an enormous success. There was stamping of feet and shouts of "Bravo!" that night. It was my first triumphant opening.

Charles Olmsted recovered and did eighteen months of flying a Spitfire overseas. Then he came back to Canada to teach others. I never saw him after he first left for England. He was killed while flying a trainer plane in Canada, on April 30, 1944. He had been married about eight months.

In spite of these contacts with fighting men, we in Canada were far from the war. However, I learned how quickly one could make a real, rather than a superficial, contact with anyone who had faced danger and had suffered deep emotional stress. Such contacts are rare even in wartime, almost non-existent in peacetime. There have been times on-stage, since those days, when I have had such contact, not with one person, but with — as it were — the whole audience as one body. But these have been rare. How can it be otherwise, on-stage or in life?

The biggest success we had at the ODL during the war was the 1941 presentation of the *Little Theatre Revue*. This was produced by Evelyn Shuckborough and Saul Rae. When Evelyn left the British high commissioner's service and returned home to England, he became secretary to Anthony Eden. I believe Saul was the first Canadian to be sent to Paris after the war ended, and he eventually became ambassador to Mexico.

In the ODL one worked not only with people from the diplomatic service, but with local residents from every walk of life. For example, there was Fred Sims, a policeman who later became a detective. When Fred was on point duty he had great flair, and if he recognized you in a car he would wave you on your way with a flourish worthy of Stratford. I heard that he was up on the carpet because of this!

It was in 1943, while I was playing a trifling role in a silly play about the movie world, called *Orders Is Orders*, that a talent scout from Metro-Goldwyn-Mayer sent me his card backstage. I was taken to supper at the Chateau Laurier's Grill and told that I was a double for Helen Hayes — a tale I had heard before and was to go on hearing for ever afterward. He was looking for a girl to play in the film *National Velvet*. For some reason they decided on an unknown called Elizabeth Taylor instead.

Some of the finest productions at the ODL during the war years were directed by Bill Atkinson, who directed our "big play" each year at McMaster. He did excellent productions of *Ladies in Retirement* and *Murder in a Nunnery*. Bill had large vision and demanded and got what he wanted out of everybody. He was a perfectionist, thank God.

Those productions were in 1945, and I had been on the board of directors for a year. I belonged to the faction that voted for quality instead of box-office appeal. Why did we have so many members who thought that only the commercial (meaning second-rate) would sell?

The first three-act play I ever directed was J.B. Priestley's *When We Are Married*, for the ODL in 1944. My mother, Elizabeth, made the 1908 hats for that production, and they were much admired by Princess

Alice, Countess of Athlone, wife of Canada's wartime governor general, when she came backstage. (It had been a benefit for the Women's Naval Auxiliary.) One hat caught her fancy because it was similar to one that she had had in her trousseau. We were always proud of our costuming at the ODL. For a play of this period my old Mr Punch books at home were our encyclopaedia, as well as a collection of photos Elizabeth kept of girlhood friends, all so elegantly dressed they might have been princesses themselves.

The great innovation I aimed at in my first production was to get all the actors to come to rehearsal *on time*. I had waited endless hours for people to arrive at the ODL. My first summer holiday after I had started teaching had been as a paying apprentice at the Mohawk Festival in Schenectady, New York, and the head of that summer theatre, Charles Cobourn, of movie fame, had been an ungentle gentleman who had made mincemeat out of any student who arrived late for any occasion. "An actor is always fifteen minutes ahead of time!" But it seemed the mark of the amateur actor was to arrive late, or not at all, and to neglect to learn the words.

The member of my casts who helped me to cure some ODL actors of this insouciant attitude was Eric Workman, a professional singer who was teaching singing in Ottawa during the war. He always called me "Madame Directress," was always on time, and, because he had presence and commanded respect, set the pace. Eric did *not* always remember his words, but at least he could always think up on the spur of the moment even better ones, a talent I have never had. Eric was to be the Instrument of Fate in my future at the Canadian Repertory Theatre.

The ODL presented about six major productions a season. These ran for one week each. The sets, under the direction of Bill Adkins, and the furnishings and props, under the direction of Bill Burrett and Avis Croteau, were always first class. I think the standard of presentation and performance was unusually high for an amateur theatre. When I was in England in 1949 and people would say to me, "Of course, you have no theatre in Canada, have you?" it used to make me quite angry, because our work at the ODL during the nine years that I had known it was much better than some of the work I saw in England at clubs and in "rep."

In 1947 the ODL put its production of Noel Coward's *Blithe Spirit* into the Dominion Drama Festival. Since its first choice for Madame Arcati was not available, I was asked to take over the part. We took the play first to the Eastern Ontario Festival, in Brockville, where Sterndale Bennett gave me the best actress award. After that we went to the finals in London, Ontario.

But before we went there I had a lesson in Toronto at the recently renamed Royal Conservatory of Music with a teacher from England called Herbert Scott. I never met anyone who looked less like what one expects of a great teacher: a tiny, plump fellow, who looked like a comfortable village shopkeeper. He was a great teacher and much of what he said illuminated what had been obscure to me before. He worked with me on how to get inside a character. A few nights later when we presented *Blithe Spirit* in London, I was so inside Madame Arcati that I lost a lot of my drive, and I was not as good in the part as I had been at Brockville. As a result, I was judged one of the three runners-up for best actress. One must never be so much in the role that one forgets one's drive, or one's technique.

For that performance of *Blithe Spirit* in London we had no dress rehearsal. Our leading man, Bobby Wall, of the British high commission, was grounded in Gander, Newfoundland, and eventually he flew a most circuitous route in order to make the evening performance. What a charming man and actor he was! Mrs Douglas Blair and Michael Meiklejohn directed the production.

Besides these major productions we also had the work of the ODL Workshop, founded by Julia Murphy, Eric Stangroom, and Michael Meiklejohn. One-act plays were done, and classes were held whenever there was a teacher around who was willing. On occasion the workshop presented a full-length play. The most lasting contribution of the workshop, and its most important, however, was the annual play-writing contest, which was in the hands of Mrs Gladys Watts. We always produced the three top winners, and that was how in 1947 I came to direct Robertson Davies's *Overlaid*.

I was president of the workshop for a number of years. My job was to get to know everybody and arrange the Sunday evening programs, finding directors and helping directors find the right actors. Often a few days before the Sunday evening of performance, I would receive a woeful phone call to distress me with the news that "our effort has fallen through." Then we would try to cook up something quickly to take the place of this promised gourmet dish!

My telephone was the bane of my life. I would sometimes rise five times during dinner to answer it.

"Is there a play on at the Little Theatre this week?"

"What time does the play start tonight?"

"Could you suggest five men to walk on at the Capitol tomorrow night in the opera that is coming to town?"

I was often asked by the National Film Board (NFB) to help it find actors for its films. Never did it suggest that I might play a role myself, which was disappointing, because it paid. We did not have to belong to the Association of Canadian Television and Radio Actors (ACTRA) in those days, of course. On one occasion some NFB producer and his crew came to my apartment on Cooper Street to ask me for advice in casting *Who Will Teach Your Child?* I assured them that it was useless to ask me to find teachers to act for them, because teachers cannot necessarily act. Anyway, I could hardly go up to a teacher and say, "The NFB is looking for someone to play a snarly-type teacher, and I have suggested *you!*"

I convinced the NFB that there were ODL actors who would be much more suitable, though they were civil servants and not teachers by profession. I found that I could think of absolutely no one to play the leading role, however. As they were leaving, I said, "How about letting me play the leading role?" There was an awkward pause. I was then asked if I could take a test for it on Friday, and I said that I would find that a most suitable day. "After four."

This could not have been nicer for me, because the lead teacher in the script had to throw a fit of hysterics, and when I blew into the NFB that Friday after four I was primed for such a scene (all teachers are ready for hysterics by Friday afternoon). They seemed impressed. "Could you just do that *again?*" they asked.

I did it again. Easy as winking. And that was how I got a part in a little film that went all over the world.

I was telephoned one evening while I was at dinner and asked if I would go over to the Little Theatre (the ODL's home) to receive the Governor General, His Excellency Viscount Alexander of Tunis. The senior lady on the board of directors, Mrs Louise White, was not available. So I climbed into my black velvet and little pearls.

Standing at the top of that great red-carpeted entrance staircase in the building that was to burn down in 1970, waiting for HE to arrive, I was as nervous as I had ever been on an opening night. At last the doors below me were thrust ajar, curtain was up, and Himself entered! A most handsome man, with fine blue eyes, and undoubtedly with a sense of humour. First of all I was embarrassed to be standing on a higher level! He had to look up at me. Suddenly I wanted to declaim

> The raven himself is hoarse
> That croaks the fatal entrance of Duncan
> Under *my* battlements.

I felt he was double daring me to *do* something. My tongue clove to the roof of my mouth. Nearer he came, his eyes never leaving me. Turning ignominiously into Third Waiting Woman, I did what was expected of me by convention, and so bored myself to death. "Good evening, your Excellency." I lacked the courage that comes of character and star billing.

Mr John Aylen and I had been instructed earlier to see HE and his guests to the front of the theatre, get them all seated, and then retire to the back. We made a solemn procession down the aisle. Lord Alexander seated each of his guests in the front-row seats that had been provided. When all were seated, and not one empty seat remained, he gave me a quizzical look. Then he stared at the governor general's chair, an imposing piece of furniture in the centre of the aisle. He stared at this for quite a while. Then he looked back at me, grinned, and with a bow offered me the chair. I bit my lip and shook my head. He shrugged, and sat down.

My final directorial chore for the ODL was a production for the workshop in 1948 of a poetical play, *This Way to the Tomb,* by Ronald Duncan, which had been brought to my attention by Eric Workman. For this, Ted Baker of Ottawa's Exhibition Commission designed and painted two handsome sets, identical, the first in colour to express the medieval *life* of the locale, and the second in black and white to show the death of true faith in the twentieth century.

I had a splendid cast. Ian Fellows was excellent as St Anthony, but the best performance to my mind was given with great simplicity by a fellow from the NFB who did not believe a word he was saying, being, I think, of the Communist persuasion. None of the three brothers believed. Eddie Nunn, playing the brother who symbolizes Intellect, told me he thought the whole thing a lot of bosh. However, he confided to me later that during the second and final performance, at the point in the second act when he had to kneel before the Tomb, he came all over strange and found himself deeply moved. We had a party on the stage afterward, and I spent the entire time playing confidante and mother confessor to members of both cast and audience who wanted to tell me about their religious feelings. It was an evening of surprises.

We used to have good parties on-stage after final performances. Deep inside me I was restless and unhappy much of this time, but one can live a good life in spite of that. I always stayed till the last dance. The height of honour at the ODL was to be invited during the party to Bill Adkins's little sanctum down in the basement, beside the paint shop. There, sitting on ancient rockers or on stools, we old cronies would take a wee drop together. It was very cosy.

It was after one such jolly, roistering evening that I climbed the stairs to my sitting-room and by the light of one lamp, at three in the morning, took out and examined thus the other side of my coin.

Élan Vital

The dead are urging me, colourless mould
Pulling me down towards the silent boon
With soft, mournful fingers: 'The story is told
And the brand is burnt out, now or too soon.'

Call me, O future! Let me not feel
The tide of negation through darkness and strife
Roll forth to engulf me here where I kneel
At the altar of death. Let me want life.

It must have been about that time, in the spring thaw of 1948, that I walked one day the eight-minute journey that took me from my home on Cooper Street, near the Driveway, to the Parliament Buildings. Snow was still on the ground, but there were as many patches of grass as there were of snow. Spring was coming. Impulsively I took off my shoes, undid my stockings and rolled them off, and walked all around that Daughter of Parliament in my bare feet. Barefoot in my country. I re-established my belonging to the Earth. It was a ritual, and in the performing of it I was released.

CHAPTER 5

SUMMER SEARCHINGS

You have to get a long way away from any part of your life in order to evaluate it. Then sometimes what seemed at the time a vain and profitless phase will be recollected as fruitful, a time that you can look back on with affection, or even with profound thanks.

I once had an unexpected flash-back from the subconscious while sitting in the dining-car of a train. It had been raining, and the light, now that the rain had ceased, was glorious, put there by the brush of the heavenly Renoir. I was appreciating the light, when suddenly, for no reason I can account for, I saw, in what seemed to be one eternal second, a full fifteen years of my life. It was my life in Ottawa. For much of that time I had not been happy, but now I saw it fresh and glowing, like the landscape after the rain. It was all shining.

Strangely enough, and in contrast, the wartime summers, when I escaped from Ottawa and burst forth "to do my own thing" as best I could, remain somewhat pathetic in recollection. They are the saga of wasted time, of a young person trying desperately to grasp at a life of expression in the theatre.

The summer of 1940 I took my earnings and went as an apprentice to the Mohawk Drama Festival in Schenectady, New York. In those days one paid, and paid a lot, to be an apprentice. The festival was at Union College, on a most beautiful campus, with good dormitories and fine gardens. The theatre was a huge, open-air stage, with canvas around, but not over, the audience.

The festival advertised that it accepted only a few senior students, but actually there were a great many of us, mostly "rich kids," whose parents visited in chauffeur-driven limousines. At my first audition I was asked, "Where did you learn such voice production, such diction?" From Clara Baker. Later, when I objected to a week of sweeping out dressing-rooms as part of my training, relations cooled.

But there were some fine teachers there, in mime and in technical work, such as lighting and make-up. It was there that I first learned make-up from a fine young character actor named Ralph Clanton. Someone advised me that my diction was so good that it made my work too intellectual. He said I ought to have experience playing "the other side of the tracks." This was very good advice, but I was not going to be able to get this experience for nearly ten years. I told Walter Hampton, who was with us for a couple of weeks playing Richelieu, that I had been criticized for having diction that was too good.

"Is your diction better than mine?" he asked.

"Oh, no, Mr Hampton!"

"Then I shouldn't worry."

I had a small part in *Peter Ibbetson*, with Dennis King, who was charming. Twenty years later I was to play again with him in Robertson Davies's *Love and Libel*, under Tyrone Guthrie's direction. Cornelia Otis Skinner was there, but she was aloof. Beulah Bondi, the film character actor, showed us home movies (just as, thirty years later, I would show my theatre home movies at Stratford to the young fry.) Charles Cobourn, as head of the enterprise, big cigar in mouth, ruled all with an iron hand. He played Bottom in *A Midsummer Night's Dream*, our final production of eight.

Amelia, as a young thing of the court, wore a bit of white chiffon, and a lot of Armenian bole, which would not come off completely, no matter how many showers I took a day. At the opening of the play I had to run on-stage and meet in the centre a returned-from-the-wars soldier, who took me by the waist and lifted me up in his arms, full length, and carried me off-stage, obviously with the worst possible intentions. He was the only fellow in the company who could have lifted even me that high. He had had army training.

If we were not on-stage, we students were expected to appear in the audience on first nights in pretty evening dresses. One night the lady in front of me turned and said, "And where do you come from, my dear?" I told her. She stiffened, "Oh! A *warring* country!" I remembered her on December 7, 1941 when I was attending an afternoon showing of the Ottawa Film Society and a man rushed out on to the stage to announce: "Ladies and gentlemen, the Japanese have attacked Pearl Harbor!"

54

There was a woman who came to the Mohawk Festival to get actors for her company, which toured the classics to schools. She was said to be related to the great Tree family. I was warned that she was a martinet who paid poor wages. Her advice to me was, "You may as well accept the fact that you are too small to get anywhere in the theatre." Years later I heard that Eileen Herlie, being told she was small, had replied, "I'm nine feet tall on stage!" I said nothing to the Tree lady, but I thought, "Nuts to you!"

One got to know some very good actors. I was so excited all the time I scarcely ate any of the excellent meals in the beautiful dining-hall. I liked being called Amelia by everybody for the first time in my life. But it was far from the realities of the war, and far from the realities of the theatre as I have known it since.

I made one lasting friendship, with J.P. Wilson, who was to come often to the Royal Alex. He had been born in Yorkshire (in the *East* Riding, he told me, as if my *West* Riding was the other side of the moon); he had appeared in over thirty of Shakespeare's plays and had been in three productions of *The Merchant of Venice* with Ellen Terry.

In the final week of the festival my friend Leith Ferguson, who had recommended Mohawk to me, came down to visit, and she and her fiancé, Ross Macdonald, drove me back to Canada. I had one dime in my purse when I got back to Ottawa.

By the summer of 1941 it seemed frivolous to ask permission to take money out of the country to study theatre in the United States, and anyway, restrictions were severe, so I took a course in radio writing at the University of British Columbia, in Vancouver. This was my first trip out west.

The best part of that summer was the train journey, with a stop-off at Jasper. In wartime the trains were packed, of course, and there was a wide selection of interesting acquaintances. So many gallant members of the armed forces to carry luggage for a girl and to chat over the quite delicious meals in the as-they-used-to-be dining-cars. There were upper and lower berths in those days, and large wash-rooms at the ends of the corridors. No roomette nonsense, where a manual is needed to understand how to make things work, and where the toilet is lost under the bed once a small person has succeeded in getting the bed down.

The summer was worthwhile because Anne Marriott, the Cana-dian poet, became one of my best friends. On the way back east I had a week at Banff and hated it. It takes more than a week to acclimatize oneself to mountains. I felt hemmed in. I prefer the seashore and the prairies. Banff was so crowded that we who were at the Banff School of Fine Arts were packed into digs. I slept with a girl I had never met before, and two other strangers were in the other bed! In the daylight, I got to lying on the platform of the railway station just to see the trains going east. The fault was in me, not in Banff. But it was torture in voice class to have to sit and listen to Canadian school teachers trying to sight-read Milton, and murdering him.

I had two summers in Toronto, 1942 and 1943, hanging around the Royal Alex. Frank McCoy had a company doing weekly stock. The actors would rehearse for about six days without "the lead," and then the Star would arrive from the United States for the last day or two.

I had made friends with an English married couple who were in the company, the Wilsons. These two had spent years travelling with the Lunts. They had probably spoken to Frank McCoy about me. It was a Saturday night that he asked me to play the maid in *Old Acquaintance*. We rehearsed my part on Monday afternoon, and we were opening that night! I was gratified to find how easy it was to get the feel of the house and to make my voice carry. Of course, the acoustics are marvellous at the Alex. I was paid ten dollars for the week. "I'll bet you're getting peanuts," said one of the crew, "and you're as good as any of them." The cast was kindly. The leading man apologized because he didn't know where Ottawa was or *what* it was. He was feeling sick, and the actors said that for some reason actors always got sick when they played Toronto.

One Saturday night Mr McCoy called me in and offered me a huge role in *The Pursuit of Happiness*. He asked me to read it for him. He handed me the script, and it was "sides." This meant that I got only my own lines, and a cue of three or four words from the end of the actor's speech before each of my own. Thus I did not know what any of the conversations were about. I was desperate, because it was already Saturday midnight and he wanted me to open the following Monday evening, in some other city! The man must have been mad. I went immediately to the Wilsons backstage, and they said to turn him down. I did.

The next season at the Royal Alex was run by Robert Henderson. I accosted him boldly and asked him if I might sit in and observe his rehearsals of *Hamlet*. (Mr Henderson was doing a high-tone classical season.) He replied that he could do better than that, and he offered me a role as a lady-in-waiting, at five dollars a week. I jumped at the chance!

I soon discovered that the male extras in the company were receiving eight dollars a week. Men and women extras were alike unhappy about their pay because they had all resigned from duller jobs to work in *Hamlet*. They came to me and asked me to speak on their behalf, since I was a rich school teacher on vacation and wasn't dependent on my five dollars. I spoke to Mr Henderson, and it ended with Henderson getting me onto his side to placate the rebelling extras!

He was also clever at handling crowds on-stage, and I watched his methods closely. He commended me for my crowd reactions, just as Miss Mather had done at school when I was in *The Pied Piper*. The only words I had were crowd responses, the "rhubarb, rhubarb, rhubarb" nonsense that old actors say, and so I decided to write lines for myself to speak in the crowd responses. I wrote them in blank verse and memorized them. This drew me to the attention of the star, Tom Rutherford, who was playing Hamlet. A pale, handsome, courteous man from Virginia, Tom Rutherford was an especially fine Hamlet, and I was ready to worship at his feet. At the end of my vacation I had to leave the company early, and on my last night he took me to what was the early Winston's then, a little coffee shop, and then home in a taxi. When my landlady opened the door and saw Tom Rutherford on the doorstep, carrying my theatre suitcase, she "nearly died!" What happened to him? I never heard of him again. I have his autographed picture, among my souvenirs.

It was not easy for me at this time. I wanted desperately to learn, and from people who really knew. I had been picking up tricks ever since I went to the theatre when I was a child, but I wanted the very best technique. Where could I learn it? And where, if I ever did learn it, could I put it to any use? Would I ever be able to get out of teaching? Of course there was radio in Toronto, but how did one get into radio? I looked up "Radio" in the yellow pages in the Toronto phone book and made phone calls. I remember having an audition — was it with Howard Milson? — and he said as he came out of the booth, "A voice like Tallulah Bankhead!" So who cares?

What I wanted to do was *create something*. I certainly did not want to sit in office anterooms waiting to be noticed and to be given little parts. I did not want to act *that* badly! I remember standing in Ottawa, at the corner of Cooper and Elgin streets, and I felt *flames* coming out of me, I was so desperate to get on with the job! Around 1945 my mother, with splendid insight and perception, had given me a box of oil paints, and I discovered in one afternoon that I could forget in paint both disappointments and heartache. How did she know that where there's paint there's hope?

I took lessons then with Henri Masson, that gentleman of outspoken charm, and he told me soon that I should continue painting because I had the ability to paint my feelings, and he said that this was rare. "Of course, we are only a young country," he would say as he walked between the easels. "My God!" he would add, *"we have been young so long!"*

Schubert sang of music, "Du holde kunst, in zie, mein hertzen zeiten!" That was how I felt about painting. It saved me.

In the summer of 1946 I was able to go back to New York, this time to study acting. What a deal of running around you had to do in those days to try to get off the ground as an actor! Imagine a doctor who constantly goes off to study surgery because there are no hospitals in his country! Where is he going to operate? On the kitchen table, I suppose.

I decided to study in New York with "The Great Teacher," Frances Robinson-Duff. Mrs Baker had already worked with her. Duff was the teacher of Katharine Hepburn, and she also boasted that "people say Ina Clair gets her French blood from Duff." Miss Duff had taught at the Comédie Française for seventeen years, although she was not French but American. Her mother had taught Caruso his breathing, the method that Duff herself taught.

Duff's studio on the fourth floor of her grand town-house was adorned with pictures of her and her mother with great folk like Caruso. The house was elegant. There was a butler, and a secretary. Duff was expensive. The private lessons, forty-five minutes long, were nine dollars, a lot of money in 1946. Sometimes during my forty-five minutes Duff would take time off to choose which hat she was going to wear when she went out: the secretary would bring them in, and here I was paying nine dollars to help her decide! She even gave lessons while she ate, seated at an exquisite little table, a meal to make the mouth water as one contemplated one's own dinner in Shrafft's or Chock Full o' Nuts.

Duff was sixty-eight and not well. She could be beastly to me in my private classes; I think women bored her. She would say, "If you don't get this breathing right, I shall refuse to teach you!" Once she wept throughout my lesson because all the people in the pictures on the studio walls were dead, and she was left alone. I was sorry for her that day. She had what I thought was a huge bosom, but I discovered at one lesson that this was not her bosom but her diaphragm, which had grown extremely large and powerful from teaching breathing. She had me put my hand down her dress to feel her breasts, which she boasted were like those of a young girl. And so they were. The boys told me she went through this routine with them, too.

She was a handsome woman, always elegantly dressed. Her control of her body and her knowledge of how to use it to show what you were thinking and feeling were quite astonishing. She could stand before me and without a sound, merely by taking up a pose, wring my heart. This was the kind of thing that I had seen Nazimova do on-stage; make one move, take up one pose, that would speak the whole scene. Duff told me, "The great actor plays a scene on one gesture." I had seen Laurence Olivier do just that in *Oedipus Rex*, when he told how he had murdered Laius at the place where three roads meet.

Duff taught the importance of the *note* on which the words ride. She could awaken an emotional response of any kind just by making sound. No words — words denote sense. Tone denotes feeling.

She would be so angry with me in my private lessons. I was working on the potion scene from *Romeo and Juliet*. "You aren't feeling a thing!" she would howl at me.

"I am, Miss Duff! I am!"

"No you are not! I don't believe you. Get *inside* that little body of yours! Get *inside* it!" But at that time I didn't understand what she meant.

I had a lovely room in a huge apartment on Riverside Drive, living with sympathetic people. I was always crying. They all said they had never in their lives seen anybody cry so much and hoped never to see anybody cry so much again. I was a living fountain.

It was not because of Miss Duff that I cried. But it *was* wretched to be so unhappy and yet to express nothing, apparently, in my work. What was the matter with my acting, anyway? When I was full of pain inside, why did she say I was not inside my body? But all the time, in spite of my misery, I never failed to notice what was happening to my breathing, what my muscles were doing, and what I felt in my arms, and legs, and in what *part* of my arms and legs, and so on. All grist for the mill, as Mrs Baker would have said.

In contrast to her treatment of me in private class, Miss Duff was most pleasant to me in group classes. I think the presence of the boys, some of them back from the war, mellowed her. If any of the tall ones in a scene with me bent over me because I am short, she would bark, "Don't bend over her! She's not a midget!" And then she would say to me, "Turn slowly around," and as I turned she would say, "A pocket Venus!" and the boys would grin. This flattery was the one pleasant thing about a summer in which I was constantly lost, unable to find my way in my work, or in my life, even lost eternally on the streets and in the subway, constantly walking in any direction at all so that people would not notice that I didn't know where I was.

Duff was wise in that she did not let me do roles like Victoria Regina, which she said I could do standing on my head. She was disgusted with my Roxanne in *Cyrano de Bergerac*. "You accept a compliment like an Englishwoman. This woman is *French*. She acknowledges a compliment with grace and pleasure!" Then she would digress. "Nobody can act unless they are French or Jewish." And I would smirk to myself, because my father's mother had a Jewish father. So there, Miss Duff! Her great credo was, "Always the too little. Never the too much."

That summer I haunted the Thalia film house, where they showed French films. I was enamoured of French actors, especially Louis Jouvet, Harry Bauer, Françoise Rosay — as well as of all the actors who came to Ottawa in Les Compagnons, under the leadership of Father Legault.

Something came out of my inner torment and struggle that summer in New York. The German poet Heine wrote:

> Who never ate with tears his bread,
> Who never through night's awful hours
> Sat weeping on his lonely bed...
> He knows Ye not, Ye Heavenly Powers!

That summer of 1946 was not the first time I had eaten with tears my bread, and it was not to be the last, but it was the last time I ever shook my fists at Heaven. Maybe in my teens I had read too much Thomas Hardy, for I carried a strong resentment against whatever powers controlled the direction of my life. Then suddenly that summer I said to Heaven, in the words of a character in *Pericles*, "I cannot get much lower than my knees!" and for the first time I did not mind being brought to my knees.

Then such a tranquillity came to me. It was like the peace you feel at a theatre after you have really been shaken by a great drama. In high school we had read Hugh Walpole's *Fortitude*, the sort of novel that some people make fun of. Somewhere in that book the protagonist calls to the Elements: "Make of me a Man, to be afraid of nothing, to be ready for anything, love, fame, success ... to care nothing if these things are not for me! Make me brave! Make me brave!"

You can laugh at that as much as you like. When I was able to say that, I was over the worst part of the climb. It takes a long time for some of us to grow up. I think we spend too long a time in schools.

In an essay on Stephen Leacock, Robertson Davies writes: "In truth, only technique can be mastered; art masters those who serve it in any form." I think that 1946 was the summer that I accepted in my innermost core that we are here to serve, and not to serve ourselves; that for some reason one had to pass through the darkness of despair before one could serve; that this was all part of the initiation. If you believed in a further shore, and I did, you had to jump into turbulent waters to reach it, or else stand for ever shivering and grumbling on the shore. You musn't balk at how much the waves buffet you; only by the struggle to keep yourself afloat and to keep your heart high would you be able to serve.

"Love the art in yourself and not yourself in the art."

CHAPTER 6

BRAE MANOR AND THE
CANADIAN ART THEATRE

In 1947 the ODL engaged a professional, Malcolm Morley, to direct *Joan of Lorraine*. I had a small role in this production, and Malcolm asked me if I would care to go to Montreal during my summer vacation and play First Fairy combined with Peaseblossom in a production he was going to direct of *A Midsummer Night's Dream*. It was to be presented in the open air on the Mountain. This expedition was to change everything for me.

I arrived in Montreal without accommodation. I went to the YWCA, and discovered it was full. It recommended a house to me that was about $1.75 a night, which was what I was ready to pay. I arrived at this address, and the door was opened by a little man in a very dirty apron. The room was not much bigger than a walk-in closet and had a couch with a light over it and, by the opposite wall, a wardrobe. For some reason I did not unpack, except to take out a nightgown. During the night I kept feeling funny, and I would pull the string above my head to switch on the light. Finally, baffled by my restlessness, I got up and went over to the mirror on the door of the hideous wardrobe. My left arm, from the elbow up, was a mass of weird bulges or bites! I ripped off my gown, jumped into my discarded underwear and suit, didn't bother with garter belt or stockings, and, leaving my suitcase behind, I was out of that place "swifter than arrow from the Tartar's bow!"

It was still dark night. I walked and walked and finally found myself at a Ford Hotel. I staggered to the desk and asked if there was a room. The clerk gave a world-weary but slightly puzzled look and said there was not. I sat down to wait till seven, when the coffee shop would open. Then I poured my woes into the ears of the waitress, who said that a similar catastrophe had happened to her and her husband and their children when they were down on their luck.

Unburdened somewhat, I marshaled my forces and set out into the unknown to look for a room. I pounded on the door of what turned out to be a sort of hotel-night-club. Was it called the New Yorker? The door was finally opened, after my persistent knocking, by a stout, sleepy, and voluble Frenchman in his dressing-gown. I told him the tale. "Well," said he, "I dunno where I can send around here a nice girl like you!" (Oh, God! Oh, Montreal!) Then he brightened. "A moment! There *is* a place, a big apartment, very nice. I'll phone". There was nothing crooked about him. It was a fine apartment, clean and beautifully furnished, and had a splendid little room, so cozy, for three dollars a night. (I couldn't keep that kind of spending going for many days!)

To an elderly friend, Mr Primm, I now appealed, and he took his car for my suitcases and took me to a doctor, who said *he* really didn't know *what* it was on my arm. But I knew! Then I was deposited at my clean abode. And I took a bath.

Nobody in Montreal seemed to want to rent rooms by the week. Finally a Jewish lady, living alone, gave me a room for twelve dollars a week in a street off Sherbrooke near Guy.

The two juveniles in *The Dream* were to be played by Bruce Raymond, of the Canadian Art Theatre of Montreal, and a seventeen-year-old, Christopher Plummer. The "rude mechanical" who played Moonshine in the play-within-the-play was played by a young man who struck me as being immensely talented. Silvio Narizzano seemed to be popular, yet he was very shy. Nevertheless, he and I became friends at once. He had attended Bishop's College and after graduation entered his father's business for as long as he could stand it. This was the Saxonia Fruit Preserving Co., which we always referred to as the cherry business. His father, who had been born in England, was interned during the war, along with Montreal's mayor, Camillien Houde. Silvio used to laugh about his dad and Houde doing road work together and say that it had done his father a lot of good to get out of his office chair and exercise. Silvio was a person of occasional extraordinary exuberance, and the extrovert side of his nature was fresh air to someone like me, who had been respectful of decorum all her life.

One evening after a performance (we performed come wind or weather), young Plummer walked me home to my rooming-house.

He was very good company, mature, urbane, relaxed. Outside my door he invited me to the movies for the next afternoon and said he would pick me up. He never came. That evening, at the scene of our revels on the Mountain, he said casually, "Sorry about this afternoon, Millie. When I left you at your door last night I never thought to look at the name of the street. Of course I couldn't phone you because I didn't know your landlady's name." I thought this was pretty cool from such a young feller, but I liked the fact that he didn't make a song and dance about it.

Silvio and I thought director Malcolm Morley a sort of teddy bear. He was physically somewhat rambling, his frame rather large, the trousers slung low and for ever being heaved up. We would have tea with him in a restaurant, and he would grumble disconsolately about his work, smiling a sideways smile. We felt sorry for him, and we were annoyed that he aroused this sentiment.

As soon as *A Midsummer Night's Dream* closed, I was invited to go to Brae Manor, Knowlton. Malcolm Morley had offered me a role in one of his own plays to be put on there, and also in a production of *The Little Foxes*.

Brae Manor Playhouse was situated in the Eastern Townships of Quebec, near the Vermont border. The whole town was beautiful, and Lake Brome was nearby. The playhouse had been started in 1936 by Filmore and Marge Sadler. Both worked at the Montreal Repertory Theatre, where Filmore was director of the theatre school. But it was only a winter job; they were both looking for something to do in the summer. So they bought a large, old house in Knowlton and for four summers put on plays in the hall of the local Lake View Hotel.

At the end of that time, they had become so much a part of the summer scene that a group of Knowlton residents came forward with the offer of an interest-free loan to build a permanent playhouse. With that encouragement, the Sadlers built a small, simple 200-seat theatre across the lawn from their home, winterized the old house, and moved down to Knowlton year-round. They usually did eight or nine plays in a season, and by the time the Playhouse closed in 1956, it was the longest-running summer theatre in Canada.

The actors who played there were largely from Montreal, and most of them paid to come. It was a holiday doing one's favourite thing, acting. At the time I was there, you paid for your room and board, and all the actors and crew slept on the second and third floors of the old house. As the Sadlers were Christian Scientists, there was no drinking in the house. But who needed it? We had buns and cocoa or coffee at night; we sang around the piano, and the conversation was always stimulating. Sunday suppers we ate outside under the trees. Outside, too, we would have a reading of the next play, and during the week you could see Leo Ciceri (and later David Haber) out on the lawn in shorts, building the set, or painting the flats in the sunshine.

They were preparing *Our Town* when I arrived at Brae Manor. It was suggested that I go to Brome Lake beach to while away the afternoon. I got into my new, pale blue two-piece bathing suit, from the Laura Thomas Shop on Ottawa's Sparks Street, and someone drove me to the beach. It was deserted, but out in the water someone was swimming. I waded out, not very far. The swimmer rose like Neptune from the water and came toward me with a wide welcoming grin.

"Hello. I'm John Colicos."

I had heard of this difficult young man. He was nineteen, the prize pupil of the voice teacher Eleanor Stuart, and he was preparing to become a classical actor. He was reputed to be cocky and quarrelsome, and here he was, the very pink of amiability and masculine charm!

"I'm Amelia Hall. I can't swim."

"Then let me teach you to float."

And John did. Of course I forgot how afterward, for I am a great coward in the water. (I am the pupil of several noteworthy swimming instructors, including Herbert Whittaker and Leo Ciceri. I still sink like a stone.)

After our amiable session in the lake, Colicos and I encountered some young Brae Manorites, and I realized, from the youthful tartness of his tongue, that he had perhaps shown deference to me as an Older Woman. Dreadful thought!

The next day Silvio Narizzano arrived — a delightful surprise. The month ahead promised to be blissful. Silvio had been asked to play Leo in *The Little Foxes*, which Herbert Whittaker was directing. It was a fine cast that Herbie had chosen. Filmore Sadler was to be Ben, Colicos was Oscar, and I was to be Birdie, with Silvio playing Leo, our spotty, under-handed son. Betty Wilson was to be Regina, and Leo Ciceri her gentle invalid husband Horace. This was the first taste I ever had of being in a production in which everything seemed to go right.

Before we started on *The Little Foxes*, the very same people appeared in a play called *The Beacon Light*, written and directed by Malcolm Morley. In this production nothing seemed right, simply because we did not trust the play. This was my first attempt at learning lines in one week, and I made a disaster of it. I *remembered* the lines, but I was so terrified that I wouldn't remember them that instead of *listening* to the other actors, the absolutely vital requisite of the actor, I kept saying my own lines over to myself while the other actors were talking. It was hell! I decided that if this was what I was going to do when learning a play in one week, then I would stop acting.

Fortunately, in *The Little Foxes*, I was so carried away by the performances of the others that I had no trouble entering into the role of Birdie, and the lines became second nature, as they should.

At the close of the first scene John Colicos had to give me a slap across the face just before the curtain came down. Herbie had John practise this slap by lining up all the company and having John take a swipe at each and every one. This was in order to save my face. Each night, as the curtain came down on this scene, John would clasp me to his manly chest and say, "I'm sorry! I'm sorry!" The audience believed that the slap was faked, but I was able to prove to them for a week afterward that it had not been faked, for John's handiwork was still be seen across one cheek. (In 1964 John told me that he had learned since how to do it so that it didn't hurt at all, but I told him that I would take his word for that. No demonstration.)

The stage was so small that when the family walked on to the "living-room" set, supposedly out of the "dining-room," in reality we had all been waiting back of the dining-room doors in a space the size of a small cupboard pressed intimately against one another and stifling our giggles. The playhouse itself was small, and it was possible to hear on stage any remark that was made in the audience.

One night at the height of Birdie's tragic scene with Horace, in which she gets drunk on wine, I heard an old lady whisper with loud disapproval, "That's her *seventh* drink!" In this scene Birdie tells Horace that all her married life with Oscar she has longed to have just one day's happiness, to have, as in her girlhood, "just one *whole* day." I recall with nostalgia going downstairs to the dressing-room after this scene and beholding Silvio and John, my husband and son in the play, sitting with tears in their eyes: "*We* did that to you." Then the three of us would listen breathlessly to the big quarrel, held offstage, between Betty Wilson and Leo Ciceri (Regina and Horace), so real that it hurt. There were no lines written for this scene; Betty and Leo, dear friends in real life, just made them up at every performance.

Though the good air of Knowlton assured sound sleep, I regretted the time wasted in sleeping. Sunday mornings everybody slept in. Everybody but me, for I would tippy-toe around the bedrooms to see if anyone was awake. "Millie, stop percolating," admonished Filmore.

I roomed with Betty Wilson. One afternoon when Betty came into the room for something, I was standing there in a trance. "Betty, I have just realized the most amazing thing! Just now I have been alone for fifteen minutes, and that is the first time since I came to Brae Manor that such a thing has happened. Except for going to the bathroom."

"Would you like me to leave?" asked Betty.

"I mean it is such a joy, to be all the time with people who like the same things, people who are all so alive. I have never before been part of such a *family*."

And that is the saving grace of the theatre: it is a family. Non-alcoholic drinks and sandwiches at night, and all of us singing "Come to me, my melancholy baby," or "Oh, how we danced on the night we were wed!" Memories of Brae Manor!

I stayed on for two weeks after I had finished performing. I had my room to myself, since Betty had gone to New York to rehearse in Judith Anderson's *Medea*, but I turned the room into a painting studio, and, secure among friends, with the necessary leadership and discipline of life supplied by my hosts, I whiled away the hours with a dilettante's joy. Leo posed for me in my attempt at a Gauguin, my own red and white sarong around his loins, and John Colicos joined me in my studio to draw without a model. He is an extraordinarily good draughtsman, and I recall his execution (!) of a decapitated head with a rat crawling over it as admirable in everything but subject matter. "Why did you have to choose such awful subjects?" And John would grin, all expansive good humour.

Back in Ottawa I had a lot to think about in the autumn of 1947. In one summer I had met at least four people who were as serious about the theatre as I was: Christopher Plummer, Silvio Narizzano, John Colicos, and Leo Ciceri. Then there was Betty Wilson, already experienced in New York and London, who had thought well of my work. These people were *more* serious than I was, because they were determined to do nothing else but theatre.

I thought the Sadlers an ideal couple, living an ideal life. It had been courageous of them to take the step of moving from Montreal to Knowlton and starting this enterprise. I longed to have such a life ahead of *me*.

Was it too late for me? After nine years of teaching high school I decided it was time to do what I wanted to do. I wasn't at all courageous. I just knew I had to make the break. In the spring of 1948

I took the inevitable step.

"Harry, I have decided to quit at the end of this term."

Harry Pullen looked at me with lively interest, but without surprise.

"What are you going to do?"

"I don't know."

"Well, it's always been obvious that your heart is in the theatre, but that may not work out, unless you can create your own opportunities. Why not take a year's leave of absence, and then, if you change your mind, we'll be delighted to have you back?"

A leave of absence had never entered my head. I wanted no roads leading back, but Harry Pullen's was a kindly offer, and I would have been stupid to refuse.

So it was left at that. I would depart for the unknown in June 1948, and if the taste of freedom soured, I could return in September 1949. From nine years of teaching, $5,000 had accumulated in the Bank of Nova Scotia on Bank Street in my name. I could exist on that, if necessary, for two years (fantastic as that seems now).

Some time later I bumped into an acquaintance in a Rideau streetcar. "I hear you've gone and given up your wonderful job as a school teacher. I can hardly believe it. Holy Mary, you'll be breaking your poor mother's heart!"

How could this concerned lady know that if I appeared to have been struck by stage lightning it was my mother who had hurled the bolt? A restless life we'd lived, crossing the ocean five times in search of a life. And in all that travelling since I was seven, I had been taken to the live theatre, when it was available, in whatever place we happened to be. The one house I have always felt safe at home in is the playhouse.

Once my formal education was finished and I had secured a good job in the teaching profession my mother knew that she had come to the end of her long, lonely climb: she thought she had obtained her goal. What we were both soon to learn was how passionate were her feelings about the theatre. You can't break your mother's heart by throwing over a secure job with a pension if she has a sense of adventure and wants you to find your own way. And so we both prepared for a new life.

At about that time I received an offer from the Canadian Art Theatre, known as the CAT, to join it for the summer season of 1948, and again I would be based in the Eastern Townships of Quebec. Joy Thomson, a wealthy Montreal woman in her twenties, had founded this organization in Montreal and ran it single-handed. Joy had heard

68

about me from Silvio Narizzano and Bruce Raymond, who were her lieutenants.

They worked from an erstwhile funeral parlour on Monkland Avenue, in Notre-Dame-de-Grâce. The building housed rehearsal hall, workshops, and two apartments, in one of which Joy lived with her husband, Edward Asselin. The CAT ran a school of acting for youngsters and presented plays for children at various halls in Montreal on Saturdays. The actors were young company members as well as experienced Montreal actors. Joy was now planning her first summer theatre. I had met her only once before, at a party at Silvio Narizzano's in the winter of 1947, when I had visited Montreal to see the Dublin Gate Players. She was an attractive woman, humorous and shy, and she said nothing to me then about her plans for the summer. It was Joy's way to speak through other people, and eventually Silvio wrote to tell me of her offer of summer work. I was not to be paid. That I took for granted! Only four members of her company would have a salary, and that a small one.

The plans for the locale of this summer theatre had changed several times over the previous year. The CATS had finally settled on the Eastern Townships. The company was to live at Rock Island, next door to Stanstead, and we were to open the plays there, playing Friday and Saturday nights at the Haskell Library and Opera House in Rock Island, and then tour during the following week, to the bar at the Lantern Inn, Magog, and to the town hall at North Hatley. For the first time I had some insight into the problems of finding theatres and sponsors. When Silvio and Bruce were "casing" one local town, a resident had told them, "We had some films last winter at the town hall, but they flickered." Silvio assured him that the CATS did not flicker!

The Haskell Opera House was built in 1902. It was a charming, tiny theatre, seating about 400, with a fine chandelier, languid nudes painted around the gilt proscenium, and a balcony from which plaster Cupids peered benignly at the stage. At that time there was an exquisitely painted roll-drop curtain depicting a nineteenth-century Venetian scene, and a set of delicately painted flats. There was little if any wing space and a paucity of dressing-room space or room for props or furniture. Backstage we were walking all over each other and over the props, many of which were damaged before they could be returned to their owners.

The most extraordinary feature of the Opera House was that it was built in two countries. The audience sat in Canada, and the actors played in the United States. Such was the position of this building that in order to drive the truck round to the fire escape to pack it with flats and furnishings, or unpack it, we had to drive through Customs.

On the nights when we played at the Lantern Inn, we set up our flats and props right on the bar floor. Some members of the audience sat at their tables on a slightly higher level. The rest were almost in our laps. On occasion a waiter bearing drinks would stroll right through the set! Not only comedies were presented here, but dramas, like *Gaslight*. In *that* particular opus, I recall sitting down in the first scene and realizing that I was sitting on a large hammer which I had left on the chair myself after helping Arnold to rig the lights. Arnold was about sixteen, certainly no older, and one of the best stage managers I have ever met. He gave me the title that year of assistant lighting man, and he revelled in ordering me about in the nicest possible way. We had to make up in the two small washrooms, and dress there too. In the intermissions we hovered around these washrooms and chatted with the patrons of the bar.

I had tried to learn all I could at the ODL about stage lighting, and I had taken many turns at prompting and doing sound effects. Now I was beginning to realize that there was much more to the iceberg than what showed above water. There were boards and committees to tackle, advertising to sell, sets to be constructed and painted, props to be cajoled from the unwilling, tickets to be printed, transport to be arranged. There seemed no end to it. And Silvio had said that they were looking for a company of about ten actors, culled for their technical as well as acting ability. Undaunted, I had signed on, except that there was nothing to sign in those days. One gave one's word.

I had contemplated a summer of lovely leading roles, and my spare time devoted to painting. I set forth with a moderate wardrobe and my easel, paint-box of oils all shiny new, and some real canvas on which to do justice to the lovely, rolling vistas of the Eastern Townships. I painted one picture. Being new to landscape painting, I chose an enormous panorama, but I was allowed to work on it only one afternoon!

I found myself out selling advertising in Sherbrooke. I was so nervous at approaching Sherbrooke businessmen in their offices that I was defeated before I had opened my mouth. After one ignominious day at this sport, I was demoted to travelling to the small towns of neighbouring Vermont and asking if I might put posters in store windows. This was more in my line, because it offered some of the joys of holiday and sightseeing. I was not so well equipped for the job of asking farmers if I might tack a poster to the tree or post outside the main gate, because most of the Eastern

Township farmers I interviewed had no English, and in spite of nine years of French I didn't dare stick out my French tongue. My smiles usually drew frowns, which puzzled me sorely, since one of the pleasures of my life in Ottawa had been the friendships I had made with my fellow French Canadians.

In the evenings when we were not playing I tried to help paint sets. After our performance at Magog or North Hatley I would help, willing but weak, carry things out to the truck. Actually little was asked of me. Others had the hard tasks of borrowing or making costumes, borrowing furnishings and props, or carrying the enormously heavy light board down the fire escape of the Haskell Opera House, which was on the second storey of the building, above the Haskell Library. The boys would pack all these heavy objects onto the truck before we went off to Magog or North Hatley for the evening performance, and after the performance was over, at eleven o'clock, they would pack them back onto the truck for the return trip to our base at Rock Island. Usually we arrived home at three in the morning. There was always a ten o'clock call for rehearsal the next day.

The problem of accommodation had been nicely settled by renting a large frame furnished house for the fellows. We girls had the second floor of Mrs Belman's house, and that consisted of three bedrooms. One bedroom held a double bed and another twin beds, and the third three single beds. I was third girl in this crowded room, with its one small clothes cupboard. I never unpacked. Then, by a bit of ear-to-the-ground work, I discovered that the single room with its double bed was about to be vacated, and I quickly staked my claim while no one was looking.

Joy Thomson was in the room with the twin beds. Joy was a night hawk. After we would get back from our out-of-Rock Island performances, Joy would keep her room-mate up till five, playing cards or checkers. I was glad to be in my room alone, because I was having a struggle to keep awake night after night. I had always been a Cinderella; all my lights went out at midnight. But in the mornings I was first up. I would awaken Joy, and after she had cleaned her teeth and climbed into her jeans we were out to breakfast and then to the theatre before ten, ready for rehearsal, and Joy would fume because the others were late!

Joy was a rare person. Of medium height, slim as a boy, she had glamour and chic in her expensive clothes, when she was dressed for an occasion. Her usual attire was blue jeans and a sweat shirt, and she looked well in them. She had a flashing, radiant smile and lovely eyes behind strong glasses. She conversed with an idiom that was entirely her own, and most of her company easily slid into it, which I thought foolishness on their part. "All the actors talk like Miss Thomson," a Rock Islander said to me, sorrowing. Joy's words were accompanied by wild, wonderful gestures. A delight in familiar company, shy in private, she was a despot at rehearsal. Directing a play she'd sit puffing intently on "an old bent cigarette" in a black holder, demanding that her blocking be preserved down to the last square inch, because she had already designed the lighting for the tiny, eighteen-foot "pros opening" stages and she knew every sight angle. God help you if you didn't remember how to hold your head so that the spotlight would hit your face!

Joy was a brilliant set designer. For these small stages and to facilitate travel, she had incorporated into the sets "set pieces" that worked as furniture and yet could be used as storage boxes on the truck. I can see her now in my mind's eye, stippling a flat, climbing with the agility of Tarzan to fix a spotlight, roaring at somebody who had been stupid. She never allowed a prompter in the wings. She thought little of actors, though she was a fair actor herself, and her poor opinion later took on a sharper edge. I was sorry about this, because I think that if you are in the theatre in any capacity you ought to feel love for actors, for the good actors, who, I think, are seldom fools or rogues. As for the phoneys or the would-be's, they admittedly are a poor lot.

Joy and I had great respect and liking for each other. I found her an excellent director, and I did good work for her. When she was directing me, for the most part she left me to my own interpretation, falling about with delight if I was inspired by her appreciation to come forth with a funny piece of business or an amusing line reading.

According to Joy, she had escaped from various expensive girls' schools. In New York she had been a classmate at drama school of Marlon Brando, one of her best friends. There were hopes during early 1949 that the great Brando would come and do a play with us, and I would not have been at all surprised if he *had* come. Joy was a Pied Piper. Her apartment in the Monkland CAT-cum-Funeral Parlour building was simple and utilitarian and scrupulously neat and clean. I made raids with Joy on her mother's fine house in Westmount, her mother being at the summer place in Como, and as we pussy-footed around like secret agents Joy "lifted" various expensive items, whisking them away to use as props, squealing the while, "When mother sees this piece on stage, she'll shriek and fall off her seat in a dead faint!"

I think we all revered Joy, though at times we could have shaken her. You might be playing the leading role in a show that she had designed, painted, directed, and produced, and after the opening-night curtain came down she never would make the traditional director's pilgrimage to your dressing-room to hug and kiss and say, "Well done!" This was not Joy's shy way. I used to take off my make-up, and change, and then go into the bar, and there would be Joy at a table, peering at me with her bright, near-sighted eyes through a fog of smoke, and she would grin from ear to ear and say, "Millie, you *mad woman*! Have a drink." That meant she was absolutely delighted!

One of our most popular productions was *Dirty Work at the Cross-roads*, and it was in this play that I had a most embarrassing accident. As I have already mentioned, the Haskell Opera House boasted a fine roll-drop curtain. At the end of one scene I stepped forward onto the apron of the stage as this curtain rolled down behind me; then, while the set was being changed, I entertained the audience with my soul-stirring rendition of Marie Dressler's song, "Heaven Will Protect the Working Girl." As I got to the end,

> You can keep your upper classes,
> Take back your *demi-tasses*,
> For Heaven will protect the working girl!

I gestured triumphantly and swept out off the stage through the down-right wings, and making a swift turn I nipped back onto the stage behind the roll-curtain to start the following scene. Somebody handed me my hat, and, as I was putting it on, the curtain started to roll up. Now, I was standing with my back to the curtain, and as it began to ascend the hem of my long cotton dress caught in the roll, and the curtain wasn't the only thing that started to go up! Because it was summer I was wearing under the costume only the briefest of panties and a bra. As the audience shrieked its merriment, I saw my whole future flash before me and wondered what would become of me. Would I go right up with the curtain and hang like a skinned rabbit? Or would my gown be ripped from me? Or would my body be horribly broken? These questions were never to be answered, because someone had climbed up to the man on the curtain perched on his platform above the stage, and suddenly with a crash the curtain, and my skirt, came down. Five seconds to marshal my wits, and the curtain was up again. Somewhat breathless but bold, I declaimed my opening line, "How strange it all seems," and the dear audience had the grace to applaud.

The Opera House was also used as a lecture hall, and on the nights when we were not there it was sometimes used by geographers who were assembled for the summer at Stanstead College nearby. The geographers were delighted to have the diversion of theatre, and it was at a party they gave us that I met a man I had admired since I was twelve, the great explorer Stefansson and his young wife. I also made a lasting friendship with Dudley Stamp and his wife. These charming people were interested in Canadian theatre from then on, and we corresponded for twenty years, till his death.

So many other friends came into my life that summer. There was Mary Sheppard, who played the villainess in *Dirty Work*. She acted later at the Canadian Repertory Theatre in Ottawa. Then there was Mary Forde, the daughter of Francis Forde, the Australian high commissioner. Mary had a bright mind that hopped agilely about, and when she had a long wait backstage she *had* to fill the time with life and imagination; so she would usually write. Soon her immediate environment would fade from her mind, and she was liable to miss her entrances.

A favourite Mary Forde story is set during our presentation of an English farce. On Mary's one and only entrance she was to say cheerfully, "Hello! I'm Poppy Dickie." This entrance came very late in the play; Mary had been a long time in her private world, and the quick transition proved to be too much for her. Entering cheerfully, looking luscious, she chirped, "Hello! I'm Poppy Dickie! ... Oh! ... Am I?"

Two other lifelong friends I made that summer were Jeannette and Arthur Virgin of New York City and North Hatley. One night, after the first of our weekly performances at the town hall in North Hatley, a gentleman appeared at the foot of the apron while we were packing up the set and asked if we would like to come to his house for a bite and a drink before setting forth to our base at Rock Island. We accepted, and that was how we came to know the Virgins. They had a lovely old farm-house in North Hatley. Years later Arthur was to buy an old barn nearby and fix it up as a theatre for any company that might play there.

We had two cars that summer to transport the company, Joy's, and a convertible belonging to one of the other actors, Jerry O'Brien. We also had the red truck which carried the sets and props. It was my custom to travel always in the cab of the truck. Much jolly singing filled the after-midnight air as Silvio and Arthur Voronka and I sped along the roads. Once we actually had a night off and decided to go by truck to visit the Brae Manor Playhouse of the Sadlers, at Knowlton, where Malcolm Morley was directing *The Rivals*. The play was opening that night.

Silvio had but a vague idea of the way to Knowlton, and we stopped many times to ask farmers for their advice. "You turn right at the big tree past the third barn and then you see a road on your left and you don't take that but ..." On and on they would drone, clinging to a piece of the truck so that we had to hear them out. Finally we hit what had been recommended as a short-cut (for the time was growing close to curtain up), and this proved our undoing. In its heyday, this road must have been a small stream, now dried up, and we continued over its rocks and boulders past virgin bush for many tortuous miles.

When we finally made Knowlton, they were well into the middle of the play. Chris Plummer was the star of that evening, because he had saved the day. The actor cast as Young Absolute had been taken ill, Chris had been phoned in Montreal, and he had come at once, learning that long role with its difficult eighteenth-century prose on the journey down! Malcolm Morley was so impressed that he asked Chris to join the company he was forming in Ottawa called the Stage Society, under the production banner of Hugh Parker. Plummer was eighteen.

When that summer was over I took a week's vacation in Montreal, dyed my hair with henna just for fun, thinking that henna washed out, went camping with Silvio and his sister Yola and Arthur Voronka, and washed my hair in a lake and found that henna does *not* wash out. So back to Ottawa as a redhead, where I received a severe reprimand from Bill Adkins, my good friend at the Ottawa Drama League. I began to suspect that people were wondering if I was Going to the Bad.

CHAPTER 7

THE GLASS MENAGERIE AND THE EDINBURGH FESTIVAL

After the euphoria of the summer of 1948, I had to come down to earth and confront the limitations of full-time life in the theatre in Ottawa, on leave from teaching. Julie MacBrian Murphy and Marian Taylor were starting a children's theatre and theatre school, and I decided to join forces with them. We got the use of the ODL workshops, and we collected together a company of young and older actors to present plays to children in high school auditoriums on Saturday afternoons. Dorothy White kept watch over our finances.

We opened with *Alice in Wonderland,* a static production that had the youngsters squirming. Next we presented two one-act plays, *The Stolen Prince* and *The Crimson Cocoanut,* and the children loved these, sitting like mice through the first, completely absorbed by the pattern and stylization of the Chinese opera technique, and screaming with excitement during the *Cocoanut* farce. I found myself spending fifteen hours a day down in the basement workshop, enjoying designing my own little sets and painting them, or making props out of two-ply. Our actors were not paid, and though at first there was some indignation on their part because I wouldn't put up with lateness or people not learning their lines pronto, their attitude changed when they saw the results of hard, pro-type work. Mary Burns, daughter of General A.L.M. Burns, was a very hard worker and a splendid actress. Bob Rose was later to become top director of commercials in Toronto at Robert Lawrence Productions. Lillias Cameron, a stalwart of the ODL, came to us as well, bringing her musical Scottish voice, her love, gaiety, and enthusiasm.

Our funds came from the **twenty-five-cent** admission that the children paid on Saturdays. We presented each play for three or four Saturdays. At the end of each month Dorothy White paid out bills, and Julia, Marian, and I were doled out the remainder as our pay. I *think* that one month we made sixty dollars each, another month thirty dollars, and another month nothing each. Dorothy White received nothing but love.

Space and liberty seemed to be beyond my reach in this situation. But just when I was beginning to tire and fret, a Knight in Shining Armour rode up, or to be literal, phoned up, all the way from Montreal. He was Herbert Whittaker, of the *Montreal Gazette*. He was going to do a production of Tennessee Williams' *The Glass Menagerie* for the Montreal Repertory Theatre. Would I be interested in playing Amanda, the mother? MRT would pay me an honorarium to cover some of my expenses while living in Montreal.

Would I?! Joy Thomson had shown great faith in me as an actress. Now another Montrealer was giving me an even bigger chance. Christopher Taylor, seventeen years young, had said of me once at the ODL that I was 75 per cent technique and 25 per cent nothing. And that had been very true. In my heart, I knew that I was now ready to be 25 per cent technique and 75 per cent *guts and heart*.

Silvio was to be the son, Tom, and Herbie had designed a set that reflected both the harsh realities and the memorable quality of the play.

My first acquaintance with the script of *The Glass Menagerie* came at the reading of the play, which took place one afternoon at the MRT. My feeling at the end was: what is it all about? This little world of Amanda and her children seemed completely alien to me. Of course I did not let on. What could I latch on to that would give me a beginning in understanding Amanda? Well, she was *tired*, and so was I. I had been sick, and I walked without energy, my weight going to my heels. This would be Amanda as she returns home, having discovered that Laura has not been attending her classes at typing school. Not much to start on!

Tom's frustration, working at a job he loathed, was a situation I could grasp, as well as Amanda's inner, but unspoken misery for her son's situation. She was frustrated, too. Her love for her children, her courage, her stupidity, her hope springing eternal, her prodigious energy on her children's behalf, her escape into memory to defeat and deny the awful truth of her inability to cope — all these things seem so obvious to me now, but back then they had to be discovered. They were all there in that glorious script, in the idiom of the speech, in the orchestration of the moods. I learned the lines meticulously, sitting on a radiator all day in my very cold Westmount boarding-house room, for we always rehearsed in the evening. I was cold and lonely and far from home, except when I entered the warmth of the Narizzano home, when Silvio and I would retreat to the drawing-room to rehearse our fight scenes and make such a rumpus that his mother would come to see why we were at each other's throats. This was a good sign, because it meant we sounded *real*.

Half-way through rehearsals we changed captains, because Herbie had accepted the call to be drama critic for the Toronto *Globe and Mail* and had to leave at once. We were fortunate in his successor, Roberta Beatty, one of the most respected theatre people in Canada. Bobby was a woman of elegance and sophistication. She was a professional American actor who had married Julius Cohen, a Montreal stockbroker, and she was valued as one of Montreal's best directors. One of the things that Bobby taught me was not to dissipate my energy on stage, to hug it inside my centre, which is what Frances Robinson-Duff had probably been getting at in New York in 1946, when she had accused me of not being inside my body.

I was slight and young to be playing Amanda, but I didn't trouble much about my face. As for my figure, we pinned a large bath-towel around me as a sort of foundation garment, and I filled out very nicely. What I had in my favour besides my fellow actors and my director was my vocal technique, because the part calls for a big voice and a wide range.

The first night was the most important opening I have ever had. I have had more glamorous opening nights since, but none has ever been a *beginning* for me as that one was. Every night, and I think there were eleven, was a revelation. The people who came backstage afterward had often been crying. Throughout the performance we had been aware of that kind of audience tension which finds relief in laughter. The people who came backstage were solemn. "My God, you were so much like my mother!"

It had never occurred to me during rehearsals that Amanda was typical of mothers, though I ought to have realized, since she sprang so readily, once you were on to her, from the guts and from the heart, that she must be a sort of archetypal figure. This constant comment filled me with awe.

The play could not be held over. It had not been seen by hordes of people, because the MRT was a house seating under three hundred souls. That made it an ideal playhouse for that particular play. In a small house, experience can be the more readily shared. Many years later Montrealers who had seen the production had not forgotten it.

During that lonely time in Montreal, when I had the daytime to myself to think about the play, I realized that I must decide whether to return at the end of my "sabbatical" to the security of the Ottawa Collegiate Institute Board. I had had a letter of inquiry from Frank Patton. I sent a half-hearted suggestion to him that I would like the board to consider whether it could create a job for me in which I would travel round to all the high schools, teaching nothing but speech and drama. I think Frank, in his wisdom, must have realized that I was undecided in myself, and a letter came back saying that the board could not see its way to this. There was nothing left for me to do but tender my resignation. I can still see myself standing at the mailbox on a Montreal street corner, lingering while all earth held its breath, until I finally dropped the fatal envelope into the jaws of His Majesty's post-box.

The die was cast. Now I was going to have to wake up to the stark fact that the honeymoon was over. In between rehearsals and performing in *The Glass Menagerie*, Silvio and I walked endlessly through the Westmount and Montreal streets, wondering how one could ever make a living in the theatre. All around, people seemed to be prospering. Was there no place in Canada for such as we? I remember passing windows of offices downtown and Silvio and I staring through at the office workers chained to their desks, and Silvio shouting "Hi, sucker!" while I hurried away.

I had been invited back for the 1949 summer CAT season, and it had been arranged that I was to live in the apartment with Joy and Eddie. Joy was not going to be with us, as she was expecting a baby before the season opened. After the baby arrived, she and Eddie would move out to her mother's house, and I would have the apartment to myself.

This summer we were to be based in Montreal. We would tour every two weeks to North Hatley, to the Haskell Opera House at Rock Island, to the Lantern Inn at Magog, to Lennoxville, and to Ste Adele, Pointe Claire, and Laval sur le Lac. The company was to consist of seven permanent people, and we were to travel in one car and the truck. The senior members of the company were Bruce Raymond, Silvio Narizzano, Arthur Voronka, and myself. The three junior members were Neil Madden, the stage manager, Elspeth Bagg, the assistant stage manager, and Jackie Buck, who acted as well as doing other chores.

Early one morning before we started touring, Eddie knocked on my door to awaken me and announced, "Millie, I am taking Joy to the hospital. I won't be back. The apartment is now yours. Have a good summer." After I got up, I found on Joy's work-table the cutouts she had made that morning so that the wallpaper to be stippled onto one of the sets might be completed by us after she had gone. She had taken care to finish her work before going to give birth to her baby. Wonderful girl.

It seemed less fun all the time. We rehearsed from ten till one in the morning. When the others went out to lunch, I went upstairs to have a snack, just as I had done when Joy was there. Now I was alone, and it was the only quiet break I had during the day.

While I was living alone in the apartment, my mother arrived from Ottawa, intending an overnight visit. She was so appalled to find us working such hours that she stayed a week to look after me. The climax of her visit occurred one night when she stood on the stairs going down to the workshop (or funeral chapel), where Silvio and I were painting flats at three o'clock in the morning, and announced dramatically, "You children stop this at once! You are killing yourselves."

I remember so little about that summer. We travelled a lot in the car, which usually broke down on the way home, but I can recall almost nothing about the countryside. I remember being desperate for a mature woman to talk to. The other two girls in the company were in their teens, exceptional girls, but given to weeping, or so the boys told me. I had got *my* weeping over in private.

In mid-summer a light appeared on the horizon. Early in 1948, during the period when I had been deciding to stop teaching high school, I had appeared for the ODL in a one-act play by Robertson Davies called *Eros at Breakfast*. We had presented this at the Dominion Drama Festival, which had taken place in Ottawa that year. Now the ODL was asking me if I could go in the play to Edinburgh to perform during the 1949 Festival. All expenses would be paid, and we were to be the guests of the Scottish Drama League. We would leave in mid-August.

I was beside myself with excitement. I had promised Joy that I would be with the tour for a ten-week season, but in the few weeks remaining they could well do without me, and I knew Joy wouldn't refuse me the chance to perform at such a prestigious festival. I packed up for Edinburgh in great anticipation.

The little reconnoitring force of Canadians arrived in Edinburgh in August 1949, not to take the British stage by storm but to test the temper of the natives toward Canadian theatre. It was comprised of Robertson and Brenda Davies, Gwendolyn Burden Blair, Michael Meiklejohn, Carl Lochnan, Ian Fellows, Bob Rose, and Amelia Hall. The cast and two directors had travelled over on the *Empress of France* and rehearsed on the billowing waves. Grant Macdonald had designed the decor, and our sound effects man, Geoffrey Evans, who had returned to England in late 1948, now joined us in Edinburgh to do his stuff.

It was raining that morning in Liverpool, and I heard one lady aboard remarking to another, "We're home, dear!" In the station the porters pushing luggage carts cautioned loudly, "mind your nylons!" I laughed and could have wept, too, because of all I felt to be back home in England.

We had been met aboard ship at Liverpool by the British Council and driven around to see the unexpected delights of Liverpool, and the bomb damage, and to admire the social planning of Lord Leverhulme's Port Sunlight. We were shown a magnificent new concert hall, and the man in charge, after displaying the perfection of the acoustics, remarked, "I suppose this is nothing to what you have over there." I was touched by his humility and naiveté.

In Edinburgh we were billeted in a university residence. People from the Scottish Community Drama Association were in charge of us, and Robert Buchanan and his wife, Christina, were our special guardians. They had two little boys, one of whom had played the week before in *Macbeth*. When Rob Davies asked this child what role he had played, the boy replied, "You wouldn't know the part unless you'd read the play."

With the company of Norwegian amateurs who performed a one-act play along with ours from August 22 till September 10, we were so much entertained that on occasion I began to flag and fail. One early morning, beginning a special bus tour of Edinburgh under the guidance of an eminent academic, I fell asleep in the front seat, in ten minutes, right under the gentleman's scholarly nose. On another occasion, as I was leaving an ugly modern restaurant building at Loch Lomond, along with two Norwegian friends, photographers began to click their cameras. I was astonished and flattered that so quickly in the theatrical profession I was making my name. But when I saw one of these pictures later on, I realized that the cameras had been whipped out to record two Norwegian giants with a little thing in slacks walking between, standing no higher than their waists.

The highlight of our visit was Tyrone Guthrie's production of a sixteenth-century Scottish satire, *The Three Estates*. This was presented in the Assembly Hall, with the audience seated around three sides. Thus this hall inspired Guthrie with the idea of a theatre such as he and Tanya Moiseiwitsch created in 1957 at our Ontario Stratford. I was amazed at Guthrie's handling of crowds. How hilariously funny he had made the play, and how clear the satire, although the language sounded almost foreign to our ears. If only I might work with such a director, I thought, never dreaming that in four years' time I would do just that.

In this production I saw Douglas Campbell for the first time and appreciated his versatility when I saw him the same week playing in *The Gentle Shepherd*, presented at eleven o'clock at night, after all the other theatres had closed. At ten o'clock I arrived at the Assembly Hall, which was not a theatre really, but a beautiful, eighteenth-century Assembly Room. The building was surrounded by a queue. One word from me that I was from Canada, and those near me were more concerned about *my* getting a ticket than about getting one for themselves. The word was passed on, and so was I, till I was at the head of the queue! I got a ticket and it cost one pound. Stunned by this large expenditure, when intermission came I decided against spending on refreshments and kept to my seat. Too late I learned that a champagne supper was served at intermission to holders of one-pound tickets.

On our final playing day in Edinburgh, we were given a farewell luncheon, and the master of ceremonies stood up and said, "All we can say to you Canadians is: welcome home!" The Scots all sang, "Will ye no come back again?" and since this seemed to call for a reply, I started our lot singing:

> Yes, we will come back again!
> Better loved we have nae been!
> Yes, we will come back again!

(I for one did go back, in 1956, with the Stratford Festival Company to play a wordless part in *Henry V* under Michael Langham's direction and to play a daughter of Oedipus under Guthrie's direction, both plays presented in the old Assembly Hall.)

On September 13 and 14 we were in Glasgow, playing at the Athenaeum Theatre, under the auspices of the Glasgow Torch Theatre Club, along with our Norwegian friends and their play. *Eros at Breakfast* was given a better reception there than anywhere else. The Glasgow audiences were great. The respected English critic Philip Hope-Wallace, of the *Manchester Guardian*, wrote about us in the *Globe and Mail*:

> Let us face it. The Third International Festival of the Arts, which has just finished in Edinburgh, was a success. Canadian participation in it was not. Not,

that is to say, a success which called attention to what Canada could offer in an international concourse ...

It was in every way a pity that this excellently cast and excellently played production of *Eros at Breakfast* cut so little ice. Robertson Davies, its author, was a disciple of Tyrone Guthrie, one of the festival's special heroes, and on that score alone one might have supposed a greater general interest.

But the searchlight of publicity played elsewhere and at least one admirer of the Canadian amateur theatre movement must have felt that almost any other town (or Edinburgh at any other time) would have extended a more inquisitive welcome, and provided a better setting, for this slight but highly diverting little one-actor.

The performance though in fact amateur, was a good deal more professional than some of the acting seen during these three weeks. By all accounts it was superior to other performances hitherto seen in Canada, but it did not draw the crowds or the notices it deserved. The whole company is to be congratulated and, though it is late in the day to single out special performances, no one who saw Miss Amelia Hall as Hepatica can doubt that at its best Canadian acting has style. Her performance was a little gem of sharp comedy.

After Edinburgh, I decided to visit London. Eric Workman had warned that after the First World War London had gone downhill and that after the Second War the city had lost the last of her charm. Well, London had charm for *me*. But I arrived, in mid-September 1949, undecided whether to be a tourist or an actor.

Because I had no idea how long I would stay, it was necessary to be careful with money. On the advice of someone at my Bank of Nova Scotia in Ottawa, I had come abroad with pounds instead of dollars. No sooner had I set foot in Britain but the pound sharply devalued. I pinched pennies, cancelled my planned trip to Italy, and eventually returned to Canada with most of my money still in my pocket. Which was a pity. Like Noel Coward's Carrie, Millie was a Careful Girl.

Two weeks at the Central Club YWCA, Great Russell Street, convinced me that its services had not recovered since the war; after eleven days I complained that my bed had not been changed. My plan for morning ablutions was to wait till the rush of work-a-day traffic was over and then claim the bathroom in peace. This was a forlorn hope, for tacked to the bathroom door was a notice stating that this door was only unlocked between such and such hours.

Flying from the nest of the YWCA, I took a large, ill-furnished room in Hampstead. Having learned that the proprietor was connected with the Boltons Theatre Club, I felt I was reaching out to touch the hem of Thespis's garment. Actually I saw this Boltonian only once, when he came up with a requested iron, and thank God I had the grace to accept it without complaint, though it was solid iron and could only be heated on live coals of which I had none.

How cold we poor, thin-blooded Canadians are in England in autumn! It took a good three hours of the gas fire's efforts to make that large Hampstead room habitable. I would escape momentarily from my bed in the morning to turn the gas on, and then the bed would claim me until I could accept the room's temperature. Next stop was to pluck up courage to venture out into the arctic corridor that led to the bathroom.

I possessed two sleeping outfits. The first was a large flannel nightgown plus heavy skiing socks. When laundered, this outfit hung on a cord in a corner of my room for three or four days and nights while drying, and meanwhile I slept in my second sleeping outfit, my skiing underwear, which I had had the foresight to bring. Returning to my room at night, I would pull up my bed to within two feet of the gasfire, and bend over the fire, my fur coat on my back, the bed open in the hope that I could heat it, reading famous murder trials for two hours till room and bed seemed warm enough! Then out with the light and under the covers. In ten minutes every tooth in my head would start to ache.

Mornings the best thing to do was to get outside as soon as possible. Mornings were usually quite lovely. There was that lyrical English mistiness, and the smell of autumn, as welcome as the smell of autumn in Canada, yet quite different. It was intoxicating. It lifted my spirits. Outside it was not cold.

Canada House was a home to all of us who were visiting, and the sight of the Red Ensign there at Trafalgar Square, and the Scottish voice of the big doorman, all spelled out welcome. Here we left messages for one another, picked up mail, read papers from home.

A Streetcar Named Desire had just opened at the Aldwych Theatre, starring Vivien Leigh, Renée Asherson, and Bonar Colleano and directed by Laurence Olivier. Tickets, except for rush ones to the gods, were impossible to obtain. So I arose at six in the morning and arrived at the box office by eight. First in line. At one o'clock the box office opened. In the mean time we queuers would get acquainted. People asked me, "How do you like this old London of ours?" I told them truthfully that if ever I was completely alone in the world I should feel least lonely of all in London. We relieved one another to go for coffee or to go to the loo. The morning was nippy, and my feet, shod in elegant nothings, were very cold. Yet it did not matter. At one o'clock I bought my ticket, which guaranteed me a queue stool.

At six o'clock I was back with my ticket to pick up my stool, and we all sat in the alley, two by two, in line, waiting for the box office to open to sell us our tickets to the gods. While we waited we were entertained by some of London's street performers — jugglers, vocalists, instrumentalists alone or in trios or quartets — and each passed the hat around at the end of his act. The one I will always remember was a Dylan Thomas type with a fine voice who recited Andrew Marvell. Loudly into the evening air he proclaimed that "The grave's a fine and private place / But none, I think, do there embrace." Then the side doors were flung open, and we scrambled, hell for leather, up the steps to get a good seat on the benches. The play, the performances, were all worth the long vigil.

Robert Beattie introduced me to Bonar Colleano in a restaurant where every other face at the luncheon tables seemed to be known to me from English movies. During the long run of *Streetcar*, Renée Asherson left and the role of Stella was taken over by a Canadian actress who had been sent to study at the Royal Academy of Dramatic Arts by the IODE in Saskatchewan. The rest of us in Canada had not yet heard of Frances Hyland.

I immersed myself in the London theatre that fall of 1948. There was *Daphne Laureola* by James Bridie, with Edith Evans and a young Peter Finch. Edith Evans, drinking brandy after brandy and at last walking across the stage, supposedly over a covered bomb hole, so magically drunk and so drunkenly graceful that one wanted to call out, "Let her walk again! Let her walk again!"

There was Peggy Ashcroft breaking one's heart in *The Heiress*, with Ralph Richardson, and a maid played by Pauline Jamieson, with whom I would act six years later in *The Merry Wives of Windsor* at the Stratford Festival. And, although I did not know it, Peggy Ashcroft had a little son who one day would direct Eric House and me in *Little Murders* for Theatre Toronto.

At the Lyric were John Clements and his wife Kay Hammond, both with charm to burn, playing *The Beaux Stratagem* by Farquhar. Paul Scofield, elegant Isobel Jeans, and Ian Hunter were in *The Seagull*, while Flora Robson cast her magic over a play called *Black Chiffon*.

85

At the Globe, John Gielgud, Richard Burton, Claire Bloom, Pamela Brown, Harcourt Williams, Peter Bull, Esmé Percy, and others equally good were in *The Lady's Not for Burning*. Afterward I went round to see Gielgud, with an introduction from Herbert Whittaker, and stayed about twenty minutes, while he talked animatedly nineteen to the dozen, much of it about his idol Edith Evans.

And when I could no longer endure life without the sound of some Canadian voices, I went to hear Barbara Kelly and Arthur Hill in Thurber and Nugent's *The Male Animal*. Afterward I went backstage. I cannot recall why; maybe I wanted to say hello to a fellow Canadian. If so, I must have lost courage, for I just stood about. Yet it had not been difficult to pay my respects to Gielgud.

Then there was *Death of a Salesman*, with the well-known film actor Paul Muni as Willie Loman. The English audience did not seem to be sympathetic toward Willie. At any rate, around me people were critical of the American way of life and seemed to lack compassion for the awful tragedy of the American Dream. I remained in my seat till the theatre was empty and then walked to the tube with leaden feet.

It was about this time that I met a young man from Montreal, to whom I had an introduction. He told me how to go about "doing the rounds" in London. He introduced me to *Spotlight*, a magazine for actors, which listed useful information, such as the names of agents. I wrote to many of these, sitting in my Hampstead room, and the results were satisfying, probably because of the splendid notice that I had received from Philip Hope-Wallace when we were in Edinburgh. I quoted that review in my letters. This lad from Montreal had no work himself. He lived from hand to mouth in a tiny room, frequently borrowing. It seemed to me that I would prefer to accept any kind of honest work that would bring in money, rather than live like that.

Soon after, I got a telephone call from Kenneth Carten, the agent of Myron Selznick (London) Ltd. He had been the most pleasant and well-bred of the agents whom I had gone to see. He had looked a long time at the few pictures that I had taken him of myself in plays, and now he had a job he wanted me to inquire into at Kew.

I set off to the Q Theatre, opposite Kew Bridge tube station. This small theatre presented revivals of West End successes. The week of October 25–30 it was going to do nine performances of *The Glass Menagerie*, and it needed an Amanda. That was why Kenneth Carten was sending me to see the director of the production, Terence French.

At the Q I was handed a published copy of the play, the same edition that we had used at the Montreal Repertory Theatre. I chatted to Terence Noble and the manager of the theatre, Mrs Jack de Leon. She thought I was too young; Terence French didn't. I was offered the role at a fee of ten pounds. No audition. I was quite surprised. As I left the theatre, French ran after me and handing me a *typed* script, said "This is the version of the play that we will be using." I was on my way to a quick dinner and then to *Cosi fan Tutte* at Sadler's Wells. On the bus, on the tube, while at dinner, in the intervals at Sadler's Wells, all this time I was reading French's script; *Cosi fan Tutte* was merely an unfortunate interruption. I longed to finish the script and quickly know the total, horrible worst. Radical changes had been made; scenes had been added or merged, speeches had been deleted, and anything very American and so not to be understood by the English had been cut out!

At the first rehearsal, French and I spent the entire day arguing. A deceptively mild man, he refused to budge an inch. He said calmly that he had been stage manager for the Gielgud production starring Helen Hayes and he knew what did not work. Even Helen Hayes could not get away with the jonquil speech, so how could anyone else? He had used his own version on tour, in which he himself had played Tom (ghastly thought!) and Betty Love, now in *Salesman*, had played Amanda, and it had been very successful.

I returned to my Hampstead digs and phoned Kenneth Carten. "Mr Carten, I cannot take part in the murder of a masterpiece."

In his quiet, English way Kenneth Carten reasoned with me. He asked me to realize that not every day did an actress come to England from abroad and within two or three weeks land a role like Amanda. He begged me to put up with the script. I did. Looking back, I marvel that I was allowed to work, for I did not belong to British Equity, nor to any union. I was paid ten pounds, which was not bad.

I discovered that professional actors rehearse in horrible places. We were in a wretched room above a pub. The Tom in our production was Walter Crisham, a well-known revue artist, often partner to Hermione Gingold, and he was a lot older than I and had grey hair. That did not matter. What was disconcerting was that he did not seem to care a fig about the play. It was just another engagement before something important came along. However, he was the master of a dachshund that was completely theatre-broken, and this dog would wander around the wings but never, ever, walked onto the stage. That *did* impress me.

Amanda's daughter, Laura, was played by a fine American actress called Helen Backlin. Helen had been in the long run of *The*

Chiltern Hundreds and was doing well in London. Helen and I flatly refused to do one little two-handed scene French had added. The Gentleman Caller was an actor who had played the role in the tour of the provinces. When I asked him why he was staring at my forehead on stage, he informed me that no actor ever looks into another actor's eyes!

The first night, Kenneth Carten came back afterward, which someone told me was a great honour. He said he had preferred this production to the one in the West End. He thought I would be very foolish to return to Canada.

During the course of that week's nine performances I had only two other visitors, those nice people, the Dudley Stamps. I could have hugged them. My "erstwhile colleague," as he called himself, Saul Rae, of our External Affairs, and his wife, Lois, got my written appeal to come the day before we closed, and Saul was abed with flu.

Betty Love came backstage after the last matinée and visited everyone but me, the stranger within the gates.

Meanwhile, letters from Silvio kept me in touch with what was happening in Canada. There was talk of setting up a new company in Ottawa, to be called the Canadian Repertory Theatre. It appeared that Silvio had been asked to join it, as he wrote:

> It seems Malcolm Morley kept quite a few of the old gang [from the Stage Society] up there. Probably because they had built up a following and it would give a sense of continuity to the new company. Bruce says I should join them because from financial end the company is good. He says he can't reveal all (a real business manager attitude) but he implies their program and plans are big and well heeled. I will go if Morley calls me (I think)...
>
> Malcolm offered you $30 and only acting. He also said in his letter that you were definitely joining him.
>
> Before I forget, Doreen Lewis said 3 weeks ago that she would like a definite answer from you middle of November. If you say YES she will have work for you Xmas term. If NO she must look and plan for a replacement — ...
>
> I hope so much for you because of everyone I know you have done the most and deserve the *mostest* and have had so little in return.

But I don't like your being in London alone, unless of course you're having a mad time and living in SIN (which I hope you are). And I wish you were here to have long talks with.

I will be happy if you can find some way to stay and happy the sooner you return.

It was news to me that I was joining the Canadian Repertory Theatre! But one thing I did know — I wanted to go home. *The Glass Menagerie* closed on October 30. I had received an invitation to visit Oslo, to meet Norwegian actors, and a few days later had an audition with H.M. Tennent, who seemed impressed. But I had been in London seven weeks, and that was enough. It was time to go home. So I said a fond good-bye to my relations in Leeds, took passage on the *Empress of France*, and was back in Canada by mid-November.

PART THREE
THE CANADIAN
REPERTORY THEATRE
1949 — 1953

CHAPTER 8

UNCERTAIN BEGINNINGS

When the ship docked in Montreal, in mid-November 1949, Silvio met me and took me off to the Narizzano home in Westmount. That night, sitting at dinner around the groaning board, lively with family and friends, I told the sad tale of how much I had hated the production of *The Glass Menagerie* at the Q. Silvio was mocking me, saying I now sounded terribly British, when the telephone rang in the hall cloakroom and behold! it was for me.

The caller was Malcolm Morley, from Ottawa, and he had tracked me down to ask if I would play Aunt Abby in his coming production of *Arsenic and Old Lace* at the newly formed Canadian Repertory Theatre (CRT), in Ottawa. Rehearsals would start on November 30, and the play was to run December 6-10. Malcolm had seen me as Aunt Abby at the Canadian Art Theatre when we played our season at Rock Island, the summer of 1948.

I said that I would like to come and do the role. That would give me two weeks to finish my Montreal visit and go home to Ottawa and see mother. But I fully expected to return to Montreal to do some teaching for the Montreal Repertory Theatre. Instead I went to the CRT to play for one week and stayed over four years, with no holiday.

What was the Canadian Repertory Theatre Society Incorporated, and how had it come into being while my back was turned in England? To answer those questions we must first take a look at another organization, the Stage Society of Ottawa.

The Stage Society was founded by Hugh Parker, a former RAF intelligence officer who had arrived in Ottawa in 1946 and deplored the lack of indigenous professional theatre even in the capital of Canada. Hugh Parker soon became active on the Ottawa theatre scene. In December 1946 he wrote and produced for the Ottawa Drama League a Christmas pantomime called *The Crystal Garden*. In April 1947 he stage-directed at the ODL a production of *Joan of Lorraine*, directed by Malcolm Morley. This gave him the opportunity to discuss with Malcolm his plans for a repertory company in Ottawa.

This company became a reality in late spring of the following year, and on May 10, 1948, the Stage Society opened its first production, *While the Sun Shines*, by Terence Rattigan, at LaSalle Academy on Guigues Street. Seats in the orchestra were a dollar and those in the balcony were fifty cents. Twenty-nine people turned up opening night. Among those who had been invited but who did *not* attend was Viscount Alexander of Tunis, the governor general. Nine weeks and nine productions later, when the same play was repeated, the governor general and his wife were in the house, along with two hundred members of the diplomatic corps. By then three hundred Ottawa citizens had bought tickets for the second set of six plays (six dollars for six), and "Canada finally had a professional theatre that was a going concern," reported *Time* magazine.

The second season had started on September 21, 1948; thirteen or fourteen productions took the company into early January 1949. Christopher Plummer joined the group for this season, and for the first three weeks he did chores backstage as well as appearing on-stage. Robert Barclay also came, while Jacqueline Fielding and Betty Lewis and young Richard Lamb played occasionally. At Christmas, Peter Sturgess, who had been understudy to Robertson Hare, England's leading farce actor, joined, and Gertrude Allen also made her first appearance. Evelyn Goodier was appointed general manager, and Dale MacDonald was in charge of publicity. Sam Payne, John Atkinson, Joyce Spencer and John Hardinge had joined the company at the beginning of 1949, and somewhere along the line that spring Penelope Sparling came in as scenic artist, with Paul Charette as carpenter.

Right from the beginning, the financial position of the Stage Society was precarious. Hugh Parker himself acknowledged that four individuals had given the society substantial financial help. According to Beatrice Whitfield, Dr Yates, an Ottawa chiropractor, contributed $1,500, and she herself donated $600 when the Parkers were nearly broke. Mr H.S. Southam, publisher of the *Ottawa Citizen*, and Charles Southgate, of the International Paper Co., were the other benefactors.

Hugh Parker also thought that some of the problems of attracting support derived from the building itself. The only theatre the society had been able to find was the auditorium of the LaSalle Academy, a Roman Catholic boys' school. At that time the space was not in use, and when the Stage Society rented it, it consisted of a bare stage, space down in the basement, and none of the backstage facilities that most theatres of even modest size provide. Parker also felt that the location was too out-of-centre for Ottawa theatre-goers, especially in winter, though, goodness knows, it was only ten minutes away from the Chateau Laurier.

It is difficult to pinpoint the exact time when the financial crisis began to become public knowledge. Certainly, by the summer of 1949, during the third season, Penny Sparling realized that her weekly cheque was not making its usual appearance. Patrons of the theatre became aware of the actors' plight, and some brought food to the theatre. On July 6, Hugh Parker sent out a circular letter, asking for donations to clean up the standing debt of $3,000.

While all of this had been going on, from May 1948 until September 1949, I had shown little interest in the Stage Society. I had seen perhaps two of its productions, when I had returned to Ottawa from the Eastern Townships in the fall of 1948 to almost non-stop toil at the Junior Theatre. I did not ask Hugh Parker for work, nor did he offer any. As soon as possible in 1949 I returned to Montreal and was away there or in England till after the death of the Stage Society.

Although I scarcely knew Hugh Parker, and never worked for him, I acknowledge a debt to him because he got a professional theatre started in Ottawa. Perhaps it is just as well that he did not realize how very difficult a task he had set himself, or he surely would never have taken the first step. Perhaps like so many "ideas" men, he was lacking in business expertise. But even had he been clever in the handling of money, even had he been fairly well off himself, he would not have found the road an easy one.

He was the first to roll the stone up to the top of the hill. It rolled down and all but crushed him. It was fortunate for a great many people in Canadian theatre that someone else, namely Charles Southgate, had come along who was foolhardy enough to attempt to roll the stone back up again, he too hoping that it would become the cornerstone of a national theatre.

For it was the feeling in certain quarters that while Hugh Parker was to be commended for having brought together a group of very talented people in the hope of building a professional theatre, his lack of financing skill was causing the money to be swallowed up as fast as it came in. With the demise of the Stage Society, however, those who had given it financial support did not wish to see the end of professional theatre in Ottawa. All the people who had worked so hard, and eventually for so little financial reward, were left "stuck there like sitting ducks," as Mrs Charles Southgate was to describe it to me long afterward. Mr Southam suggested to Charles Southgate that if Charles would put up $2,500 to back another theatrical enterprise, he himself would put up $5,000. So they went to the Bank of Nova Scotia and gave their note for these amounts.

The new organization received a federal charter of incorporation on September 9, 1949. Thus it was that exactly one day before the curtain came down for the last time on the Stage Society, the Canadian Repertory Theatre Society became an established fact.

Mr. Southam was to be the sleeping partner, Charles Southgate, our very active patron and guide. Charles Southgate had come out to Canada as a young man before the First World War. When the war started he joined the 21st Battalion and went overseas with the 2nd Contingent. He became a staff-sergeant and then was wounded, after which he was attached to the Medical Corps and stayed in England till its office was closed. During this time he met and married Violet Richardson, whose family were friends of the Southgates. He and Violet came to Canada in 1921, and he remained a year with the Medical Corps, as an accountant closing up the books in Ottawa. At the end of that year he was demobilized and took up his accounting career again with the Beaver Co., first at Lachine and later in the United States.

In 1927 the Beaver Co. amalgamated with another firm and Charles was out of a job. He was fortunate to be taken on by International Paper. He and Violet were delighted, because they had longed to return to Canada. After three years in Montreal, by 1930 they were back where they had started, in Ottawa, where Charles became assistant sales manager and eventually president of the sales company of International Panel Board, a subsidiary of International Paper.

The first public announcement of the formation of the new theatrical company was made not by the sponsors but by Malcolm Morley, on September 19, 1949. He announced that the entire company of the defunct Stage Society had been taken over by the Canadian Repertory Theatre Society and that the winter season of this company would open in October.

The CRT first opened its doors to the public on Saturday, October 1, 1949. The play was *Quiet Weekend*. The program introduces three men who would constitute the CRT's management committee: Malcolm Morley, Reginald Malcolm, and my old friend of ODL days, Eric Workman. Malcolm Morley would serve as director of the plays and also as general administrator. The other two members of what was sometimes called the operating committee would act in an advisory capacity.

All three had been in the theatre all their lives. Malcolm Morley had worn many hats: writer, actor, director, critic, adjudicator. He had become known abroad for his work at the Everyman Theatre, Hampstead, of which he was director from 1927 to 1931; there he had produced Ibsen and introduced to the public Strindberg's *The Father* and a number of European playwrights. In the United States he had worked in films and on-stage, and in Canada he had adjudicated at the Dominion Drama Festival and, of course, had directed in Ottawa and Montreal.

When I joined the CRT, Reggie Malcolm was ill and not in evidence. After a long career in the British and the American theatres he had retired to Ottawa to live with his son, but the Stage Society had claimed him and he had become its senior member. Reggie's acting debut had been made at the St James's Theatre in London with Sir George Alexander. During his years on the English stage he had appeared with such great names as Henry Irving, Mrs Patrick Campbell, Sir Gerald du Maurier, and Dame Sybil Thorndike; in the United States, under the sponsorship of the Theatre Guild, he had toured with Philip Merivale and Gladys Cooper and had acted with Katharine Hepburn, Helen Hayes, and Ethel Barrymore. Reggie was the greatest raconteur of theatre stories that I have ever heard. Theatre was his life's blood.

Eric Workman had established himself as a singing teacher and concert artist in Canada when he settled in Ottawa during the war. He had an imposing appearance — large pink face, snow-white hair, a dignified carriage. As Eric looked, so ought a duke to look. He had sung opera and given recitals in France, Switzerland, Holland, Italy, and in his native London, where he had played the lead in the original *Lilac Time*.

The tenure of this triumvirate was going to be brief at the CRT, but I did not know that when I arrived at LaSalle Academy. Something else I did not realize for weeks was that in the cellar, like a diamond hidden in the earth, was someone whose influence on CRT was to last for a longer time, though, alas, not long enough. This was the designer, Penny Sparling.

Penny came out from England early in 1949 to stay one month in Montreal with her Canadian relatives. At the end of the month she didn't want to leave, and she heard of Malcolm Morley's association with the Stage Society in Ottawa. Malcolm offered her the job of scenic designer and painter at thirty dollars a week. She was delighted. At her first arrival she had fallen in love with Ottawa. During the war she had been in the British Women's Land Army, and immediately after peace was declared she went to the Old Vic, then in Liverpool, and asked to be put to work as a student. There she learned theatre backstage. When the Old Vic returned to London, the Liverpool theatre was taken over by the Liverpool Repertory Theatre, the oldest rep company operating in England. She became its scenic artist.

At LaSalle Academy, Penny found herself working in a cellar below the theatre, in a huge room with an earthen floor; the light was so poor that there were sections of that cellar that she never could explore. Equipment was scarce, and nobody, Penny used to say, at that time in the Stage Society, really knew anything about set painting. She had two helpers — the little carpenter Paul Charette, with his wit and his perpetual grin, and a huge half-Indian boy called Bert, with whom she enjoyed some wild canoeing on the Ottawa River. Bert was amazed that an English woman could handle a canoe so well.

Rats scuttled about in the dark corners of the paint room. "The rats and Paul and I cohabited," as Penny put it. In spite of this, these three oddly assorted people enjoyed life in the cellar. Admittedly the uneven floor made it difficult for Paul to get a true angle when he was working wood, and the "size" which at that time was used to mix paint came in such big toffee-like chunks that four hours were needed to melt it on the tiny electric burner Penny installed. Stage flats are made of canvas stretched over a wooden frame. These flats were painted with water paints that have to be mixed with size. If the set called for a handsome embossed wallpaper, Penny, unlike Joy Thomson, did not use a stencil for the patterns — that would be too slow and cumbersome; she would simply create the pattern with her nimble brush. She never used the colours as they came out of the tin but blended the powders till she got what she wanted. She liked blue or buff for a background and found green flattering to actors, as I do myself. For comedy she liked a light background and for drama a dark one.

If the paint job on the flats could not be completed in one day, that same batch of paint had to be reheated the next day, and overnight the colour would have altered and they were in trouble. Sometimes discrepancies in the colour would not show up till the flats were on the set and lit, and then Penny would take them back down to the cellar and do the work over again. The flats at the Stage Society had so much paint on them that it would "go cancerous" and peel off. Normally flats are discarded when they reach this point of deterioration, but there was no money for new flats and Penny conceived the idea of scrubbing them down with hot water. The flats had to be placed on trestles, since the ceiling of the cellar was too low to stand them up, and as Penny and Paul and Bert splashed about with hot water on the ageing flats it ran off on the dirt floor and formed mud! From then on, large heavy planks were put down and they walked on these. The many coats of paint under the application of hot water blended together and formed a base for the next fresh coat of paint.

Penny said that no matter what suggestions Malcolm made to her about the colours he would like on next week's set, he always ended up wanting a sort of mid-brown. This became a company joke.

Penny was at the Stage Society when there was not money for the salaries, but it took her a while to notice. She was enjoying herself, and had met David Geldart, production manager for the Film Strip Division of the National Film Board.

It does not surprise me in the least that Penny was at home in a canoe. She had the eyes of one who looks over wide outdoor vistas, a dreamer's eyes, and she was immensely practical. There was something of the wood nymph about Penny, and the house in the countryside outside Ottawa, which eventually she and David were to build, was a suitable background for Penny, under wide skies and surrounded by trees. She was vivacious, outgoing, frank, and honest, yet elusive and secret: very English and young for ever.

When I arrived in December 1949 Bruce Raymond as business manager seemed to be the one fixed star in the behind-the-scenes firmament. Credits in the early programs show there had been some shuffling around of personnel, but Dale MacDonald had finally settled down as assistant to the business manager, as well as actor; David Haber was stage manager, and actor on occasion; Claire Perley-Robertson was property and costume mistress; young Charlie Brennan was assistant to Paul and Penny; and Joyce Spencer, a London cockney, was assistant stage manager, and acted as well. The two electricians, Roy Sylvester and Don Torney, were the only people who worked at something else "in the daytime," and they appeared at the CRT for dress rehearsals to do the lights.

David Haber had arrived at the CRT in late 1949 for the second production, J.B. Priestley's *An Inspector Calls*. He had studied ballet in Quebec City where he had lived with his sister, and ballet was his first love. From ballet he had turned to drama, and that had taken him for the first time to Brae Manor Playhouse, where he had found his forte in stage management. That was in 1948. He was to return to Brae Manor every summer after that, and he was to help Madge Sadler run the place after Filmore died, until the property was sold in 1956 and the theatre there was pulled down.

Most of the actors who had been with the Stage Society stayed on. They were joined by others. Anna Cameron arrived after education at Elmwood School in Ottawa, Brae Manor Playhouse at Knowlton, some study in New York, the Lorne Greene Academy of Radio Arts in Toronto, and Hart House Theatre in Toronto. Gwen Dante of the Army Show was at the CRT on her intended way back to England. Janet Fehm, from Catholic University of America in Washington, DC, where she had worked and studied under Walter Kerr, was the only American.

When I reported for rehearsal of *Arsenic and Old Lace* at LaSalle Academy, the CRT had just opened the play *Petticoat Fever*. In its cast were Anna Cameron, Derek Ralston, Sam Payne, David Haber, among others, and my dear old friend from the ODL, Lillias Cameron, playing Little Seal, an Inuit, in what I was informed was an outrageously smelly costume. David Haber also played an Inuit. I saw one performance, and in the last act, when some of the actors "broke up" and giggled a lot and were more amused than the audience, I was *appalled*.

By this time the CRT had already produced seven plays, and Malcolm Morley had directed them all, one a week, each running for six performances, Tuesday to Saturday, with two performances on Saturday.

My salary at the CRT was to be twenty-eight dollars a week. This was just about one-quarter of my earnings during the last year I taught high school. I believe this was the general salary for women under Malcolm's management. Betty Leighton started out at the Stage Society at fifty dollars a week and at the CRT may have received forty or forty-five. I suspect that the other women received the same pittance as I did. Malcolm had a large cast of women permanently in the company. During the weeks I worked under his management the company grew to include Joanne Baker, Gertrude Allen, Betty Leighton, and Barbara Field, and there were guests such as Jacqueline Workman, Lynne Gorman, Beatrice Whitfield, Norah Hughes, and Kay McVicker.

The actors included Sam Payne, the Englishman John Atkinson (a fellow Yorkshireman), Peter Sturgess, and Derek Ralston. On occasion others were jobbed in, such as the two management members, Eric Workman and Reginald Malcolm.

It was while we were rehearsing *Arsenic and Old Lace* that I learned that Brian Doherty was bringing his production of the same play to the ODL's Little Theatre, shortly after the close of our CRT production. I knew that Malcolm must have been aware of this fact, and I was led to suspect that he had decided to do the play for that very reason: to get it on ahead of Brian. I was angry with my old friend; he ought to have appreciated that the more theatre there is, the more theatre thrives. I was all for stepping out of *Arsenic,* but of course I didn't. I could have, because we had no contracts at that time, but one's word is more binding than a piece of paper, and I did not make the grand gesture. Perhaps it was just as well to learn right away that in the theatre many people you like are going to do many things you don't like.

I must confess that I can recall nothing of opening night. It presumably went off well. Malcolm asked me to stay on indefinitely. The following play was to be Sutton Vane's *Outward Bound,* one of those modern morality plays in which a group of people are shut up in one place and a Being appears who interrogates them. We were all shut up in a ship, which one presumes is the Ship of Death. I was to play a rich old girl called Mrs Cliveden-Banks, and I needed that English accent that Silvio had claimed was more pronounced since my trip abroad. My effusive opening line in act I was to a young man played by Derek Ralston. "I saw your name on the passenger list; so I came to the bar at once! And here you are!"

I was absolutely terrified on opening night. It was one thing to appear in *Arsenic and Old Lace* as Aunt Abby, a role I had played before with success, but another thing to rehearse in six days a brittle role demanding finesse and sophistication. I felt I was on trial. All went well, though, because in that first scene in the bar Derek *willed* me to succeed. He was a most generous actor, and always so well prepared, that he gave me the confidence I needed. Week after week Derek was doing long roles, and always his lines were solid. Know your words, as the old actors would say.

It was during this production that I began to develop a talent for character make-up. For Mrs Cliveden-Banks I made up my face with grease-paint, all light and shade, to look very old. I put pink on the lower lid above the eyelash to make my eyes look pink and old. Then I powdered over this old face with talcum, John Atkinson having told me not to use tinted powder on a character make-up; then I made up this old face with dry rouge, eye-shadow, lipstick, and false eyelashes! I don't recall what I did with my hair (we had no wigs), but I probably covered it with a hard red dust, or gold dust, which I'd wash out every night. My clothes were elegant, perhaps made out of the tat we kept around the nether regions of the CRT. All this must have been effective, because on opening night, when I was all ready and nervously sitting in the so-called Green Room, Bruce Raymond hurried through like the White Rabbit on some errand, turned and said, "Good evening," and went on his way. Ten minutes later he came through again, stopped in front of me and exclaimed, "It's you! I thought you were some elegant visitor."

Anna Cameron and John Atkinson played a pair of pathetic lovers, and in one scene, when Anna came on-stage in a state of panic, seeking her lover, and calling "Henry! Henry!" the theatre cat strolled nonchalantly out of the cabin door. She sat on the apron of the stage, washed herself, yawned or just watched through the whole dénouement of the play, while white-haired, dignified, handsome Eric Workman, in the guise of the Reverend Mr Frank Thomson, interrogated all us misguided or sinful souls.

It was necessary at LaSalle Academy to have a theatre cat. When I arrived I was told horrendous tales of rats that were so bold that they appeared on the proscenium apron during performances, but I cannot vouch for this. Certainly we had a cat most of the time that I was there. If the cat wandered on-stage during a performance, an actor would take her up gently and eventually hand her over to David Haber in the wings. During the years that I directed at CRT, our cat would on occasion come and sit with me and would lick my hand or arm, and I would break into a rash, or sneeze. I have much respect for cats, but for a long time I was allergic to them, perhaps because I had never made their close acquaintance, my mother being one of those of whom Shylock speaks: "Some that are mad if they behold a cat."

About this time I wrote Silvio to announce that I was not enamoured of the CRT, that it was "tatty." He wrote back to say sternly that I ought to stick with it for a while and it would do me good:

> Let's rationalize. You are interested in Theatre with a Capital T. The closest you will get to it in Canada is right there in Ottawa. Yes, I think the CRT is 5th, 4th, 3rd rate but it is (let me repeat) it *is* professional. I think that it can teach you a hell of a lot. I think you're better than what it offers. But it still can teach you a lot. It's just about the only type of experience you haven't had. A couple of months of it, half a year of it, even a year of it — what then will you not be able to tackle? O yes it's frustrating, O yes it's sketchy, o yes

each production isn't what you want it to be. But what a time to crystallize, to know and discover what a production could be, will be.

Now Montreal. What about it? Teach here? You've done it all before and know that you can do it again. Direct some groups here? You've done it all before and know that you can do it again. If you have to feel noble in order to do good work why not take this attitude: the only way the CRT can become tops or National is for it to have the best. The better it is the bigger the audience, the bigger the audience, the more money, the more money the possibility of better actors being employed etc., etc. ...

There were many things that disturbed me about the company. I didn't like actors coming to rehearsal looking as if they had not had time to shave or to put on make-up. Some looked like that. Just as on-stage you ought never let the audience see that you are working hard, so in life you shouldn't look as if you are about to drop dead. I was revolted by the downstairs quarters, where two dressing-rooms, one for the men and one for the women, had been panelled off from the disorderly Green Room. This whole area needed a good cleaning out, and redecorating. It was incredible how much litter had collected in the short space of two months, since the CRT had opened. Sam Payne was for ever taking a broom and seeing what he could do about the Green Room floor. "If seven maids with seven mops swept it for half a year ..."

Malcolm Morley had his own little corner, an office in a tiny windowless room, which, after he left, we were to make into the storage room for costumes. Here Malcolm sat most of the day, writing (so Bruce once claimed) about thirty personal letters a day; or else he was trying to decide which play to do next week. I always marvelled that the scripts arrived in time for rehearsals, if it was true what I was hearing about Malcolm's inability to make up his mind. He was not always present at rehearsals. He sketched in the blocking the first day and then left it to the stage manager, David Haber, for two days, before he returned to look us over. David was a wonderful audience, but when you have only a week in which to rehearse you like to have the director there all the time.

We next did *Little Women*, and I got to play Aunt March, who is about eighty-five, a good part to play, and only one scene, too. But it is hard to be playing Aunt March when you feel like bursting out of your cage and playing Jo.

I was for ever deciding what I would do with my nose, my hair, my figure, for the next character part. I would even make plans before I had read the play, and after reading I would have to begin all over again. How I longed, though, to be under forty for a week! Nay, under fifty! It was not so much that I pined to wear pretty clothes and to look beautiful, but I wanted to have wings occasionally and to move and speak with grace and speed. We are as old as we feel, and an actor on-stage feels the age he or she is playing and can carry that feeling off-stage, too.

It must have been while I was playing Aunt March that I went off after the show one night to a New Year's party at the Australian high commissioner's. As I left the theatre in my evening attire and on the arm of a beau, Malcolm grinned and said, "Your heart is young and gay, eh?" I regret to admit that I was not amused. It is wretched to be tied to character roles simply because you can do them. After all, one can play such roles for years and years till the day one retires, if ever one *does* retire, but the younger roles one cannot go on playing indefinitely.

At that time all the Canadian actors, or almost all, were young. We played all ages. How fortunate we were, in that one respect, here in Canada. We stretched ourselves in every kind of role, becoming every age from twenty to a hundred, and those of us who could encompass variety in styles and in age benefited and grew in theatrical stature.

CHAPTER 9

THE THREE OF US

We were now well into January 1950. I do not recall when it was that Eric Workman first broached to me — at a gathering at his own house, over a drink in the corner — that he and Charles Southgate and the other members of the CRT's board of directors were anxious to reorganize the whole thing and place young people in charge, Canadian young people. He asked me if I would take on the role of director of the CRT.

I was astounded. I knew that Eric himself had liked working under my direction at the ODL, and indeed much of my success as a director I owed to him, because, though I was young, he had *treated* me as a director. I now explained that since I was new at professional theatre, and the actors in the company had been at it professionally longer than I, some of them much longer, I did not know how they would accept me. I told him I would think about it.

When next I had an opportunity to talk to Eric, I suggested that it might be a better idea to have two directors, and then we could take turns directing and thus not be overburdened. Under this system both directors could also act on occasion, if needed. I expressed to him my trepidation about accepting this job behind Malcolm Morley's back, because he had been my friend and the instrument in taking me to Montreal and opening up a whole new world for me in theatre. Eric said that if a new policy were not agreed upon the CRT would surely die, and this I could see.

In the mean time the CRT chugged along. In *No Time for Comedy*, by S.N. Behrman, and the last play Malcolm directed, Betty played one of her smart, sophisticated roles, and I was, of all things, the black maid, surely one of the last people in the world to play in black-face! It seems incredible now that back in 1950 we could not get a black actress to play it. I had a trying time mixing blue and brown to try to get myself the right colour. Clementine is a good role, and I was inadequate.

I do not know when Malcolm was told about the new plans. I believe he received a letter. I think he must have been immensely relieved. He had felt himself trapped at the CRT. It must have been for him a hard come-down from his earlier years, to be directing and managing a company so thinly staffed for the production of weekly stock, and in a country where it was not easy to entice people into the theatre. Those who had talked with him daily claimed that he believed the enterprise was doomed to fail. He had seemed to be half-hearted about the whole venture. He later married and went back to England, from where he often sent me loving messages by friends.

The new plan was that Sam Payne and I should be joint directors and Bruce Raymond would continue as business manager. This triumvirate would be the management. We three would also sit on the board, plus four others: Charles Southgate, president; Gordon Hughes, vice-president; George Perley-Robertson, lawyer; and Kenneth Hossack.

This triumvirate was celebrated in a song devised by Derek Ralston, which went like this:

> I get no kick from Sam Payne,
> Amelia Hall doesn't thrill me at all,
> Raymond is only a Schmoo!
> But I get a goose out of Bruce.

Actually the company received us very well. I was quite surprised when one member said that I was the most mature person in the company, and so ought to lead it. It gave me confidence to hear that, whether it was true or not.

The astonishing feature of the board of directors was that it seldom met. We three were left on our own to plan. We were never badgered. Never having been in the position before, I did not realize how lucky we were! Of course, the most amazing thing of all was that we were actually *on* the board ourselves! This was in 1950, and yet in 1967 I was at a meeting called by the late, astute Peter Dwyer to see what could be done about theatre in Toronto, and one of our recommendations, for all artistic enterprises, was that artists be on the boards. Are not hospitals run at least in part by doctors? Why are there no longer actors on theatre boards? I was told in 1970 that I would have been invited to be on the board of the National Arts Centre, but this idea had been turned down because I might on occasion perform there!

One of the first priorities for the new management, clearly, was to encourage a regular audience, responsibility for which fell heavily on Bruce Raymond's shoulders. The program in those early days consisted of a single folded sheet of heavy paper with ring holes cut in the fold to encourage the customers to keep and file them. On the front cover was the CRT crest, and below it the words "The Crest of Good Theatre." Almost from the beginning, the back page carried an ad for Ogilvy's department store, and above it appeared the CRT manifesto:

Your Canadian Repertory Theatre

is Ottawa's 'own' professional repertory company, and one of the few all-professional theatre groups in Canada. Its weekly plays are designed to provide, at popular prices, legitimate stage entertainment of a high calibre to the theatre-going public of the nation's capital.

However, important though the providing of entertainment may be, it is not the sole reason for ' CRT's ' existence. It has a dual function — the providing of stage entertainment and, more important still, the building of an audience that attends the playhouse through a love of theatre.

By creating in our city a consciousness of the value of drama in our cultural life, and by providing careers at home for at least a few of our country's actors and actresses, the Canadian Repertory Theatre feels that it is contributing in no small way to the growth of the inevitable National theatre.

Next, Bruce began his practice of putting inside the folded program a "Prompt Sheet," which gave the public information about plays to come. These chatty, informal bulletins were valuable in creating in our audience the feeling of participation in the future of the CRT. Here is part of the first "Prompt Sheet," on February 21, 1950:

'C.R.T.' Changes Policy!!

Three weeks ago, you and your friends assisted us in completing a survey of what you want most in your own community Theatre. You chose certain plays for us to produce, you made suggestions, and even complained a little. From that moment forth, the C.R.T. changed its policy. You, the audience, became the determining factor in running your Theatre and we, the artists and management, determined to work harder than ever to bring to Ottawa plays worthy of your interest.

Our problem is to get more Ottawans to come to the C.R.T. plays. Once they come, they usually come again. In spite of our advertising in the newspapers, radio, handbills, and direct mail, we believe 'word of mouth' advertising is the most important. If you really enjoy our plays and want us to continue to serve you with good wholesome entertainment, won't you please tell others —

START A REAL HONEST WHISPERING CAMPAIGN!

The price of admission in 1950 was hardly prohibitive. On Tuesday opening nights there were special discount prices of *three shows* for $2.85, $2.15, and $1.80. From Wednesday to Saturday there were special discount prices of three shows for $3.25, $2.40, and $2.00. Thus a single person could attend three opening nights for as little as sixty cents a performance, or could attend three Saturday nights for as little as sixty-seven cents a performance! Saturday night was the most popular, and opening night the least; perhaps an audience thought we'd know the words by Saturday night! Of course, our productions *were* at their best by the end of the week, but we were not as a company weak on our lines at the opening.

The first production decision that Sam Payne, Bruce Raymond, and I made, as soon as we knew that we were to be the operating committee, was to send for Christopher Plummer to come back to Ottawa. Chris had become a matinée idol while working with the Stage Society, but Malcolm had refused to have him at the CRT. Bringing him back for the opening production under the "new management" was a decision that pleased the public. Chris was an actor who could give headaches to management, which was why Malcolm did not want him back, but, as a member of the Stratford board of governors once remarked to me, "When I see him on stage I don't give a damn about the headaches!"

The opening play was to be *The Glass Menagerie*, and Sam was to direct it. The setting that he and Penny Sparling decided upon was dark and enclosed, like the set that had been used on Broadway. I have played Amanda six times, but never in a set that I liked as much as the set that Herbert Whittaker designed for our production at the Montreal Repertory Theatre. That set had a dream-like quality.

The first night was a memorable occasion. The audience began to applaud right at the beginning, as Christopher walked down the aisle through the house to climb the fire-escape steps of the set onto the stage. Years later Sam Payne recalled that opening night, "and the tumult caused when the lights went up on Chris, smiling as only he can, at the audience who appeared to idolize him — or so it seemed — as he came back to the theatre in that play." There were cheers and a standing ovation at the end, and jonquils were handed up to me, and champagne backstage, "in appreciation of a fine cast for an exceptional performance." There was a little set of glass animals for me from Eric Workman! "May these wee beasties bring luck on the first night of your new venture. May you go on and prosper for many moons to come." From Silvio Narizzano in Montreal (my son, Tom, in the Whittaker production) came a telegram addressed to Mrs Amanda Wingfield, c/o Bruce Raymond, saying, "Hello. Goodbye," and signed "Father." Among the good wishes was a telegram from my mother:

EVERY SUCCESS TO AMELIA SAM BRUCE AND THE COMPANY OF CRT.
ELIZABETH ANN

I thought: "Isn't it lovely! Everything will be like this from now on." Present to cheer us were Charles Southgate, Reginald Malcolm, and Eric Workman.

The glow did not wear off altogether — it was rekindled at the beginning of March, when Silvio sent me a very complimentary letter, and told me what Chris had said to him, and the remarks of both pleased me mightily:

I think I wrote you a letter which I never mailed
which was devoted to extolling your Glass Menag-

106

erie. To be brief I think you were not *good* because this is a term we are always applying to actors when they surprise us by being better than we expected. I knew what to expect, but instead I discovered something like, I suppose, pouring your heart out over a collected work of Van Gogh's reproductions and years later taking that trip to New York, walking into the Modern Museum, climbing the steps to the V.G. Room, entering into focus and suddenly there it is — there it is. And was it the way you expected? (turn page for answer) 'NO'.

I think Chris paid you a wonderful compliment, though it is rather discouraging for us mortals. He said, 'When you play with Millie you don't have to act. You just re-act.'

Your performance had SURPRISE and this is the whole secret of acting. Surprise! Surprise! Surprise! You're probably mad now and think I'm talking about sensationalism. No. I'm talking about imagination.

The review *The Glass Menagerie* received from Lauretta Thistle, Ottawa's most knowledgeable critic, and one not easily given to superlatives, was further cause for rejoicing:

Ottawa hasn't seen such a magnificent piece of theatre for months. The Canadian Repertory Theatre's performance of The Glass Menagerie last night was a momentous achievement.

Magnificent and *momentous* are high-powered words, not to be tossed off lightly, but nothing less will do to describe this presentation. This is a fine play, written with rich insight and sensitive feeling for the complexities of human relationships, and it offers opportunity for imaginative staging. These challenges have been met with brilliant success by the young actors and by producer Sam Payne.

From those first moments when Christopher Plummer as the narrator prepared the audience for something a little different from the conventional play, to the last moving scene when he eased us back to reality ('There my memory ends, and your imagination begins') the performance had a magic quality. This was exciting theatre. .. The writing of Amanda's part is superb, of course. This richly etched character, so bereft of spiritual resources and so incapable of facing reality is an acting 'plum'. And Amelia Hall was the actress who knew how to exploit its possibilities!

Perfectly convincing in her rages, she was equally impressive in her moods of infuriating martyrdom and self-accusation. ('My devotion has made me a witch.') The changes in her face as she felt the fraying rags of her gentility slipping from her, or as she snatched them back to shelter her self-esteem, were something to marvel at; here was an actress whose transformation came from within.

Christopher Plummer's return to Ottawa could hardly have been made in a more favorable role. His delivery of the prologue, interludes and epilogue was eloquent, unselfconscious, and sensitive to the poetry of the lines. He had the skill to handle the high-tension scenes with his mother. And always he projected the sense of his helplessness, his confusion, and his despair at ever finding that peace of mind which was 'lost in space'.

Derek Ralston's performance as the Gentleman Caller, the symbol of hope deferred, was also a great triumph.With great sensitivity he traced the character of the Caller — a limited fellow, able to perceive suffering, anxious to help, but incapable even of solving his own personal problem.

And what of the poor colorless little figure, the girl who lived in the dream world of glass animals? Janet Fehm gave a superlatively good performance, one that will live in the memory of this reviewer for many days.

Staging and lighting were as important as characterization in this play, and they were equally well handled. Imaginative use of different sections of the stage, blocked off by lighting, added immeasurably to the vividness of a most absorbing evening.

Cheers, tremendous applause and curtain call after curtain call assured CRT that Ottawa welcomed this venture into the works of Tennessee Williams. Judging from this enthusiasm and from the unusually large first-night attendance, we can venture to predict that the public will demand that this play be held over for at least another week.

Immediately after *The Glass Menagerie*, Sam directed Rose Franken's comedy *Claudia*, with Janet Fehm and Anna Cameron, while I was preparing for my first directorial assignment. This play was to be Ruth and Augustus Goetz's *The Heiress*, an adaptation of Henry James's *Washington Square*, about a young woman who loses her lover when her father threatens to disinherit her. This was the play that I had admired so much in London, with Peggy Ashcroft as the affection-starved Catherine.

I don't recall where the costumes came from for *The Heiress*, but they were good. We did not have the luxury of our own costume designer, wardrobe, and staff. Whatever costumes or modern clothing the public donated to us were kept in inadequate quarters below stairs, but for costume plays we usually rented from Malabar's. Penny's drawing-room set was excellent. I have never known a designer better at interiors.

Yet I was disappointed in my production, because I remembered too well the perfection of the London presentation. Jacqueline Workman Hyland played Catherine. I had directed her at the ODL before she had gone to study at RADA in London, after which she had worked in England and then had married. Tall and beautiful, she had a charm and vivacity that came from her French mother. But while Jacqueline was rehearsing this role she seemed abstracted and listless, and I felt it must be some personal concern that was sapping her vitality. I knew that she was capable of much more than she gave. It is a strange fact that sometimes, when an actor is feeling deeply some personal emotion, his or her work will suffer on stage. One must always be more aware of the character one is playing than of oneself. There are those who practise the so-called Method who will not agree with me. An actor must not be swamped by his or her present state of being. He or she must be energetic enough for the conscious mind to be alert, and relaxed enough for the unconscious to break through.

In weekly stock one has to learn fast. People like Derek Ralston and Betty Leighton were fantastic studies. As all our regular audience knew, Sam was not, and most of the time the public did not mind his occasional fluffs, because of his great warmth and charm.

I suffered at rehearsals because, as Catherine's father, Dr Sloper, he was having such a bad time with the lines of his biggest scene and because he was so angry with himself. I discovered right away in this first production that the one great headache for a director of weekly rep is an actor having trouble with the words.

The critics liked the play, and I was not displeased myself. I had just wanted it to be superb, that's all.

The Saturday-night performance was sold out. So an appeal went out in our next Prompt Sheet:

> Saturday night continues to be our capacity house. May we suggest that some of our Saturday patrons come earlier in the week? We always feel sad turning away people who can only come to the Theatre on Saturdays. Of course, Season Tickets are one sure guarantee of a seat every night!
>
> So many letters have poured in demanding another week of *The Glass Menagerie* that we are sorely tempted to make an exception in our no-holdover policy. A few more letters will decide us. Have you any opinion on the matter?

February 28 we opened *The Voice of the Turtle*, but I was busy preparing Patrick Hamilton's *Rope*. This drama of suspense is about the deliberate murder for kicks of a young man by two of his friends, who invite the dead boy's family to a buffet supper which they serve from the box in which the body is lying.

I had decided that the room would be green. I then heard that green was a most unlucky colour to use on a set. I ignored this superstition and continued to ignore it through the years. At the National Gallery of Canada I went to Kathleen Fenwick, in the prints department, and got permission to borrow reproductions, framed, of paintings that I thought would give "class" to the apartment. In England the previous winter I had seen *The Third Man*, which hadn't yet reached Canadian movie houses. I was determined to use *The Third Man* theme, which nobody in Canada seemed to have heard. Finally I tracked it down in Myre's Music Shop.

I thought that Plummer and Ralston were delightful in *Rope*. Since one of them has to play the piano, we provided a grand piano on stage and had the pleasure of hearing Chris play. The critics were not enthusiastic about the play. R.B. Coates of the *Ottawa Journal* wrote: "What weakened this play was the preoccupation with detail. There was too much business with the lights and too many trips to the sideboard for whiskey. At times it developed into a parade and the audience became more engrossed with watching the whiskey level fall in the decanter than in the outcome of murder for a thrill." He seemed to think *I* had written the play!

The houses were disastrously poor. Bruce Raymond tried to comfort me with the news that even the local cinema had done rotten business with the Alfred Hitchcock film. I couldn't keep away from the theatre, ready to choke at the sight of the tiny house.

Right after *Rope* I tackled Lillian Helman's *The Little Foxes*. This ought to have been pie, since I had already had experience of the play in Whittaker's splendid 1948 production at Brae Manor. When the books arrived from the royalty house, they consisted of a tattered old prompt script, typed, and "sides" for the actors. I foresaw disaster, and to avert it I invited the cast to my house for their evening off, a sort of party (!) and I handed out the sides, and we read the play out loud, so that we would all know what the thing was about. Anna Cameron had the role of Regina, Sam and Derek were the heavy brothers, and Chris was my lounging, pimply son, for I was to play Birdie as well as direct. John Atkinson was the invalid husband of Regina.

In this production I did the unforgivable thing — I brought my own problem on to the stage, to sap my vitality and my creativity. Swimming as I was in a sea of personal and professional worries, and never having time for a good cry (always a tonic for me), I decided that in scene 1 in which Birdie is too miserable and frightened to say a word to her in-laws, I would let myself have a nice, quiet cry in the corner. I did just that. This CRT Birdie bore no relationship to my Brae Manor Birdie, who had raised a tear in the eye of one or two of my fellow actors. When I had played the Brae Manor Birdie, I had been relaxed and happy.

We pulled out of the tatty doldrums of that production the following week with the blessed reappearance of Betty Leighton as the silly movie actress in *Personal Appearance*, directed by Sam, while I played the tiny part of the actress's secretary, my mind on *Rain*, which I was directing the next week.

Gertrude Allen now rejoined the company. I had not met Trudy before. She was from Welland, Ontario, and like myself had studied with Clara Baker. She, too, had a degree in Speech and Drama from the Toronto Conservatory. In 1946 she had won the Brickenden Medal as best actress at the Western Ontario Drama Festival. Trudy had worked at the Stage Society in 1948 and had appeared in the fall of 1949 in the first CRT presentation, *Quiet Weekend*. She was small and had lovely brown eyes, a good figure, and a splendid voice.

111

The physical atmosphere of a play excites me. I plunged into *Rain* with gusto, agog to create a mood of heat and rain and eastern torpor. This play is founded on a short story by Somerset Maugham. Christopher Plummer played the onlooker, Dr MacPhail, and he was the spitting image of the middle-aged Maugham. Chris never used much make-up, though in this play he did put on a beard; but he could be completely believable as a middle-aged man, even if he had to wear his own clothes. He was nineteen at this time.

The second day of rehearsal, Wednesday, I produced the sound effects of rain and tropical birds, as well as Sadie's gramophone. Chris complained that it was impossible to concentrate on the lines amid all this clatter. I was adamant, saying that we had to get used to the background sounds at once, or they might "throw" us at the technical rehearsal. I suspect I was just enjoying being thorough. At the CRT, from the second rehearsal day on, we always worked with props. Of course the actual props that we were to use on the night did not appear till Sunday or Monday, and indeed sometimes not till the last rehearsal on Tuesday morning, but there always had to be a substitute.

Betty Leighton, in a complete reversal from the extrovert actress she had played the week before, was the missionary's wife, such a compassionate study of a repressed woman that I remember it above all the other performances.

Anna Cameron as Sadie was at her very best as the girl reformed by the missionary. I had decided when I was casting for amateur plays that actors are often at their best when you cast them against what people think of as their "type." Anna was always being cast in extrovert types, like the Sadie of the first act. But it was when we glimpsed her as the reformed, almost angelic Sadie that she shone. Any producer who type-casts actors knows nothing of acting and not very much about the human psyche.

Everybody had to be commandeered into this production. Stage manager David Haber and Bruce Raymond were army types, property mistress Dorothy Hamilton was a native girl, our dependable friends Ivor Jackson and Joan Hossick were natives. Even Trudy Allen, who was always at her best when smartly gowned, was good enough to cover her face and arms and legs with native tan as Sam's native wife. Lynne Gorman, who lived in Ottawa, came into this production, the first time I had directed her since ODL days. She was one of our best and most popular and most reliable actresses. There were two sinks in a corner of the Green Room downstairs, but we boasted no shower, so these heroes and heroines had to wait to wash off after they returned home. Pretending you are in the tropics at the end of March in Ottawa *is* heroic.

When she was ten, Amelia studied elocution with Vere Blandford Rigby, and in 1927 appeared as Cinderella in one of Mrs Rigby's "Recitals." (Inset) Amelia at age seven, taken in Leeds, England, during one of the periods in her early childhood when she and her mother returned to England.

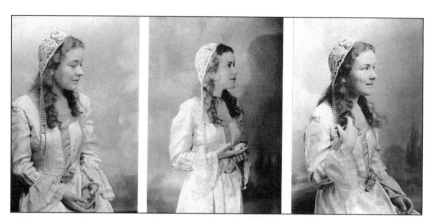

Amelia as Juliet in scenes produced in 1933 by her voice teacher Clara Baker.

Graduation from McMaster University in 1938.

Amelia as Madame Arcati in Noel Coward's *Blithe Spirit*, the Ontario Drama League's entry in the 1947 Dominion Drama Festival. *Photo: A.A. Gleason.* (Inset) Mrs Clara Baker, taken during her retirement, in 1971.

Governor General Viscount Alexander of Tunis visits backstage at a production by the Stage Society in Ottawa.

When the National Film Board were looking for someone to play a neurotic teacher in their film *Who Will Teach Your Child?* Amelia suggested she play the role, and the film was a great success. *Photo: William Doucette*

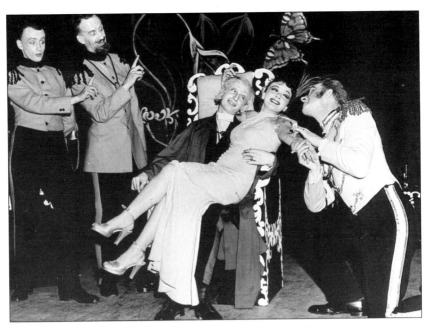

In 1949 Amelia went to Edinburgh with the Ottawa Drama League to play in Robertson Davies's *Eros at Breakfast* at the Festival. *Photo: Capital Press Service*

The Canadian Repertory Theatre team in action: William Boyle, author of *Days of Grace*, Sam Payne, and Amelia Hall. *Photo: Bill Newton*

(Above) The 1950 CRT pro-
duction of *The Glass Menagerie*: Christopher Plummer
as Tom, Amelia Hall as
Amanda, and Janet Fehm as
Laura. *Photo: Robert C.
Ragsdale*

(Right) Amelia Hall in one of
her favourite roles — Nora
in *A Doll's House,* seen here
with Eric House as Dr Rank
in the 1951 CRT production.

The CRT company, 1949-50: l. to r. Gertrude Allen, Derek Ralston, Amelia Hall, Dorothy Hamilton, Christopher Plummer, Betty Leighton, Dale MacDonald, Janet Fehm, Sam Payne, Bruce Raymond, John Atkinson, Charles Brennan, Penelope Sparling, Paul Charette, David Haber.

The CRT company, 1950-51: l. to r. Bob Barclay, Silvio Narizzano, John Howe, Mary Sheppard, Donald Glen, David Haber, Jane Graham, Bruce Raymond, Amelia Hall, Sam Payne, Penelope Geldart, Paul Charette, Gertrude Allen, Eric House, Ron MacDonald, Peter Sturgess, Michael Gardner.

(Above) William Hutt, Bill Shatner and Barbara Chilcott in the 1952 CRT production of *Castle in the Air. Photo: Bill Newton*

(Right) Leif Pedersen, who came from Denmark to join the CRT, and served as stage manager until 1954.

A rare quiet moment at home, when Amelia could indulge in her favourite hobby. *Photo: Bill Newton*

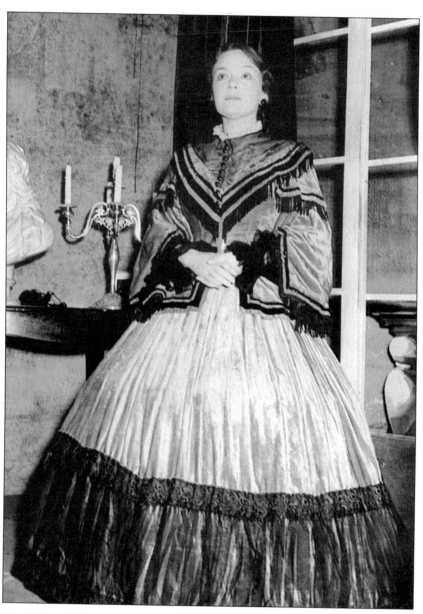

To celebrate the coronation in 1953 the CRT mounted an ambitious production of *Victoria Regina*. Here is Amelia as the young queen.

Stratford 1956: former CRT actors gather for a group photograph. L. to r. back row: William Shatner, Christopher Plummer, Richard Easton, Donald Davis, William Hutt. Front row: David Gardner, Max Helpmann, Ted Follows, Amelia Hall, Eric House, and Bruce Swerdfager.

With Tyrone Guthrie at Stratford. In the midst of construction of "The Tent," Amelia and Judith Guthrie are dressed for a reception only one week before opening night.

The first Canadian and first woman to speak on the Stratford stage: Amelia Hall as Lady Anne and Alec Guinness as Richard III. *Photo: Peter Smith*

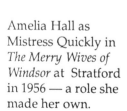

Amelia Hall as Mistress Quickly in *The Merry Wives of Windsor* at Stratford in 1956 — a role she made her own.

Always popular with young audiences, Amelia is surrounded by students in her dressing room at Stratford, 1964. *Photo: Peter Smith*

Amelia's mother Elizabeth was an indispensable support in the frantic life at the CRT. This dramatic photograph of Christopher Plummer as Antony in the 1967 Stratford production of *Antony and Cleopatra* is inscribed with affection to Elizabeth. *Photo: Douglas Spillane*

Emily Carr, in the play by Herman Voadon, was one of Amelia's favourite, and most successful, parts. *Photo: George Lilley*

Queen Victoria again: with John Wayne as Lord Chippendale and Frank Schuster as the butler in a CBC TV sketch, Christmas 1975.

Amelia Hall appeared at Niagara-on-the-Lake for several seasons. Here she is seen in the 1975 production of Shaw's *Major Barbara*. *Photo: Robert C. Ragsdale*

The cast of *Tartuffe* at Stratford, the last time Amelia appeared on the Festival stage. *Photo: Robert C. Ragsdale*

In 1975 Amelia returned to Delta Collegiate in Hamilton for the school's 50th anniversary concert. This photo was taken during rehearsals.

By this time Holy Week was upon us. We were eventually to learn that it is wise to close for Holy Week, but at this stage we were full of good intentions and did our bit by presenting a play with a religious theme, *The Servant in the House,* by Charles Rann Kennedy.

My personal mood had been much more holy while we were rehearsing *Rain,* for I had stood in the balcony excited by the atmosphere we were creating and thanking God in little prayers that soared to Heaven on the wings of my joy that I was at last doing what I wanted to do. I was already aware that in spite of the problems, worries, and disappointments that each production brought, it was a heady excitement to have fallen into this wonderful way of life, in which every week, or at any rate every week in which I was directing, I could inhabit a completely different world. I think the director is more aware of this than is the actor. Directing, if you do it conscientiously, uses all your powers — your seeing, your hearing, your feelings, your knowledge collected over the years. You relate what you are doing to the other arts, to music, to painting. You carry the play around with you every minute till you hand it to the audience on opening night.

In the spring Sam directed five plays. We did not take turns directing; it really all depended on which of us was needed to play a large role, and of course sometimes a particular liking for a play would make one of us ask to direct.

One of those plays, which opened on May 2, was the first Canadian presentation of Terence Rattigan's *Playbill,* which consisted of two one-act plays, *The Browning Version* and *Harlequinade.* The film of *The Browning Version* had not yet appeared, and nobody in Ottawa seemed to have heard of this singularly moving play. Chris Plummer's performance as the middle-aged, unsuccessful school-master was extraordinary. During his moment alone on stage, when he breaks down and cries, I used to stand in the wings, waiting my re-entrance as his unsympathetic wife, Millie Crocker-Harris, and listening to him I would nearly break down myself.

Derek played the wife's lover. It was on the opening night of this play that Derek had not arrived at the half-hour, eight o'clock, when every actor has to be in the theatre. He arrived just at eight-thirty, in a state of great agitation. With no time to put on the moustache he was wearing for his role (probably to give him age), he drew one on his face with black pencil! I stood with him in the wings while we awaited our entrances. He made his entrance and carried on well, trouper that he was. I entered, and kissed him passionately, wondering all the while if his black-pencilled moustache would be on my upper lip when we came out of the clinch. By some freak or fortune it was not.

We must have been exceedingly busy in the intermission, getting ready for the second play of the evening, *Harlequinade*. This is a comedy about an elderly actor-manager (Chris in our production) and his wife (myself), who with their company are rehearsing the balcony scene from *Romeo and Juliet*. The Saturday before we opened, Chris and I appeared on the front cover of the *Citizen's* weekend supplement, Chris climbing the balcony as Romeo, in a terrible tattered wig, his legs enclosed in loose tights to give the impression of shrunk shanks, and me in my blonde wig and Juliet cap, my face made up to look old and then remade-up with the aid of dry make-up and enormously long eyelashes to look young.

Derek, playing the role of stage manager, walked through *Harlequinade* grinning from ear to ear and carrying a clip-board, on which he had written conveniently all his lines!

Attendance was poor. A friend of mine told me that she had a sister in Ottawa who boasted that she did not need to go to the CRT because every year her husband took her to New York for two weeks where she could see all the plays done by *professionals*. Those who did come that week could boast afterward that they had seen Christopher Plummer at the age of nineteen playing a magnificent Andrew Crocker-Harris.

Not that I was altogether pleased with Chris that week. He had a habit of coming to the theatre early, often with friends who had to be asked to leave at the half-hour, and then on occasion he would merrily fool around till nearly curtain time, when he would discover that he had insufficient make-up and could not find his costume. At the CRT we of course had no dressers. I remember Chris not being able to find all the bits and pieces of his Romeo costume for *Harlequinade*, and the frantic efforts of some of the backstage people to locate them. I can see Dorothy Hamilton in the wings helping him into his doublet, which she had searched out for him, and myself thinking, "If only these women would stop helping him he would help himself, because nothing in the world means as much to him as going on-stage and doing a good job." In truth, though, the circumstances were at fault, not Chris. An actor ought not to have to worry about his costumes.

It was our custom at the CRT to have the actor who played the leading role give a curtain speech, especially on the closing Saturday night. The speech was a thank you, and usually something was said about next week's play. In *Harlequinade* Chris gave this speech and did it in character, as the actor-manager of the tatty rep company. On the final night he stepped forth and said a few words, ending his speech somewhat in this manner: "and I hope to be back here ... one day ... with a FAR BETTER COMPANY!" This took all of us by surprise. No comment was made. I couldn't have liked it more.

Of course something had to be said to Derek about his arrival on opening night just before curtain, giving the entire company the horrors. Bruce and Sam asked me to undertake this task. We women are notably cold-blooded, and men dislike being unpleasant. It was arranged that I meet Derek the following day in what had been Malcolm's office. We were both in a state of nerves. Derek immediately announced that he wanted to resign. I longed to say, "It really doesn't matter!" But he was adamant. We would miss him very much, not only on stage, but backstage, where his sense of humour was one of the delights of life.

One night that winter I was free to attend a play at the ODL, where for so many years I had been more at home than anywhere else. Moving through the crowded foyer, I stopped to speak to one of my favourite amateur actors, whom I had directed a number of times. To my surprise, he looked at me, more in anger than in sorrow, and said, "So you've gone over to the CRT." There was also a day of Ottawa sunshine when I met Herbie Fripp, president of the ODL; looking at me with those flashing blue eyes that could come across the footlights like a neon sign when he acted on stage, Herbie croaked at me, "Millie, I could kill you!"

Did this mean that ODL membership had gone down? Funny if it had, for I have always felt that the more theatre there is, the more each theatre thrives. But as time went on, great rapport was established between the ODL and the CRT, and many of the actors there came to play at the CRT when we needed a big cast, and flats were lent to our designers and help was forthcoming from Bill Adkins.

Chris left us after our production of Emlyn Williams' *A Murder Has Been Arranged*. There had been in him an increasing restlessness. Everybody knows he looked like Laurence Olivier. At one rehearsal he amused himself (and us) by playing his role all day as if he were Olivier. So convincing he was it seemed almost an impertinence to give him direction. Throughout *The Importance of Being Earnest* he was very naughty, probably because the production grated on his nerves, as it did on all of us. Actors are never easily satisfied, and if they dislike the play, or the mounting of it, or the direction of it, they are difficult to placate. We all felt tatty in *The Importance*, and Chris retaliated in various ways. In a scene we shared he spoke straight out to the house; so I retaliated by doing the same. I had heard of his tricks at the Stage Society, but he had never tried any on me. In a scene with Lady Bracknell, he muttered under his breath all the time she was talking, attempting to throw the unthrowable Betty Leighton. Betty had lived through the London Blitz!

I don't know what the occasion was that prompted Sam and Bruce to ask me to "speak" to Chris. "Take him out after the performance and have coffee." We had only stepped out of the theatre and onto Sussex Street when Christopher opened the campaign by an immediate surrender, saying, before I could open my mouth, "Darling, I've been behaving like God. I'm sorry," and then a grin and a titter. We said no more. Whenever Chris became grand, a word from a friend could prick the bubble, and he was always the first to laugh.

Because he was such a quick study on his lines we let him hold his book till Sunday nights; he would learn his lines at one gulp on Sunday afternoon. There was one Sunday night when he put his head in my lap on-stage and said, "My brain is going! I can't learn the words any more!" Too many late nights, that's all, I warned him.

Chris has a great gift for mimicry. I was delighted when he "did" me as Amanda in *The Glass Menagerie*; it was so absolutely right. His pièce de résistance, though, was his Malcolm Morley. During a stop in the rehearsal of a scene, or during a break, he might step onto the apron, loosen his belt, and let his trousers droop low, and with his slim figure mysteriously assuming bulk and age he would start to tick us off, or to direct us, in Malcolm's voice. Out of the corner of his mouth, with an amused smirk, he would drawl, "You're not on Broadway YET, dear," which had been Malcolm's favourite line when he wanted to demolish us, or put us in our place.

Bruce and I together directed the last play of the season, *Dirty Work at the Crossroads*, just copying the production we knew so well from playing it in the Eastern Townships, in Joy Thomson's production. The author was Bill Johnson, and the play is not a true old melodrama, but a good comedy based on the old melodrama themes. We did not "ham it up," a form of so-called acting that I find deadly boring after fifteen minutes if I am in an audience.

Bruce once again was a rather fetching villain, who looked like Groucho Marx. We had at last got Silvio into the company, to play his old role of the hayseed Mookie Maguggins, called "Camillien" when we played in Quebec, and from Montreal we had also imported John Colicos, for Nellie's husband and true love, Adam

132

Oakhart, whose decision to go to the Big City proves his downfall. "Why, oh *why*, did I ever go to *Toronto*!" he moans at the end of one scene. A sure laugh this, because everybody in the country knew that Toronto rolled up its sidewalks at nine o'clock at night!

At least once a year we were destined to have Sam in drag. In *Dirty Work* he appeared as Mrs Upson Asterbilt, "of Rockcliffe and Kirk's Ferry." Large-size ladies' dresses were often presented to our wardrobe department, with Sam in mind, I am sure. Lynne Gorman was on hand as Ida Rhinegold, with reticule, a villainess who reforms in time to save Adam and Mookie from the oncoming train, "with the greatest mechanic effects ever seen on stage" in the form of a powerful spotlight appearing from upstage, plus terrible train noises. This spotlight blinded the audience until blackout and the suspenseful end of the scene.

If we were to hire an actor like John Colicos for only one play, why in the world would we hire him for a role like Adam in *Dirty Work at the Crossroads*? Probably because he happened to be available for those two weeks. I had corresponded with John to ask if he was interested in working at the CRT and he had replied that he would have to be paid fifty dollars a week. This was more than anyone received at the CRT and it would be unfair to pay one actor more than others, even if we could afford it. John was doing well in radio in Montreal, and he had a strong awareness of his family obligations and of his own worth and qualities for which I have always admired him. He wrote to tell me the plays he would like to do, plays like *The Only Way* and *The Bells*, which I would have liked to have done, but we could not bring in one actor to be leading man, for it was not our policy to follow the English repertory system of leading man, leading woman, character man, character woman, ingénue, juvenile. At the CRT we all took turns being all these things. But we enjoyed having John Colicos in our midst before he went off to cover himself with glory at the Old Vic, where he stepped into the role of Lear to great acclaim.

It must be remembered that when Sam and Bruce and I took over we had had no time in which to plan a season, and we could only get together and pool our ideas and then see which plays we could manage from the standpoint of availability of rights, of casting, and of technical practicability. I had wanted to do *The Heiress*; we all knew *The Little Foxes* as a good play; I had read about *Playbill* in the monthly magazine *Theatre World*, to which I subscribed from England; and *The Importance of Being Earnest* was a classic that seemed within our scope, and it had the advantage of no royalty. It was a catch-as-catch-can season; but then, to some extent, all our seasons were to be hand-to-mouth affairs, because it is not easy to find thirty or more plays a year that fit your company, your technical facilities, your budget, and your energies.

Thirty-four plays had been presented that 1949–50 season at the CRT, sixteen of them directed by Morley, ten by Sam, seven by me, and one by Bruce and me. There had been one North American première, and one première of a Canadian play. Of the eighteen plays that we had presented after Malcolm left, half had made a profit: *The Glass Menagerie, The Heiress, The Voice of the Turtle, Personal Appearance, Harvey, Elizabeth Sleeps Out, Tons of Money, The Importance of Being Earnest,* and *Dirty Work at the Crossroads.*

Only one thing had been remarkable about the season, and that was the fact that it had existed at all. We were the only professional theatre in the capital, and the only theatre in Canada that had been open for thirty-four solid weeks, never going dark. We were the only full-time professional theatre in this huge country. It was a tiny ray of hope in an otherwise lamentable state of affairs.

In the fifteenth week of that season of 1949–50 we had opened *The Glass Menagerie* with hearts full of hope for a new state of affairs. The weeks that followed had never again seen us reach the peak of hope and of enthusiasm that we had then. In spite of all our drive and vitality, hard work and attention to detail, in spite even of our attempts to clean out the dressing-rooms and the Green Room, there was something that eluded us that seemed not to be right. Was it a kind of inertia lurking we didn't quite know where, lingering on from the past? Was it a clashing of personalities?

It looked to me as if everything depended on choosing the right company for the second season, perhaps a company of people sharing similar backgrounds and aims. That company I was fortunate in putting together before the beginning of the 1950–51 season.

CHAPTER 10

A CLEAN SLATE

The 1950–51 season was the Golden Year at the CRT. When I think of that season I am elevated to the mood of Elwood P. Dowd in *Harvey*, when he says that he could almost live his life over again —*almost.*

After we had closed the CRT's 1949–50 season in early June, I had time to take a look at some of the summer enterprises in western Ontario. I had no expense account for these trips, and I was not paid my salary till we started to rehearse. As far as I recall, any work we did for pre-opening went unrewarded in money. I loved what I was doing, especially at this early stage of the game, and I was grateful to be doing my work.

Back in Ottawa at the beginning of July, I corresponded with the people I had seen or heard about and asked for pictures and synopses of their brief careers from those I had already hired. Then I wrote to Sam and Bruce, telling them what I had done.

By the time we all returned to Ottawa in September, Mr Southgate had made it possible for us to begin with a clean slate by having the below-stage area renovated and painted. Before we had left for our summer engagements, David, Sam, Bruce, and I had had a great clean-up downstairs, and I remember throwing out from the girls' dressing-room enough soiled underwear belonging to one of them to stock a lingerie drawer. Mr Southgate had ordered the construction of new dressing-rooms, with guards on the dressing-table light-bulbs to prevent further accidents, for Betty Leighton had burnt a hat and Anna Cameron had damaged her sister's fur coat by hanging them on or near lightbulbs. The floor had been painted, and a corner of the Green Room had been made into a stage manager's office for

David Haber. The horrid, windowless room that Malcolm Morley had used as an office was now the costume room.

The main portion of this understage area was comfortably furnished with donated pieces as an actors' Green Room. Arranged as it was with loving care and always kept clean during that year and the next three, it lives in my memory as the only real Green Room I have known. Traditionally a Green Room is a place for actors to relax. It is not a room in which stage-hands play poker or in which office or cleaning staff take breaks or eat meals. Therefore one cannot say that the Stratford Festival or the Avon Theatre or the National Arts Centre has a Green Room. At Toronto's Crest Theatre there was no Green Room, but in the corridor outside the dressing-rooms the telephone hung on the wall, and I used to love it when Max Helpmann would answer this phone and say, with hauteur, "Crest Theatre Green Room!"

In the CRT's Green Room was a notice board on which was tacked a sheet for actors to sign in (we had learned our lesson from the previous season), and here we hung the cast list for next week's production. In a corner behind the girls' dressing-rooms were two wash basins, and behind these were two unpredictable, erratic toilets.

The auditorium also now had an up-and-coming air, with lighter, brighter paint, acoustic tile (from Mr Southgate's company), attractive grey and blue masking on the stage, and paintings displayed on the walls. In the centre of the proscenium arch was a huge CRT crest.

The financial position as we entered our second season looked a good deal more healthy than it had at the start of the 1949–50 season. At that time, it was calculated that the operating loss was at least $600 a show—a loss that our backers, Mr Southam and Charles Southgate, guaranteed with sturdy optimism. But since the production of *Harvey* in April 1950, we had been continuously in the black.

We would open the new season with a weekly payroll of around $800. The 672 seats, selling at prices now ranging from 60¢ to $1.20, meant a possible weekly take of $3,100. But, of course, that was conditional on full houses every night, which we never, even in our most optimistic moments, expected. Nevertheless, we entered this new season with spirits high.

We had asked Silvio Narizzano back, and also Gertrude Allen. Mary Sheppard, my friend from Canadian Art Theatre and London, England, days, was back in Montreal, and we got her. Donald Glenn and John Howe were two young actors I had seen at Peterborough in the summer and had hired. These five were to be the permanent actors in the company. Altogether more than seventy people would appear on-stage during the coming thirty-five weeks.

I myself did not have a contract at the CRT. I do not recall the actors who came for the season having any kind of contract. To some who came later on, from New York City, or from Toronto for perhaps one play, I sent a form of letter-contract. All the five years that I was at CRT those employed always got their pay, on time, and got what they had been promised. Sam Goldwyn is reported to have said that a verbal contract isn't worth the paper it's written on, but verbal contracts worked well enough for us. (After 1955, we Canadian actors had to become members of Actors' Equity Association, related to the American AEA, and from then on one had to sign contracts. It was necessary because the industry was expanding. Even at Stratford the first season one did not have a "union" contract.)

The actors found rooming-houses. I never had time to visit any of these, but I used to recommend to them the house of the Misses Dalton, on Maclaren Street, I believe, where Mother and I had stayed when I arrived in Ottawa in 1939. Some of the actors settled there each season. I had worried during the first season about how poorly some of the men were eating, especially fellows like David Haber, who worked even longer hours than the rest. I was able, through Bruce Raymond, to arrange with a French-Canadian lady on Guigues Street for a hot meal to be served around her large dining-room table at 12:30 noon each weekday for most of the men. Sometimes they ate there at night before an opening, and I would join them.

As soon as we got back, Bruce plunged into work with Peter Sturgess, his assistant, and with Mr Southgate, opening the box office (where two ladies alternated services at Lindsays on Sparks Street and then manned the box office in the LaSalle "foyer" in the evenings); Bruce would arrange seat prices and season-ticket prices and bargain for advertising in the *Citizen* and the *Journal*. Meanwhile I would be reading scripts and choosing plays, casting them, and contacting actors.

We started off the season with David Haber as stage manager and John Howe as his assistant. John was ASM a brief time, and then he acted full-time, and by December Robert Barclay of Ottawa had become ASM. Bob was a westerner who was educated in Ottawa. He had worked at the Stage Society and would have left for England except for the pull of the CRT. He wanted even then to be a film director, and he achieved his ambition eventually. Bob wasn't young the way so many are young — their youth a kind of acne you hope they'll grow out of — you just hoped that Bob would never lose his youth. It was a joy to see his sensitive, inquiring, lively face.

By late February David had become production stage manager, Bob Barclay was promoted to SM, and Michael Gardiner, a young lad from Joy Thomson's summer crew, became ASM, while still helping Penny as scenic assistant. Michael Gardiner's main job as ASM was to operate the turn-table that produced music during the intervals and, on occasion, during the play itself. In the words of Penny, "he looked as if he had been kept too long under the stairs." Rather tall and slender, fair-haired and pool-room pale, he somehow conveyed an air of happy immersion in his work, as he very slowly pushed a broom across the Green Room floor. To Penny he was a Trial, dipping his brush into the paint pail and carting it limply toward the flats, "losing a pint of paint on the way!" "A theatre is no place for a young lad; he should be out in the open air," asserted Sam, shaking his head. How had he come to the CRT, anyway? Nobody seemed to know. I shook my head over the boy's diet of ice-cream sodas, sundaes, followed by hamburgers and pop.

David's new job as production manager was a blessed relief to me, because it meant he could sit at a desk and organize and could be a liaison between the director and the crew. By mid-November we had Jane Graham, Bob Barclay's beloved Jane, doing props, and these two dedicated workers took special pride in making our Green Room a home away from home for all of us. By late February Don Torney no longer came in "in the night time" away from his day-time job, to do our lights, but David took over the lights. Eventually we found that Bob Barclay was a most imaginative lighting designer, the best we ever had at the CRT.

For the season we had in all two persons in the office, two box-office ladies, and a crew consisting of designer, production stage manager, stage manager, assistant stage manager, property mistress, and scenic assistant. All others on the payroll were actors, but the office staff and the crew also appeared on stage on occasion.

We had decided that our first play would be *Life with Father*, by Clarence Day, with Sam in the role of Father Day. We rehearsed for one week. Betty Leighton had arrived in Ottawa from Deep River to play Vinnie, and the sons were to be Silvio Narizzano, Richard Lamb, George Bloom, and a fair male child I had observed taking tea with his mother in Murray's restaurant, which I had frequented during early September.

This little child looked like the young Edward VIII as he appears in pictures with his great-grandmother, Queen Victoria. I was delighted to obtain his family's permission for him to play the youngest son of the Days. I gave his mother the lines for him to learn ahead of time. I think we must have rehearsed day and night that one week (no union rules), for I recall an evening rehearsal early on in a classroom of LaSalle and this little boy, recovered from his initial shyness, spending most of that evening rubbing chalk on those felt dusters provided to clean blackboards; then he would sneak up behind one of the men and slap the chalk all over the actor's suit. He was absolutely ungovernable; so we ditched him, and I got a little girl with long curls called Faye Palmer to play the male child.

When Sam made his first entrance on opening night, September 19, appearing on the staircase provided by Paul Charette and Penny Sparling, the audience burst into applause. He was Father Day to the life. The sets by Penny Sparling (Geldart since her marriage in July) maintained her usual high quality.

The second production, Terence Rattigan's *O Mistress Mine*, introduced Donald Glenn to the audience, playing opposite Betty Leighton. That year Don became the matinée idol of the CRT. He was a big, handsome man, with a splendid voice and an air of easy, good-humoured sophistication, plus the hard-headed mind of a business tycoon. Every day he studied the stock-market in the men's dressing-room. He was born in Brazil, where he had some military training, went to school in England, and served in the RCAF during the Second World War, emerging with the rank of flight lieutenant. He held a degree in metallurgical engineering from the University of Toronto. I think he would have been a great success after 1952 had he decided to enter the then lucrative field of Canadian television, but he left acting and went into business in Toronto.

When Sir Laurence Olivier decided that if you can't beat the critics you should get them to join you, he hired Kenneth Tynan. Mr Tynan chose his own title, and thus that snobbish word "dramaturge" came into theatrical use. I did some of a dramaturge's august work at the CRT by reading a never-ending shelf of plays, and for each one I would make notes on a prepared sheet headed "Production Costs." Down would go name of play, author, number of sets interior and exterior, my suggested casting, the value of costumes required by rental (allowing two dollars per day per item), special effects required that would cost money, and my general comments.

During my Mountain Playhouse summer, armed with my Hermes typewriter, I had commented on *One Wild Oat* by Vernon Sylvaine as "Terribly funny. I laughed out loud alone. Not just humour in the situations but in the lines. Best farce I have ever read." So *One Wild Oat* became our third production. I think it was my first attempt at directing a farce. Florence Fancott came over from the ODL to play the wife of Humphrey Proudfoot (Peter Sturgess), and Mary Sheppard made her CRT debut as their daughter. I can still hear

Humphrey Proudfoot saying to her in quivering tones, "You're a *bad* girl!" Betty Leighton and Sam and Silvio were the members of the Gilbey family. In these farces, Peter always played the outraged, virtuous little man (in this case a pip-squeak goody-goody solicitor), and Sam always played the bounder, who at some point had to disguise himself in women's weeds. Vancouver's Jack Ammon was with us, and Bruce came down from the office to take part, and we had Donald Glenn and John Howe and Ann Coffin, years later of the Canada Council, who often worked with us.

I had given the role of Audrey Cuttle, the "one wild oat," to Trudy Allen. After a day of rehearsal Trudy came to me full of woe: she could never play a role of that kind, she maintained. "It's your kind of role, Millie," and she asked me if she could play the small role I had given to myself so that I could concentrate on the directing. So we switched roles. Audrey Cuttle was a plain, middle-aged female; one could hardly imagine her to have had a lurid or indiscreet past. I didn't give her much thought except for my make-up, for I had my hands full directing. It was not until I got on-stage opening night that "Millie caught on" and I realized that all Miss Cuttle's dialogue was highly suggestive, packed with innuendoes. I began to enjoy Miss Cuttle.

Lauretta Thistle in the *Citizen* reported: "There was rather more than usual first-night dropping of lines, but in this anything-goes type of comedy it didn't matter much, and Mr. Sturgess pushed the merriment index up one notch higher, when he unabashedly went over to the prompt corner to get a line. And when he dropped his moustache, tossed it into his pocket, and waved an apology to the audience, he stopped the show entirely. The audience loved it and told him so." (I'll bet Amelia Hall didn't love it! But she loves reading about it now.) The *Journal* awarded the honours to "the blousy variety queen assumed by Betty Leighton and her upholsterer."

We were proud of our production of *Born Yesterday*, which opened on October 17, 1950. I directed this Garson Kanin play, and I was helped immeasurably by the study I had made of Joy Thomson's production the summer before at the Mountain Playhouse in Montreal, and by the importation from Montreal of Henry Ramer to play Harry Brock, a tough millionaire junk-dealer. With this production we introduced the late Gerry Sarracini to the CRT, playing the hero role of Paul Verrall. Silvio was again Eddie Brock, the role he had played in Joy's production, and Donald Glenn was superb as the upper-class alcoholic lawyer who has sold himself to Harry Brock.

I had cast Mary Sheppard as Billie Dawn, the plum role for actresses at that time. I knew there was a feeling that Anna Cameron would have been a better choice: she had played the part at Knowlton that summer and people raved. But I was adamant that Mary have her chance, for she had not had a good part since she came to the CRT and it was time her figure and her talent were displayed to best advantage. Someone, certainly not a professional of the company, started a rumour that Mary was not going to be very good. This was the kind of rumour that we had found at the ODL could easily circulate if you let people into the rehearsal hall who were not in the production. It is one of the reasons why I cannot stand anyone at a rehearsal who is not in the company or a member of the crew. This rumour came to my ears, and because I knew Mary's calibre, I told *her*. We shared our anger, and we worked that much harder. One of the many advantages that Mary had toward the playing of Billie Dawn was that she had seen some of the kind of world that Billie moved through, both in Montreal and in London, England, because of her step-father's connections in the boxing business. Bruce's friendly ads asked: "With two mink coats was she as dumb as she looked or just *BORN YESTERDAY*?" At the bottom he added, "Incidentally, the Mink Coats are supplied by Devlins."

When I saw the set on arrival at the theatre on the Sunday night before Wednesday opening I was ecstatic. It was a huge hotel room all in grey, with a staircase at the back, and I do believe we had wall-to-wall, thick grey carpet!

By the standards of the 1980s there is little swearing in *Born Yesterday*. I deleted God from all the "God damns." A burgeoning theatre cannot afford to offend its audience, and our audience was easily offended. Some people, like myself, had grown up hearing scarcely any swearing. When in New York in 1946 I went to a modern American play and within five minutes of curtain up one of the characters said to another, "*Jesus*, your hands are dirty!" I was shocked. I felt that in the theatre "damn" and "hell" were as far as I wanted to go. The one piece I had ever read at that time in which I approved of the use of our Lord's name was the last line of the poem *Patterns*: "Christ! What are patterns for?" When the audiences opened their programs for *Born Yesterday* they found the Prompt Sheet, written no doubt by Bruce, and it was headed, "To Swear or Not to Swear." This is what he said:

> Among the many messages congratulating us for
> *One Wild Oat* we received a note deploring the use of
> bad language in that production. The thought oc-

curred to us that a few words on the subject of stage language would not be amiss, particularly in view of tonight's show ... Should we tamper with the accepted work of a playwright? Should we refuse to do a good play just because it uses a few street-corner phrases? After a great deal of thought we adopted the following policy: We try not to present any plays that are cheaply immoral or which use bad language for sheer sensationalism. If, however, a play is basically good theatre we delete offensive language where it is not necessary to the development of either the plot or the atmosphere as the author intended them. On the other hand, we know that our audience would not want us thoughtlessly to interfere with an author's attempt to portray a particular person or way of life realistically. If we offend we apologize. We hope that our friends will accept our productions as we offer them ...

Five hundred people seeking admission to *Born Yesterday* had to be turned away. I think the most telling compliment that Mary received for her Billie Dawn was expressed to Bruce by one of the brothers of LaSalle Academy. We never sold the balcony on Saturday matinées, and sometimes one or two brothers would slip in there, out of sight of the audience, and watch the play. After *Born Yesterday* one of these said to Bruce: "I know I'm not supposed to notice, but that Mary Sheppard ..."

Against the screams of the entire company I was adamant not to use a freshly slain rabbit in William Douglas Home's *The Chiltern Hundreds*, supposedly shot by the Earl of Lister, a lord most endearingly created by Sam Payne. We got from the museum or from a high school a taxidermist's ancient job on a rabbit, and thus the creature appeared to have gone into rigor mortis the instant it was shot! The dead fox was a fox-fur piece. Donald Glenn, carrying these across the stage in his role as the dignified butler, must have felt a fool.

It was around this time that I became distressed by some of the younger company members being careless of their appearance in public. I remembered how untidy some of the actors had been when I joined the CRT. I called the company together and warned people that we did not want the public to recognize us as actors simply because we looked shabby, long-haired, or unshaven! Not until Gerry Sarracini had left us did I discover that he thought my speech was aimed at *him*. Apparently he had no more clothes than the suit he stood up in. I had not known this. At any rate, Gerry decided to leave. He said he was dissatisfied with the work he was doing for us. Actually I think the reason was a personal one. I had been comparatively well off when I was teaching and had money saved from those more affluent times. Some of the girls had families with money, or husbands to provide, and it did not occur to me that there were fellows who might find the financial road a rough one.

Somehow, I really don't know how, I found the time to sit in the library and look for a really good play in which to star Gerry before he left us. I read or examined some sixty plays in one week. The play had to have only one set if possible, not too big a cast, and a great role for Gerry. I found what I wanted in *One Hundred Years Old*, by Serafin and Joaquin Alvarez Quintero, translated by Helen and Harley Granville-Barker.

Gerry Sarracini was thoroughly believable as the centenarian Papa Juan. It was a surprise to the audience when in the curtain call he gave a farewell speech and reverted to his own age. This gentle, almost plotless play, set in an Andalusian town, offered a change of pace from our usual fare. We actors were enchanted by it. The dialogue, Carl Weiselberger said, "like a peaceful brook, winds through three acts." Although a number of customers found this so relaxing that they came more than once, the box office was poor.

Penny had created a Moorish villa and patio, and in the distance were hills and villas. To be on that stage was a kind of winter holiday. Off-stage we had singers for Papa's birthday, Jacques Lapointe, Charles Donoghue, Roland Lefebvre, and Jacques Larfortune, and dancer Yolande Leduc played the castanets.

We had a party on-stage and backstage to bid adieu to Gerry. He seemed genuinely sorry to leave, for by now he knew that he had not let us or the CRT audience down. I sat on his knee and begged him in vain to stay. I never saw him again. He died in New York in 1957, while appearing in Peter Ustinov's *Romanoff and Juliet*. He was knocked down and fatally injured in an argument outside a theatre.

Betty Leighton returned for five more productions, and we had much fun with Ivor Novello's *Fresh Fields*, Lynne Gorman and I playing elegant, impecunious sisters, and Betty and Don Glenn playing two Australians rolling in money. It opened with breakfast on-stage, a good beginning as far as I am concerned, for I always like to eat. I played a languid, seemingly cold Lady Lillian Bedworthy ("such a ridiculous name, my dear!"), but I switched from being an old maid and as a bewitching charmer wooed Don's lusty, tough Australian, a scene the ladies in the house relished. It was what one would call a matinée piece; they don't write plays like this any more — pure entertainment, with good dialogue, charm, and elegance. I wonder if such plays will ever "take on" again?

Sam had directed *A Hundred Years Old* and *Fresh Fields*, and now he directed us in *Light up the Sky*, by Moss Hart. I have nothing but happy memories of this comedy about theatre people in the Big Time. Betty played the Star, an unpleasant lady with a veneer of "class," and I was her hard-bitten mother, Stella. My first entrance was beautifully written: enter laughing raucously, shut the hotel-suite door, and roar, "Tell them a joke and give 'em a good laugh and they like it better. I haven't tipped a bell-boy in twenty years." I was nervous opening night because the curtain line for act one was my shouting, "Gin! Goddammit to hell! Gin!" But no one in the audience took noticeable offence.

John Howe played the starry-eyed director, who cries when he is watching rehearsals and always says at eight o'clock, before curtain up, "It's Magic Time!" He had one line that the critics loved: "Am I mentioned in both reviews? I never read them ... that's why I ask." John wanted to direct and became a top director at the National Film Board. Back in 1951 he asked me at a party one Saturday night if we could give him a chance to direct. It was an awkward question. Silvio wanted to direct, and later on there were others. Sam and I had been hired as directors, and I knew that Mr Southgate wanted it to stay that way. Our one aim at the time was not to develop Canadian playwrights, nor Canadian directors, but to get an audience to come to see plays presented by Canadian *actors*. Naturally, it was not easy for talented and impatient young theatre folk to accept the limitations.

To anyone who has devised an entertainment that he or she is longing to offer to a waiting world, my advice is: don't offer it to them the week before Christmas. We quite knocked ourselves out with a beautifully mounted production of *She Stoops to Conquer*, performed with guts and high spirits, and everyone in Ottawa went Christmas shopping instead of beating a path to LaSalle.

I had told Penny that I wanted us to do it as the Old Vic had presented it in 1949, with sets after Rawlinson. I went to see Kathleen Fenwick at the National Gallery, and we studied Rawlinson prints. What Penny conceived from her contact with this source was quite beyond my wildest expectations. The stage at LaSalle Academy was only seventeen feet deep from the back wall of the stage to the very edge of the small apron in front of the proscenium arch. In order to make the stage seem much deeper, Penny made a wide arch in the back flats of the living-room set, and through this arch we could see a commodious kitchen, with utensils on the walls and hams and dried vegetables hanging from its ceiling. In actual fact this entire kitchen was only a couple of feet away from the archway and was a painting that she had done on the building's brick and plaster walls! At stage right there was a huge country fireplace and beyond it a flight of stairs. These stairs, after about six treads, reached a landing, and then the staircase turned abruptly and went right up out of sight behind the flats.

The first day that we rehearsed on this set, I was standing below the stage apron when Bruce came into the auditorium from his office among the LaSalle classrooms upstairs. He suddenly stopped in mid-sentence, and bellowed at me: "Who authorized the lumber for that staircase?" I said timidly that I had no idea and advised him to go and examine it. Onto the stage he climbed, and when he got near the back wall flats he roared with laughter, discovering how Penny's ingenuity had deceived him. The staircase was painted on the wall!

One of my favourite moments in this production was when Marlowe and Hastings are arriving and all the servants who have been listening to Mr Hardcastle's instructions suddenly scatter off-stage in all directions. Paul Charette was one of the servants. I left him on-stage till all had departed; then, realizing with horror that he was alone in the room, he gave one terrified look at the house and scampered off. Nice to see the backstage carpenter have his little moment in the limelight and do it so well.

Sam got the biggest laugh in the production on opening night. It was in the scene outside the Hardcastle house, in the garden, which Tony has deceived his mother into believing is a barren heath frequented by highwaymen. She is hidden behind a tree while Tony talks to Mr Hardcastle, who, to Tony's alarm, has come for a stroll in the garden. There is a deal of repetition of questions in this scene, and it was one of those occasions when Sam was shaky on the words. He dried. The prompter, David, came in quickly with, "I heard a voice!" But Sam didn't hear David. So Silvio whispered to Sam, "I heard a voice!" "Oh, did you?" replied Sam heartily, ready to improvise for a bit. "No, no!" whispered Silvio, "*you* heard a voice!" "Oh," beamed Sam, turning to the house, "*I heard a voice!*" Roars and applause!

During the Christmas season Violet and Charles Southgate gave their annual Christmas party for the company. We all crowded into the dining-room of their fourth-floor apartment on Cooper Street, now gone the way of all the fine old houses on that block. Seated round the table, we pulled Christmas crackers and hailed the treasures within: paper hats, ancient jokes and conundrums in teeny print on coloured slips of paper, fortunes that promised untold wealth and warned to be wary of sinister strangers, pearl necklaces and rings that turned the fingers green, little fish of cellophane that moved and curled on the warm palm, boxed puzzles that led to desperation as we tried to tilt three tiny silver balls into three shallow depressions — all these little joys of childhood Christmases. They were a relaxing respite between a hard day's rehearsing and an opening night on the morrow. Seated on the floor around the Christmas tree we received our presents, and I still open all my letters with an opener in sterling silver that came off the tree one Southgate Christmas.

We were to open on January 2, 1951, with the tender Saroyan play, *The Beautiful People*. Young Richard Lamb played the central role of the boy, and the rest of the cast consisted of Mary Sheppard and me, Don Glenn, Silvio, John Howe, David Haber, and two guests, William Fournier and William Wood. After the rehearsal ended on New Year's Eve, 1950, at nine o'clock at night, I said: "Anyone who wants to come to my house is welcome."

I think they all came, except Dickie Lamb and Don Glenn. Bruce also came, and Paul Charette. There were about ten of us, and we joined hands and sang "Auld Lang Syne." No one drank much, though I kept nipping out of a small bottle of brandy, "because it's only once a year." Someone said, "Let's read *Hamlet*!" So we did, from cover to cover, out of the three or four copies I mustered, and each had a turn at reading the Prince, girls as well. I have a distinct impression that Richard Easton and I read the scene from *Richard III* that I was to play two years later with Alec Guinness at Stratford, but what Easton was doing in Ottawa I do not know. He may have been holidaying. At any rate we must have been up all night, quietly enjoying, Bruce eventually nodding off on the chesterfield, his shoes discarded.

That was the best New Year's Eve I ever had.

CHAPTER 11

A FULL LIFE

The new year, 1951, brought us considerable success and press coverage. On January 9 we presented Robertson Davies's new play, *At My Heart's Core*.

About the play, Robertson Davies had written: "The point which I am trying to bring out is that the physical hardships which the pioneers suffered were very great, but that many of them suffered at least equal pain from the intellectual frustration which they endured."

I had first met this brilliant scholar and man of letters at a drama festival in 1947 and had stayed with him and his family that summer when I visited the Peterborough Summer Theatre. I had long been an ardent reader of his column, "Everyman's Diary of Samuel Marchbanks," which was a weekly feature of the *Ottawa Citizen*.

The play had been presented the previous summer at the Peterborough Summer Theatre, with Robertson Davies's wife, Brenda, as Mrs Stewart and Kate Reid as Catharine Parr Traill, the part that I would now play. Also in the original cast had been John Primm and Donald Glenn, who would repeat their roles with the CRT.

Brenda Davies was Australian by birth; she and her husband met when they both worked at the Old Vic, she as actress and stage manager.

The part of Mrs Stewart had been written for Brenda, and the role of Catharine Parr Traill had been written with me in mind, though I had not been in the first production. The role of Edmund Cantwell had been written for John Primm, and he came back from New York City to play it again. John was a Montrealer who had lived in Ottawa

147

at the end of the war and had been our Peer Gynt in 1946, when Julia Murphy had bucked the commercial elements of the ODL and presented Ibsen with a cast of thousands. Since then he had studied in New York with Duff and had been stage co-ordinator with the New York City Center Opera, working with Komisarjevsky.

Our production, directed by Sam Payne, drew capacity houses, and on the Saturday night a lot of people had to be turned away. Bruce reported that the play ran fifth in box-office appeal of all fifty plays the CRT had presented so far, and in the present season it was surpassed only by *Born Yesterday* and *Life with Father*. One letter to the *Citizen* thanked that paper for introducing its readers to Davies through his column; otherwise he might not have gone to the CRT to see *At My Heart's Core* and thus would have missed a grand play, well done.

On the Saturday night that Davies attended the play, he was called on-stage for a number of solo curtain calls. He said to the audience, "Ottawa people perhaps don't think there's anything very wonderful about a professional theatre working in a school auditorium. But they should remember that the Greek theatre began in a field, the English theatre began in the courtyard of an inn. It is not many years since the idea of an English ballet company was laughed at. Now Sadler's Wells is famous around the world. Good Canadian theatre is not a thing to be looked forward to in fifty or a hundred years. We have it now, and the time to support it is now. Our young Canadian artists have proved that what they want is not 'wads of money' but the opportunity to work in their own country." Of course this speech was quoted in the newspapers, where we hoped it would be read by the unconverted, or unconvinced.

Our production of *At My Heart's Core* got some extra publicity when it was mentioned in Marchbank's diary the following week:

> Saturday: To Ottawa today, to attend a performance of a play by my old friend Apollo Fishorn, the Canadian playwright. Fishorn got on the train at Smith's Falls, with a live hen in a net, and a basket of fresh eggs, which he said he was taking to the actors, who appreciate these little comforts from the farm. He also had a carpet bag with a bad catch, which kept falling open and revealing the sorriest pair of pajamas I have ever seen ... I liked the play, but joining a party of knowledgeable persons in the lobby at one of the intervals, I learned that there was too much talk in it, and not enough action. Now this puzzles me.

There are only a very few kinds of action that can be shown on the stage. Love is a great theme of playwrights, but if they try to develop it as action rather than as talk, the censor cracks down. Murder is good, but if you murder more than one person an act, people think you are trying to be Shakespeare, and complain. I mentioned this criticism to Fishorn, and he sighed, and said: 'Yes, but life is 99 percent talk. Look at the people who want more action in my play: what are they doing? Talking! What are you doing? Talking!' And sure enough, when I caught sight of myself in a mirror, he was right.

Having distinguished ourselves with *At My Heart's Core* we plunged into two unmemorable productions, a farce, by Vernon Sylvaine, called *Madame Louise* and a comedy, by James Thurber and Elliot Nugent, called *The Male Animal*. I directed the farce, and Sam did the comedy. I think I would prefer to rehearse a Shakespeare in one week rather than a farce. *Madame Louise* called for difficult props. The first was a dress designed by "Madame Louise," a male designer, played by Peter Sturgess. This dress was a three-in-one affair, and David Haber as production manager took this problem in hand and designed and made the garment himself. It was a day-time dress and you pulled a string and it became a tea gown, and you pulled another string and you had a ball gown. This creation was never patented! The second time-consuming prop was one of those money-carrying mechanisms that used to run on wires above the heads of the customers in all drapery shops. In this play the running joke was that Peter put the money into the box, pulled the string, and then walked to the other end of the short counter to take the money out, put the change into the box, and then send it back to its starting place, Peter walking back with dignity to retrieve the change. One review said, "This play is an opportunity to see an overhead cash carrier working with more speed than ever before dreamed of in a department store."

Peter played his role in *Madame Louise* in a provincial tour in England for 150 performances. He had been away from us for a few weeks during Christmas to appear in a pantomime, *Babes in the Wood*, for Dora Mavor Moore at the Royal Alex in Toronto. In that production had appeared Eric House, and now Eric played a small role in *Madame Louise*, his first role at the CRT. I sensed quickly on opening night that he had warmth, a special rapport with the audience, and would be a fine addition to the company. He played

149

the lead the following week in *The Male Animal*. This comedy deals with free speech versus football mania in an American university community. If I call it an unmemorable production, it is not to say we did it poorly; only that the theme was not one of burning interest to us in Canada.

The morale of the company week by week always reflected our degree of respect for the present production. A flash report on what we all felt about the play we were presenting could be read on the face of David Haber. Dazzling smiles reported fair weather and a wonderful show. But if David looked as if he were planning a mass poisoning and you were going to be the first to go, then he did not think much of the current play; the minute curtain was down on Saturday night he was going to rush on-stage to have his revenge and tear the whole thing apart. If David had loved the play he was loath to take it down on Saturday night, and he and I quite often stood about on-stage like lovers lamenting that never again would we stand by this particular bonnie, bonnie bank.

Charles Southgate was often away on business trips. But by Saturday night, come wind or weather, he was usually back in Ottawa, sometimes flying in from cities such as Chicago, in order to appear on Saturday night in his usual front-row seat, smiling happily. It was on one such business trip that he saw a production of George Kelly's *The Show-Off* and came home to tell me that this was a good comedy, with a fine leading role for Silvio Narizzano. I had told Silvio about Charles Southgate's recommendation but had been rebuffed: "You think I can play anything! Well, I can't. I know I won't be any good for that part; so forget it." I read *The Show-Off* and thought it one of the most naturally written plays I had ever read. The mother is a true character, as Amanda is in *Menagerie*.

We opened *The Show-Off* January 30, with Silvio in the name part of Aubrey Piper, the Show-Off, and with that role Silvio came into his own as a CRT actor. The *Le Droit* review even had the heading: SILVIO NARIZZANO, and said, "La pièce tourne autour de Narizzano, et Narizzano, fait tourner la pièce autour de lui." Sam directed, after much argument that we couldn't possibly do it because we didn't have a big, bony woman to play Aubrey's mother-in-law, Mrs Fisher. I was nervous lest he discover some big, bony actress to play the role, for I coveted it!

I have seldom enjoyed a role more. I just *felt* full of big, raw bones for Mrs Fisher. Some years later, when I saw Helen Hayes play the part, no more bony than I am, I longed to play Mrs Fisher once more. She is hard-voiced, sharp-tongued, down-to-earth, and accomplished in making a dime go a long way. A perfect foil for Aubrey. Rocking back and forth in her chair in the Fisher living- room-cum-dining-room she prefaces every stinging sarcasm to Aubrey with, "Listen, boy ..." John Primm was the father, who dies at the factory, and there is a touching scene in which this dread news arrives and they get Mrs Fisher ready to go to the funeral parlour, or rather she gets herself ready, finally producing her purse from the top of the victrola, where she keeps it secure under the lid.

It always gave our regular patrons much pleasure if we could so disguise ourselves that it took them a few minutes to figure out who we were. This happened in the opening few minutes of *The Show-Off*, when I wandered around the dreary, 1920s working-class living-room in my apron. Then, before any word was spoken (I was alone on stage), they realized who this woman was, and they burst into applause.

In the Prompt Sheet which was placed inside the program each week, we would announce about every five weeks the next group of plays that we had chosen. The business reason for keeping well ahead was so that we could sell theatre parties, which had to be arranged ahead of time. Once theatre parties had been sold, we could tell the public that such and such nights were already sold out; this looked good, and *was* good.

A club or an organization would decide to have a theatre night. If it bought the full house, it cost $300 for the 672 seats. The orchestra alone, 484 seats, cost $250. The organization was then issued a special set of tickets. It could sell them for whatever price it chose, but we recommended a dollar a ticket. The 188 seats in the balcony could be had for $125, but if they sold them at general admission prices of sixty cents the balcony cost only $75. Our box offices would also sell their tickets for a group, and our ads would bear the group's name on the day of its party. Forty-eight hours before its Theatre Night it had to send a cheque to our office for the $300, or the $250, or whatever the amount was to be. If it had decided by that time that the theatre party was going to be a financial wash-out, it could cancel. Theatre parties were a painless way of raising money, because the selling of tickets is handed over to someone else. New customers are brought into the theatre, and there is always the hope that they may get the habit of regular theatre-going.

Thus it was that by January 16, 1951, we were able to announce eight sold-out evenings coming up before the beginning of March.

There were thirty-two people in *The Man Who Came to Dinner*, by Kaufman and Hart, which we put on in February. That number includes the five boys I obtained from the choir of St John's, the students from M. Provost's drama school in Hull, and Beatrice Whitfield, Norah Hughes, and Lillian Wolfe, from the Ottawa Drama League. Young Jane Graham is credited for the set dressings and furnishings.

Donald Glenn was Sheridan Whiteside, and Trudy Allen was in her element as his sophisticated, back-answering secretary, Maggie. Mary Sheppard was the exotic actress Lorraine Sheldon, John Howe was the Noel Coward type called Beverly Carlton, and Silvio had a ball as Banjo, who of course is Harpo Marx. Silvio was very put out because I would not allow him to jump up and down on the sofa, which was elegant and *borrowed*. I cannot recall whether he heeded my warnings. I directed this and played the role of Harriett Stanley, who, it is hinted, is Lizzie Borden. This was the first time I had tried a play that involved a large group of outsiders, and I found that it was not difficult if one planned carefully, knowing when each of these would be available and arranging the rehearsal schedule carefully to fit them in, and never, *never*, deviating from it.

I have little patience with directors who do not plan exactly how long they're going to spend on each section each day. I always kept a schedule in front of me, telling me at what minute of the clock I had to drop one scene and get on with the next. Especially is this important in weekly stock, because you can then tell company actors at exactly what time their "call" is, and thus you can give them some free time, especially time to sleep in. I have worked with directors who keep the entire cast present all day, and with others who call an actor for a certain time and then keep him or her waiting for an hour. This is abuse of power and lack of planning.

Of course there are productions in which it is a fine idea to have everyone present all the time to make the cast feel the atmosphere of the whole production, but when you are doing play after play over a long season you cannot possibly take this kind of High Art approach. Guthrie never kept an actor after he had finished with him or her, but said, "Don't need you any more. Go home." I once spent an exhausting three weeks attending, with all the other actors, every rehearsal of a Michael Langham production, a twelve-hour day with meal breaks, and we were all cheesed off. The circumstances were exceptional.

The excitement of this big production must have taken its toll, because I recall walking through our next piece, Barrie's *Dear Brutus*, in a fog of high temperature. I had at last got to play a young girl, and even had I been well I would have found it dull going. Norah Hughes played the excellent character role I had turned down, and Peter Sturgess played Lob. Jennifer Anne Street was the little girl Margaret but was criticized as too robust; it is not easy to play a Barrie child. John Primm as the father got top marks. This play was a popular request, and I think that those who had requested it showed their gratitude by coming to see it. They did not bring a throng with them.

This was John Primm's final performance for us. We had a party at my house on the Saturday night, and Filmore Sadler was there, visiting from the Brae Manor Playhouse. It was always a special pleasure when others in the business, from Toronto or from Montreal, or even Vancouver, would turn up; it was an excuse for a party. Lister Sinclair would come to visit Sam, and there might be Mavor Moore or William Needles, and others that I met this way for the first time. To these parties at my apartment someone would bring liquor, but not much of it was ever consumed, and when people left the bottle would be placed on a shelf in our kitchen, against the next time.

John Primm went back to New York, and for some years he was a floor director in television. The last time I saw him must have been in New York in 1956. The great Russian director Komisarjevsky had died and had willed all his papers to John. The apartment was crowded with cartons of letters, and you made a lucky dip and out would come a letter from some luminary such as Sir John Gielgud.

While Sam was busy with Emlyn Williams's *The Late Christopher Bean*, I had a week off in order to prepare the old melodrama *Maria Marten, or Murder in the Red Barn*. I do not know where I had picked up the script for *Maria Marten*. It was a tiny, ancient paperback, printed without punctuation, in small print, on the thinnest of paper. There were seventeen scenes in all, and some of these were about a third of a page long, with scarcely any dialogue. It was a true old melodrama, written early in the nineteenth century and to be taken quite seriously. It had first been performed at the Marylebone Theatre in London in 1840. There was great pathos in the play, but the clowns were wooden and their comedy as incomprehensible to us as are some of the Victorian jokes in the earliest *Punch* cartoons.

I discussed the music for *Maria Marten* with Peter Sturgess and decided to have only recorded classical music ... certainly no hamming up on the piano. Peter had a considerable library of recordings, and I went to his digs to listen and after a while put the choice completely into his hands. We were never stopped at that time by the

musicians' union from playing recordings, either before the performance, during intervals, after the play, or during performance.
We always played music right up to curtain time and again the
minute the curtain came down. Music gives a sense of occasion. In
a place like LaSalle especially, where the lobby was drab, we had to
give the audience a lift when it got into the theatre. Music, then lights
going down, then curtain: all these things have to be delicately
timed.

Many of these recordings used week after week at the CRT came
from the lending library of records at the public library. I remember
my mother being solicitous that these be cared for, and taken back
promptly, and her especial concern about one recording that she
offered to return to the library for me; she placed it on the couch and
then in an abstracted moment *sat* on it! Records cracked into many
pieces in those days.

We decided to use movable set-pieces for the various scenes in
Maria Marten, with a cyclorama of curtains around the stage. So that
we would not waste time between scenes, and put the audience out
of the mood of the piece, Bob Barclay, the stage manager, had a
marvellous idea: to use a strong beam of light from one side of the
proscenium to the other during scene changes. The audience could
not see through the beam of light to watch the movements of the
stage crew changing the sets behind the beam, all to music.

David hung the lights on the Monday night before the Tuesday
dress rehearsal, and he and I were there nearly all night, thoroughly
enjoying ourselves creating moods with the use of coloured light.
There was always a green light surrounding the weird gypsy of Eric
House, and the hanging scene at the finale was very red!

John Howe and Ron MacDonald (a newcomer to the CRT) had a
hard row to hoe as two supposedly comic showmen at the Fair. Their
costumes, probably from Malabar's, were most authentic and Mr
Punch-like, though I did not find them particularly funny. Fortunately the humour of this play is of little import -- one could perhaps
do a cut version without it. Sam Payne, as William Corder, the
murderer, Squire Polestead's son, distinguished himself for the
vigour and dignity of his performance, which, in the prison scene, I
found most moving. Trudy Allen was most touching as Maria, and
"her vibrant voice and full-fledged personality contrived to tower
above her diminutive stature," as one critic, Bobbie Turcotte, put it.
This same Mr Turcotte lamented that Sam had no moustache to
twirl. Ah me, what is the use of research when public and critics
don't appreciate it? In the early nineteenth-century melodramas the
villain has no moustache. We had done much in our allotted time to

154

be authentic, even to footlights that looked like old gaslights and a boy with a taper coming on to light them before the play opened. The lighting in general was much appreciated, though the hanging scene was *not* and quite revolted the patrons.

I had bitten off that week more than I could chew. Or more than we could sell, for it was uncommon long.

Perhaps the most memorable event during the run of *Miranda* early in March was the burglary of the theatre, a haul that included two revolvers borrowed from the police station, and — more disastrous from an actor's limited viewpoint — a camera containing the roll of pictures we had taken, particularly of *me*, in my large, blonde wig, wearing a most beautiful mermaid tail that had been borrowed from the Brae Manor Playhouse, where I believe David Haber and Maud Whitmore had made it. There had even been a photograph in the camera of my "topless" scene, played in the moonlight, my bosom delicately covered with a fine silk flesh-coloured bra. Each evening during the run of this very light comedy David Haber helped me in the women's dressing-room to wiggle into the heavy, colourful fish-tail; then he would carry me upstairs to an off-stage dressing-room, where I changed during the performance into various Mayfair gowns; after my curtain call (in my wheelchair), David carried me back downstairs and uncorked me. The fish that I ate from the goldfish bowl were of course thin slivers of carrot: I was not a college goldfish swallower!

One of our critics commented that Peter Blackmore, who wrote this light yarn, had but one joke to stretch over three acts and that "cut glass evidence of this paucity" was the presence on-stage at one time of no less than five decanters. Shakespeare says that for lovers lacking matter the best shift is to kiss; likewise dramatists, I think, lacking dialogue find the best shift is to offer drinks.

We followed one girl with another. *Laura* had been a popular movie, a romantic thriller. I had already directed this piece in 1949 for the Canadian Art Theatre, and I remember the night at St Adele when Bruce, hidden behind a curtain of the living room set in the last act, pointed his gun at the character called Waldo, and when he pulled the trigger the gun jammed and would not go off! Sitting in the audience I laughed my head off. Nothing disastrous like that happened at the CRT, and it was good to have Bruce play again the hero Mark McPherson (the Dana Andrews role), a change of pace for him, and a treat for the audience to enjoy him in the kind of role that it had never seen him in before. He was good, casually underplaying his role. Silvio was the effete Waldo, the Clifton Webb role in the film.

Silvio did not like the way I had blocked the action for much of the last act of *Laura*. He illustrated to me on a table at the Connaught Restaurant what *he* thought would be much better blocking. I did as he suggested, and he was right.

When we had done this play on the summer circuit for the CRT some fool of a reporter had "ruined a week's run of the play by a careless revelation of the play's top secret," Bruce told the Ottawa press, and he begged them to be very careful in discussing the plot. Lauretta Thistle of the *Citizen* beseeched her readers to throttle any friend who tried to tell them the story.

Holy Week was now upon us. We presented another Emlyn Williams, *Wind of Heaven*, suitable for Easter because the story is about a Welsh showman called Ambrose Ellis (Silvio) who is looking for something sensational to promote, and he comes across a young lad in a Welsh village who can perform miracles. This twelve-year-old child was played by Terry Finlay, whose father was rector of St John's Anglican Church. The boy speaks no words throughout the play, and Terry's presence was both beautiful and dignified. In the final scene, when I was an onlooker with nothing to say, I had huge tears every performance that went plonk! plonk! on to the bosom of my nineteenth-century blouse. We actors all found the play deeply moving, and it put us into the spirit of Easter.

It was unusual how at every performance of that play, after the final curtain, we who had been in it, Silvio and Mary and John and Lynne and Eric, loath to go downstairs and get out of our costumes, would sit around the set, still held by the spell of a play that had been soothing to the soul.

As for the audiences, although Bruce had placed at the bottom of the newspaper ads in large black print, *"BRING A FRIEND,"* it was obvious that they had not done so. This was the last attempt we ever made to "bring them in" at Holy Week, though of course we never did play on Good Friday. In the following seasons we "went dark" for the whole week.

In 1956 I met Emlyn Williams briefly in his dressing-room at Stratford-on-Avon, but it never occurred to me to ask him if he remembered his brief brush with the CRT. Apparently when he was performing his one-man Charles Dickens program in Ottawa, at the Glebe Theatre, he got into a taxi outside his hotel and said to the driver, "Take me to the theatre." The next thing he knew, he was in the lobby of the CRT!

"BRING A FRIEND" is larger than ever in the huge ads that inform the world that next week the play will be *You Can't Take It With You*, by Kaufman and Hart. There were nineteen in the cast, so we had to bring in people from outside. We nabbed from the ODL Betty Lewis, because of her memorable performance as Essie when the ODL had done this play a long time before, and Miriam Wershof, to be the black maid, Rheba. We had Roger Aucouturier, also from the ODL, playing "black-face" not for the first time in his career as an actor (he worked for the civil service "in the day-time"), and Anne Garbett as Mrs Kirby.

I arranged rehearsals to accommodate all these people. Fortunately those who work for the civil service have all manner of days "due" to the sick leave and one thing and another. This was one of the great mysteries of Ottawa life to me when I was at the ODL acting or directing. It used to puzzle me how members took time off during the week's run while I was still at my desk at the High School of Commerce at 8:40 every morning, with no coffee breaks!

You Can't Take It With You is what we call a very "proppie" play. I warned Jane Graham, our property mistress, that we would have to have every substitute prop by the Thursday morning rehearsal. I think she produced them by the Wednesday morning! She and Bob Barclay had been up nearly all night manufacturing such things as "mock-ups" for the various scripts that Mrs Sycamore is writing: "my War play, my Crime play, my Sex play ..." There would even be a "mock-up" for the two little kittens, so that the actors handling these would not have to mime. Jane and Bob producing with pride all these substitute props for rehearsal is one of my warmest CRT memories.

The ingénue Alice is important to the success of this piece. I unfortunately brought in a youngster who was not adequate. Looking at the cast list now, I marvel that we did not have Mary Sheppard play it, even though she was so good as the drunken unemployed "actress," Gail Wellington. When action centres around a weak ingénue, the others have to keep picking the pieces off the floor. As we actors express it, "It's gone under the ground cloth!"

All these people who came to us from outside the regular company would be paid something. Perhaps ten dollars, perhaps twenty dollars. An actress like Lynne Gorman, who was a professional, would receive a salary comparable with that of the rest of the company. Those who came "for fun" more than for pay were nevertheless paid something. From this rule there were few exceptions (I think some of the walk-ons in *Victoria Regina* in 1953 were not paid, at their own request). It is not a good thing to have anyone working in a voluntary capacity. When those employed backstage and in the office appeared on-stage they did not receive any extra salary.

About this time, we received a fine tribute in the *Citizen* from Lauretta Thistle, music and drama editor:

> It's heartening to see that CRT is being accepted so well in the community, heartening to hear it talked about wherever you go, and to realize that it is being supported not through a sense of duty to "culture" but as something to be enjoyed. It's good, too, to hear people comparing the stage and screen performances of *Born Yesterday,* or *Harvey,* and often concluding that the stage performance was better in many respects.

In our next play, Eugene O'Neill's *Ah, Wilderness,* Mary Sheppard played a lady of the night who had met a young man played by John Howe in a bar. On the last night of this production, Bruce said that he wanted to make an announcement at the end. He came on-stage and told a delighted audience and a delighted but startled company lined up behind him that Mary and John were going to be married before the season was over! The wedding would take place somewhere between the matinée and the evening performance of May 19, the last day of our season. One old gentleman exiting that night was overheard to remark, "We seem to be becoming a real theatre-minded city, interested not only in stage plays but in the private lives of our actors."

In June 1951, an editorial appeared in the Ottawa *Citizen:*

> The enviable place which this play group has gained in Ottawa life has been established through talent, enterprise and sheer hard work. It has been made possible by the spirit of friendship, patience and always smiling co-operation to which Mr. René Provost, director of L'École d'Art Dramatique of Hull, paid merited tribute the other day. It has drawn strength from the kind of unselfish support given by ardent devotees like Mr. Charles Southgate, the honorary but hard-working chairman. It has derived in no indirect fashion from the planning skill of its organizers, who set it up as a non-profit company. It

has gained considerably from the generous helpfulness of the LaSalle Academy whose assistance to the company has been a valuable community service. Now the fruits of all these labours, good will, and careful planning are in danger. Expanding student enrolment has made it necessary for the Guigues Street school to ask the CRT to seek another playhouse .... At present only 13 professional resident stock companies operate throughout the winter in North America, it has been one of them ... It has attracted full-time actors from Vancouver, Hamilton, Ottawa, Welland, Calgary, Montreal, Quebec City and England. To guard against artistic stagnation, it has brought in first-rate guest players from other Canadian cities and has given cast members leave of absence to participate in other productions.

A common Canadian complaint is that ours is a country made up of cultural islands. As John Bird has put it, there is too much mosaic and not enough cement. The cultural reciprocity which the CRT has fostered has gone a long way towards providing that cement. This company may well be the nucleus of a national theatre. Drama-conscious Canadians *earnestly* hope it will be able to continue.

What had happened to jeopardize our very existence? The real reason, which was never divulged to the press or our patrons, had its roots in the play we presented back in April, immediately after *Ah, Wilderness*.

We had planned an innocent little comedy entitled *There's Always Juliet*, which for some reason had to be shelved. At an emergency meeting in Bruce's office in April 1951 he and Sam suggested that we do *Separate Rooms*, an American comedy with which I had no acquaintance. Sam gave me a small part in the second act. I did not read the play until the night after the opening of *Ah, Wilderness*, and early next morning I telephoned Bruce to announce, "I think this is a dirty play." Bruce laughed and assured me that if we said all the lines fast enough, the audience would never notice and would love it!

Bruce's advertisements for the CRT are in a class of their own, though there is a touch of Toronto's Honest Ed Mirvish about some of them. Most were huge, thanks to the generosity of Mr Southam's *Ottawa Citizen*. Bruce could turn all things to advantage. For in-

159

stance, the authorship of *Separate Rooms* was enough to make one expect the worst, yet Bruce made meat of this by printing at the top of a great six-inch-by-ten-inch advertisement:

A STAGE PLAY SO HILARIOUS
it took *FOUR MEN* to write it! ! ! !

Incidentally, I doubt if anyone in Ottawa, including ourselves, had ever heard of any one of the four.

I decided to be audacious and play my character, a reporter for *Household Hints*, as a lesbian. I wore a mannish suit and a felt hat and kept a cigarette in my mouth for the entire scene, except to take my one drink. Not exactly subtle playing, but a whole new look for me. The set was that of a penthouse apartment. Asked if I would like a drink, and replying that I would, but that I didn't drink much, I walked over to the small bar and put my foot up to rest on the rail with which I was obviously well acquainted in public bars. There being no foot rail at this little bar, I fell. This was my one big laugh. Taking my drink in a single gulp, I returned the cigarette to my mouth and continued to talk out of the other corner. By the time I got off-stage I was nearly asphyxiated.

Trudy had the lead in this sophisticated piece, of which I remember nothing outside my own role, except the repercussions!

Bruce had been quite right about the reception the play would receive: "A roaring success ... audience convulsed throughout. Risqué? Well, rather, but it's amusing, scintillating, and thoroughly enjoyable ..." I soon learned that the Roman Catholic bishop of Ottawa had forbidden his flock to patronize the play. Bruce claimed that the critic for *Le Droit* had written a great review but the paper had not printed it. Then came the final blow: a report had been sent to New York's *Variety* by Paul Gardiner, and the bishop had been shown the release from that bible of showbiz, in which it was stated: "Ottawa Rep Company declared out-of-bounds by RC Bishop plays to SRO [Standing Room Only]." Then the fat *was* in the fire!

It was true that business had been terrific. Poor comfort this, when Mr Southgate received notice that after the close of the present season the CRT would no longer be allowed to use the premises of LaSalle Academy. What were we to do?

I was heartened, amazed, and deeply touched when I had a call from Harry Pullen, my former principal at the High School of Commerce and now head of the Ottawa Collegiate Institute Board. Harry said that the CRT must not die, and that if we could not find a suitable home we were welcome to use any of the high school auditoriums. We could work it out somehow, he declared. Remembering that only a year before he had met me on the street and had said, "When you get all this out of your system let me know," I welcomed this indication that the thinking public were now really valuing our work.

I had faith that somehow Mr Southgate with all his charm and his devotion to the theatre, would see us through. Meanwhile, on with the show!

This was the year that Shaw died and there were Shavian revivals in London and on Broadway as well as at the CRT. It was also the year for panning the central character, Lady Cecily, in *Captain Brassbound's Conversion: The Times* gave thumbs-down to Ursula Jeans at the Old Vic, and the Ottawa *Journal* gave the raspberry to Amelia Hall at the CRT.

Sam directed *Captain Brassbound's Conversion* in April. I ferreted out the extra men to bring our male cast list up to twenty, including Grant Wheeler and Grant Munro, Jack McGrath and John Gilmour of the ODL, René Provost, and a clutch of Arabs from his Academy of Dramatic Art in Hull.

Laurette Neal, who had often done costumes with my mother at the ODL, sometimes helped in a similar capacity at the CRT, and for my role as Lady Cecily she lent me lovely summer dresses of the 1910 period. Her mother had died when Lauretta was a little girl, and she had kept her mother's beautiful dresses. They fitted me without alterations. At least I was going to look nice.

Richard Coates of the *Journal*, a man of whom we were really quite fond, spoke his mind. "But it was the central figure, Lady Cecily, whose behaviour we find difficult to understand. Far from the mannered and aristocratic lady who overcomes evil with sheer goodness, we find a woman who treats everyone like a group of schoolboys and finds it vastly amusing in the process ... This reviewer felt that Amelia Hall was badly miscast." At one point Shaw has his heroine say: *"Captain Brassbound, all men are children in the nursery"*. A couple of weeks later I sat next to Dick Coates at a dinner, and he said that he had been rereading the play and had come to the conclusion that he had been wrong.

A letter was sent to Sam, Bruce, and me after the Shaw play. It came from Cobblebrae Guernsey Farm, R R 2, Kars, Ontario, and the writer was a David M. Mann:

I am enclosing the (membership) card that I got at the CRT last week. I might add that I am a regular patron and will do all I can to help you carry on in Ottawa. I am an old man but when I was a young fellow in Scotland the spoken drama was our only entertainment and I want to be able to see it as long as possible. I might say that I enjoy everything you do; in fact, I went twice in one week to the following plays: *Light up the Sky, You Can't Take It with You, Separate Rooms*, and on the second visits I brought a car full of friends. I saw Ellen Terry in *Captain Brassbound's Conversion* in Edinburgh over forty years ago but I liked Miss Hall better, as Ellen Terry at that time was too big and heavy. I also saw William Gillette in *Dear Brutus* and liked John Primm better, although in the Gillette production Helen Hayes played Margaret and she was a dainty little thing then.

I will certainly subscribe for next season and will do all I can to get others to do the same. I am booking three (season) seats for Friday or Saturday.

The ads that Bruce devised were usually accompanied by a simple line drawing that in some way illustrated the play. There was one drawing that was my favourite, and he used it many times. It showed a theatre electrician, a funny little fellow, standing at the top of a huge ladder and adjusting his lights to hit the background of newspaper print so that the CRT advertisement could be spotlit. This ad was used for *Candle-Light*, a comedy by Siegfried Geyer, directed by Sam. "Choose neither linen nor women by candle-light." Apparently the weather had turned hot at the beginning of June, but the play was light and gay as a Vienna waltz, and the CRT auditorium was cool and comfortable.

Penny Geldart had produced one of her most attractive and luxurious sets, this time in black and white. Don and Silvio and Trudy in the three leading roles were delightful, and the entrance of Amelia as the Baroness was "a revelation." This was another instance of our trying so hard to change our appearance from week to week. I had never before had the opportunity to look glamorous on the CRT stage, and I went to work, making my hair black and sleek with carbon paper and the face very pale, with high cheekbones, a dark red mouth, and long eyelashes. It was fun to hear the buzz of "Who is she?" when I entered.

That week we entertained the *Tit-Coq* company, who were playing that French-Canadian play, by Gratien Gélinas, in both French and

English. Gélinas was known at that time to most of us as Fridolin, the revue character that had made him a household name in Quebec. He and his company looked all over our theatre backstage and wanted to know how we managed a play a week. I had seen *Tit-Coq* in both languages, and deficient as I am in French I had preferred it in that language.

Joan Hossick, the costume mistress, worked all afternoon to prepare a buffet tea for our visitors, and Mrs Southgate poured tea at the table which was covered with a large white paper cloth, on which Gélinas drew a number of designs to illustrate to me the technical problems of set changes in *Tit-Coq* and how they managed them.

That is how things stood when we came to our final production of the 1950–51 season, *The Royal Family*, by George S. Kaufman and Edna Ferber. I love this play, partly because I have such happy memories of this production and partly because it is about theatre people.

The household of "The Royal Family," the Cavendishes (really the Barrymores), is well staffed, and so we brought in Doris Stacey and Grant Monroe, and for other "downstairs people" there were Michael Gardiner and Peter Sturgess, Peter carrying a total of fifteen well-laden trays and making some twenty-odd entrances. Eric, Sam, Trudy, Mary, Ron, John, Don, and Silvio were all there, Lynne Gorman playing the grand old lady of the family, Fanny Cavendish, with gusto and with touching pathos. Beth Gillanders we brought in from Toronto to play the Ethel Barrymore role, the "Julie Cavendish" who has that lovely speech about the audience taking off their galoshes through the first act and putting them on again through the third. Furthermore, she complains, the entire audience had seemed to be ready for a TB sanatorium, all of them coughing like seals.

Our program for *The Royal Family* unfortunately does not name two of the participants. The script calls for Tony Cavendish entering in the first act from foreign parts, with two huge dogs on strong leashes, plus a servant from India behind him, bearing a parrot. If we borrowed two enormous man-devouring dogs, would they bark down in the Green Room and Ruin All? Two police dogs appeared finally at a rehearsal. I wondered if they could *smell* how nervous they made me? But apparently my nerves were as nothing compared to theirs, for when they were led onto the wings they stood there visibly shaken, and nobody could drag them on to the stage.

I was disgusted with them. "Get a chihuahua," I said to David. And he did. When Silvio walked on-stage opening night, with that little mite on a long leash, and roared his opening line, "Is there a steak in the house?", we seemed to have improved on Kaufman and Ferber. As for that parrot, no one could go near him, except David. He perched on David's shoulder whenever they were on-stage. He hated women, David warned; yet when he was in his cage on the Green Room floor, and giving me a wicked look, Mary Sheppard happened to walk by his lodging, and as he turned his head to watch her legs he gave a low wolf-whistle!

Carl Weiselberger was an occasional reviewer for the *Ottawa Citizen*. He was an erudite European, a shy man, who truly loved theatre. I think we can get a sense of the gentle Weiselberger from these extracts from his review of *The Royal Family*:

> Ever since stage-acting has become an honourable profession of actors who are responsible citizens, union members with bank books and sometimes even share-holders, actors wish to remind us that they are still very different from the rest of the bourgeois world. Thus they like to poke fun at their own sanguine temperament, their pomp and pathos, their hamming, vanities, weaknesses ...
>
> It is almost amazing how stage-director Amelia Hall, with only one week's rehearsal, managed to integrate a very large cast into a well-blended unity of characters and types (or stereotypes!).
>
> ... Lynne Gorman as the family's famous matriarch Fanny Cavendish created one of her finest roles. She dominated the scene, hobbling on her stately cane, reminiscing and still dreaming of a come-back ... Her scene in the second act describing the haunting magic of the theatre, which survives age and infirmity and illness, was a climax of poignant, tragic strength.
>
> ... We liked Silvio Narizzano's dissolute, fantastic, comical Anthony (another pleasingly bizarre Narizzano character).

May 19, the last night of *The Royal Family*, was not only the last night of the season, it was also the day of Mary and John's wedding — sandwiched between the matinée and evening performances. How in the world did Mary and John get through the matinée? The ceremony was performed at St John's Church, Elgin Street, at 6:30 p.m., and the newly-weds had to be back at the theatre before eight o'clock for make-up. Bruce had managed a special souvenir program for that Saturday night, with photographs of the happy couple inside.

Lauretta Thistle of the *Citizen* seems to have caught the flavour of the evening in her column:

> Closing night at CRT on Saturday had all the informality of a family party, complete with wedding presents and interruptions from a not too well-mannered pet ...
>
> The Saturday night audience, long known for its warmth and enthusiasm, had scooped all other CRT audiences, and collected money for a present for John and Mary Howe — a hundred dollar Savings Bond.
>
> On this last night of the season, producers Sam Payne, Amelia Hall and business manager Bruce Raymond all spoke briefly, thanking the assisting artists, the backstage workers and others.
>
> Even the flamboyant macaw who had a part in the play had his say. But his hoarse *Awrrk* sounded a sour note in the proceedings and furthermore it was badly timed. So David Haber, stage manager, banished him in disgrace.

The city seemed to have caught on to what we were doing "in the day-time," and it was reported in one paper that if readers were to follow David Haber or Peter Sturgess or Bruce Raymond through a day's work they would be relieved to return to their own job and "not to have any worries but running the nation, or bringing up six children and a dog."

During this season Sam had directed twenty-two plays, and this final play was my thirteenth. Penny had designed thirty-four of the sets, and she was the only person on the payroll outside the two ladies at Lindsays' box office who had not appeared on the stage. Most of the actors had appeared in every play, and I think that only Mary and Trudy and Silvio had had two plays off in a row, so that they could take a week away. We had not gone dark once, not even at Easter. No one had missed a performance. You couldn't miss, because there were no understudies, and I do not recall anybody in five years missing one performance.

Yet as soon as our season was over we were all going off to work elsewhere for the summer. Sam had offers to repeat his highly successful Elwood P. Dowd in *Harvey* and would be appearing for Vancouver's Theatre under the Stars and then perhaps play Elwood again at Brae Manor Playhouse. David and Trudy were going to Brae Manor for the whole season (David, as stage manager, had been Filmore Sadler's right-hand man for some time). Betty Leighton, John Primm, Donald Glenn, and Brenda Davies were going to Brae Manor for briefer periods, some of them repeating their roles in Robertson Davies's *At My Heart's Core*.

The papers announced also that Bruce Raymond, Silvio Narizzano, and Amelia Hall, "complete with new hair-do," were bound for the Mountain Playhouse in Montreal, "a comfortable spot with bar attached." That was the province of Quebec for you! At the CRT we had only a soft drink stall in an uncomfortable foyer that was a school corridor. A schoolroom served as cloakroom. Penny was off to England for a few weeks to see her family there, before she had her first baby, which was expected in October. I had taken her presence at the CRT for granted, and it was a shock to realize that the edifice was going to lose this central pillar. That unsettling thought must have been what sent me down to the cellar to visit Penny on her home ground. I had never had occasion to go down there, and I was jolted by what I saw: pregnant Penny teetering around on planks of wood that kept her feet out of the earthen, muddy floor! Penny producing all those lovely exteriors and interiors in a cellar that deserved the credit "decor by Fagin."

We never gave Penny a send-off! We were so wrapped up in the wedding that we forgot those hundred or so sets that Penny had designed and painted (some of the plays had three different sets), and we thoughtlessly did not take a second to wonder how Penny must feel at departing from a task she had enjoyed so much.

Eric House would do some work for the NFB and then would join his friends Donald and Murray Davis at their Straw Hat Players in Muskoka. We had seen their production of the revue *There Goes Yesterday* when it came to Ottawa.

It was announced that the CRT was ending the season in the black by a small margin, that we did not have a new home yet but expected to open *somewhere* on September 18, and that our 1951–52 season would end May 17, 1952. We had entertained in the 1950–51 season about 80,000 customers and had arranged theatre parties for some thirty-seven organizations.

When I think of that second season of the CRT, which was for me the happiest of the four I spent there, I remember best walking to work every morning before ten o'clock, in the fine weather of the fall or of the spring, walking past the Chateau Laurier and around the corner toward the park, through the park and on to Sussex, and by the Basilica, turning down Guigues Street and so in at the stage door. Often "the pavement danced beneath my feet." It seemed to me then that I had really lived quite a full life and that I would not feel cheated were I to die now.

Each of those thirty-five weeks had been long simply because each had been so full. Every play had been a new experience, a new life; each had created a world of its own, so that in thirty-five weeks I had seemed to live many years. I had tasted every minute.

CHAPTER 12

THE RED BARN

I made a choice that summer of 1951 that would deplete my energies and in consequence have a deleterious effect on the CRT. Bruce and I had planned to show ourselves at the Dominion Drama Festival, which was celebrated in London, Ontario, that year. To be present in best bib and tucker would be good public relations. This festival gala week took place during the CRT's presentation of *The Royal Family*; so on the Wednesday morning after our opening night we set out at eight o'clock in the morning. We flew to London, airborne in spirit as well as body because we were proud to be representing the CRT after such an artistically successful season. We could look for talent while we were there and return to Ottawa for the closing Saturday night performance. Early the next morning at my London hotel a telegram arrived that went something like this: "Red Barn Theatre at Jackson's Point available for the summer. Would you like to rent it?" It was from Brian Doherty.

I read this offer with mixed feelings. I have some respect for initial impressions, and I could hear a faint inner voice that cautioned, "Don't put your oar in! Keep your oar out!" I had an urge to tear up this unwanted intrusion. On the other hand ... ?

There were already complications enough. The scenario for the summer as it had first been conceived was that Silvio, Bruce, and I would return to work for Joy Thomson at the Mountain Playhouse in Montreal. She had requested us.

Three events during those two or three weeks of late May and early June affected my decision. There was a clipping that came to my attention from a Montreal newspaper, showing a picture of myself, one of Christopher Plummer, and one of Joy Thomson, and the print below stated that Chris and I were going to appear at the

Mountain Playhouse under Miss Thomson's management. My eyebrows were raised at this early announcement, for even in those early, pre-contract days, we liked to know exactly what we were metaphorically signing on for before we took ship.

There was next a letter to me from Silvio, now back in Montreal, listing the duties lined up for him at the Mountain Playhouse, and they seemed to embrace directing, acting, stage-managing, set-building, painting, and understudying the janitor. I was depressed when I read his letter — surely he would tell Joy where she could go?

On top of this arrived a letter written on behalf of Joy, to me, by one of her underlings, and it was written in the peremptory manner that Joy assumed when she was getting something off her chest. It was not a tone of voice that she had ever used toward me. This letter stated that for the summer I was to direct and assist other directors, and act, and teach voice production. There was no "Would you like to?" or "Will you please?" Since the end of 1949 I had been acting for $28, or $35, or $45, a week, because it was my pleasure to do so, but anyone who asked me to *teach* was doing business with a BA and an ATCM in Speech and Drama and a first-class teacher's high school certificate and wasn't going to get those qualifications from me for nothing. Having given up teaching at $100 a week, I was damned if I was going to resume it, and act, and direct, for $35 a week.

I suffered some hours of agonizing indecision before I finally made up my mind. I then composed a telegram to Joy stating that I was not going to be with her that summer. Christopher Plummer, for reasons of his own, made a similar refusal.

By the time I received Joy's letter, which she had written to me on May 25, she must already have received my telegram saying no. I had qualms and heartache when I read her letter, so different from the one I had received from her Girl Friday, and although the letter was subdued, somewhat diluted Joy, it was nevertheless expressive of the madness in Joy that I found so endearing:

Dear Millie:

A few sordid observations ... in the dark hours ... *Present Laughter* part of Joanna set ... could you have lines on arrival to save the time? ... However you and the lines don't worry me ever. Because your great scene is with 'Gary' ... we can rehearse it separately with Barry Morse ... whom you will LOVE. Also this is a good part for you to appear in first as audience has chance to see you as you ARE shall we say ... before the old-age make-up goes on ... Could you give the costume some thought? ... As you see she must be sexy and but good ... If you haven't an evening dress that will do could you drop Kay a line re. same? The pajamas are easy ... His. Next show looks to be *Skylark*. I think you as the wife ... what's her name? ... Lydia? Anyway part Gert. Lawrence played ... Can you find a copy? We haven't got the scripts for this yet Or I'd send you one. You must know the show anyway ... fabulous part with great possibilities for comedy and general audience appeal. Now what happens next is problem 700000000. Maybe *Room Service*. ... and if so all minds will snap with 12 men screaming. And naturally impossible to latch all [for rehearsing, she means] during the day I foresee you, Sil and I directing mad scenes all over the place at weird times ... so we can go mad together ... [She explains that women's roles in *Room Service* are only small parts.] Would like you to have smaller part before we do *The Man* ... so your mind won't snap. Afraid of *The Man* ... not running two weeks ... What do you think? ... Death? Is there anything else? Nooooo? Probably 60 things I've forgotten. Oh re. voice teaching [Jack] Creley can teach that ... but as he is also teaching ... Acting ... I thought you might like to take it over ... only an hour a week. However, I read your letter re. same. And that's out. Can't find your letter at the moment ... but remember that you were not against directing? Anyway we can talk about that. Soooooooo ... shall see you. Please let me know exact date of arrival, so we can have your bed set up, etc.

Oh and as you know Sil is going to be Company Manager ... Producer ... MC and etc. And it is up to us to help him keep the authority needed for this harrowing position ... especially with some of the 'guest' actors and stuff. I know that you will help in this so that his mind doesn't snap with all the responsibility and etc. You know what I mean? ...

Love to all.

JOY.

At the same time came a letter from the lotus-land of Val St Michel, an invitation from Mary and Ed Greenwood to stay with them for a few weeks. "Let us know when you will arrive, so that we can lay in supplies (brandy for Alexanders) and meet you at the station. Do come, and please us both." But I had no time for holiday-making. When you are in love with hard work and crusading you can't sit still. "I hear in my heart, I hear in its ominous pulses, all day on the road the hoofs of invisible horses, all night from their stalls the importunate pawing and neighing." Who wrote it? That describes it.

After receiving Joy's letter I felt remorse at my belated backing out of the Canadian Art Theatre. If the letter had come before I had sent the wire, who knows? Silvio also decided not to go to Montreal and, after some hesitation, decided to come in with Bruce and me in the Red Barn adventure.

Why did I accept Brian Doherty's offer? In a letter to Silvio earlier I had expressed it like this: "Why am I going to this Red Barn venture? The only reason as I can see is that I want a chance, as at CRT, of working with people I like and respect and producing a good show (not *good theatre* yet, alas, in the highest sense of that term) and living pleasantly in the country while doing it. I hope I don't lose my money and that maybe I'll make what I would have earned working for someone else. Dear me, I do sound so serious — almost Russian. I hope that something in the air, in the company, will compensate for what looks like darned hard work."

So, on June 7, Bruce, Silvio, and I, together with a few colleagues, set out for Jackson's Point, in two cars with all our luggage. The three of us had each put $500 into the venture; Silvio, I believe, had borrowed from his father, a man we all respected and liked, while my own $500 was a windfall from my mother who held an insurance policy that had reached maturity and paid off, so that my own money remained untouched. The thought never entered my head that we might go financially into depths far above our heads and be liable for all we had, and fortunately this calamity did not befall us.

During this pre-opening period we wondered if we might collect unemployment insurance, for when we worked for the CRT we were obliged to pay into this fund; we soon learned that because we were now employers instead of employees we could not collect. Thus ended the one and only time in my life I have considered going after unemployment insurance. Bruce said that once we opened we could pay ourselves a salary of something like seventeen dollars a week, and our top fee for actors would be something like twenty-five dollars. We reasoned correctly that since it was late in the season to be casting for a summer theatre no one still available would be overly demanding of money.

Before we left Ottawa we did one thing that was wrong: we raided the CRT costume room and took a few cartons of costumes with us. True, none of the costumes was valuable, and all had been donated rather than bought with CRT money, and many of them had been donated directly to *me*. But nevertheless they were not ours to take, and as far as I was concerned they carried a curse with them and on my head it fell.

We were charmed by the Red Barn when we arrived at Jackson's Point. It was about one hundred years old, and it sat in a meadow; at one side of the barn rose the white silo on which were painted the words "RED BARN," and this at night could be floodlit. The barn had been converted into a theatre two years before, and inside it was most comfortable. In the summer of 1950 Brian Doherty and his partner, Roy Wolvin, had presented original musical revues, but now Wolvin was busy in New York and Brian was engaged in making TV films.

The impression given by some of the pre-opening press releases was that Brian had hired us three to run the Red Barn, though the actual word used was "imported." (The arrangement was that we would rent the Barn from him for $100 a week; he in turn would give us his extensive know-how in public relations and introduce us to people around the lake and in Toronto.)

We were to have a three-week pre-opening work period. We had already lined up some actors in Ottawa and Montreal: Paul Charette, Michael Gardner, and Bob Barclay and his younger brother John were all present at the outset to help get the physical plant ready. Peter Sturgess would come soon, and Georgie Bloom, Dickie Lamb, and Nonnie Griffin would stay for one show, as would Christina Drever, that thoroughly professional young character actress from the Ottawa Drama League. From Montreal we had invited Henry Ramer for *Born Yesterday,* and Penn Paterson, who had been so right as the drinking lawyer in Joy's production. Penn would stay with us for most of the summer. Two more Narizzanos had been roped in — Yola and Dino. We planned to decide which plays we could do and in what order when we had got a company together. We hoped eventually to bring our number up to twenty.

Where were we going to sleep all these people? That is one of the questions that had to be settled that first weekend. There was a hotel called the Grand View, and it boasted a two-storey annex. The hotel management offered us this annex at a low rental; the company could eat in the hotel dining-room. However, at the low rent we were paying, there would be no maid service. "Not to worry," I said gaily, "I'll play matron and hand out the clean linen every week. And I'll organize some sweeping out by the ASMs." I was going to rue the day I made that offer!

Brian beamed with enthusiasm and helpful suggestions. That first Sunday we few, a sort of landing-party, were invited to come over from the Grand View Hotel at noon-hour to have a drink at Brian's cottage and meet some people. I think it was that early in the enterprise that a nagging tick of tension started inside my innards. We had a heavy load of work lined up for that Sunday (for there was going to be no time off, no free Sunday day-times or Monday nights as at the CRT), and here we were on that very first day of scheduled physical exertions, drinking *at noon*! I have already said that we seldom drank at the CRT, only at parties on Saturday nights. Nor had we ever drunk very much at the Canadian Art Theatre, in spite of all those Quebec bars; and of course nobody drank at Brae Manor. I appreciated that drinking went along with public relations, but we had no public relations department, except Bruce, and he had other jobs as well. If people were going to "take to us" and ask us out a lot, we were done for.

At the beginning of the so-called normal working week, Silvio and I climbed into a hired car and gaily drove off to Toronto. Brian had given us the use of his offices, which I believe were on Grenville Street, opposite Malloney's, near where Women's College Hospital now stands. For two days actors congregated to see us from morn till afternoon, from afternoon till night. We saw the applicants for about ten minutes each, talking with them and sizing them up, asking about availability. I was absolutely delighted when Derek Ralston turned up, and we were able to get him for most of the summer. Toronto actor Douglas Marshall was available immediately, and since he seemed right for Father Day, that helped decide us on our opening play. Others that we hired for brief engagements were Muriel Cuttell, Carol Starkman, Guy Purser, and Terry Bolton; but Joan Watts, Daphne Goldrick, Phyllis Malcolm-Steward, Norma Renault, and John Frid were to come for longer periods. On his way to California, a most personable young man called Timothy Moxon from England agreed to stay. We *nearly* captured Anna Russell! She breezed into the office, absolutely delightful, giggled a lot, said she'd love to come, but her miserable agent would not let her work for under $100 a week. Very wise agent.

By the third or fourth evening we had interviewed them all and could return to the Red Barn and get on with the job. Our business meetings at Jackson's Point became curiouser and curiouser — three people tied together for a three-legged race. The fever of tension I had suffered that first weekend now had Silvio in its grip, and he came out in spots of apprehension about Money. There he showed more sense than I, who vaguely supposed that all might be well in that department. Silvio no doubt feared that if we went deep into a hole only his generous father could pull us out, and that would be shameful.

I suppose we would all three have liked to have pulled out before the first play got under way, but we were bound and committed. I do not mind at all being alone and quickly move out of any association where I sense I am not wanted. It was agony not to be able to walk away. One luncheon meeting I exploded with a loud, "You make me so MAD!" and left the dining room, a sudden object of interest to a number of inquiring eyes. I rushed out to the annex and up to the second floor where, locking myself in the large communal bathroom, I proceeded to overcome emotion by washing the floor. Loud footsteps along the corridor, and banging on the door: "Don't be a fool! Let me in!" So I unbolted, and Silvio and I glared at one another and no peace was made.

We could not agree on the Billie Dawn for *Born Yesterday*. I wanted someone whose work we had seen; Silvio wanted somebody new and sensational, some sexy piece from New York who would turn them on. A Toronto columnist, Stan Heller of the *Telegram*, was suggesting Barbara Hamilton. Silvio had his way. We looked at glossy prints from New York and we chose Dolores Dawson. She was not a bad choice.

By June 22 the players had arrived, and Silvio plunged into the job of directing *Life with Father*. I played Vinnie, and the children were Robert Barclay, Richard Lamb, George Bloom, and a little seven-year-old called Terry Bolton. Terry came from the Sterndale Bennett Canadian Theatre School in Toronto and he had never been away from home alone before. His interests were baseball and poetry, and he was particularly fond of Christina Rossetti. His mother had read poetry to him and his five-year-old sister ever since they were tiny things. He gave me a signed drawing of an Indian which I still treasure. Terry arrived knowing all his lines, and he never once complained or made a nuisance of himself the whole two weeks he was with us. However, at the dress rehearsal, which went on far after midnight while Silvio was giving us notes, Terry, sitting next to me, suddenly piped loud and clear: "Miss Hall, do you know why I forgot that line? 'Cos I'm TIRED!"

Douglas Marshall did not have Sam's warmth as Father Day. But who has? Vinnie is a lovely role, and I got some good reviews. Lotta Dempsey had given us a great boost:

Groping back from Jackson's Point through the frightening meshes of a dense white fog Saturday, one had time and enough to think back on the opening performance of the Red Barn Summer Theatre ... In spite of the grim circumstances, the performance of *Life with Father* seemed even better in retrospect than it did at the all-absorbing time, and we decided that if all the presentations are to be as finished and entertaining as this one, we will journey north regularly. Not only were Douglas Marshall and Amelia Hall delightful as Father and Mother Day, but the latter has that special quality of stage charm about which Sir James Barrie used to write, and which no really loved actress among the great has ever lacked. Young George Bloom as Whitney, age about 10, was practically our favourite actor of the evening. It is one of the most likeable shows of the year.

Not much had been said about Silvio in the reviews: all he had done was design the set (which meant doing a lot of the building and painting as well), play the role of the Reverend Dr Lloyd, and direct the play! As I reminded him, often little notice is paid the director of a stage play unless it has been a disaster; so be pleased.

During the week of *Life with Father* I had toured the annex, peering miserably into the bedrooms where it seemed an axe murderer had been at large. All sheets and every pillowcase where a male Day had laid his head was blood-red with the grease-paint and cold cream that we had used on our hair. (Rose MacDonald of the *Telegram* had mentioned that the family redheads looked oddly damp!) I stared at that gory scene and pondered, as women have before me, on the nature of the male. Ought I have lined up the male Days after each performance and *forced* them to wash their hair?

I had another experience that week that shook me. We had brought Richard Lamb from Ottawa to be with us for the season. He had distinguished himself at the CRT, and as Pinocchio he had appeared for the ODL at the recent Dominion Drama Festival to great acclaim. I tenderly watched over this young plant. Now Dickie asked me if he could speak with me. He seemed greatly agitated. We went out of the annex to seek privacy on the lawn, and there he unburdened himself: he wanted to get out of theatre and establish himself in the civil service where he would have A PENSION. I managed to assure him that he must leave us at once if that was what he wanted. (Perhaps he was seventeen, surely no more.)

Had our wranglings somehow been picked up by Dickie's antennae? I also worried about the young apprentice Warren Wilson, whose father in the CBC had sent him to us, entrusting his son to my care. I have continued to wonder through the years what Warren thought of us. He has now long been a writer, and with the CBC himself. One day I came upon the letter his father wrote to me on July 18, 1951: "Dear Miss Hall: Will you please forgive this very tardy letter of thanks for the great kindness you and other members of the cast showed my son Warren when he stayed with you? Since his return he has given me several glowing accounts of the good times he had and of the interesting work and responsibilities with which he was entrusted. This has been his first real experience of legitimate theatre and I am pleased to tell you that it has now come to stand much higher in his estimation than either screen or radio."

We were following *Life with Father* with *Charley's Aunt, Elizabeth Sleeps Out, Born Yesterday, Arsenic and Old Lace, Harvey* and *The Man Who Came to Dinner*. I suppose we had intended to do eight plays, but our season had been a little late in starting and we did only seven. We were also attempting Brian's 1950 schedule of performances Monday to Saturday, with a 7.30 and a 9 o'clock performance on Saturdays, but after a while we reverted to only one Saturday performance.

At the Red Barn, summer-idling young charmers with nothing much to do were discovering our encampment and the assets we possessed — the Barclay boys, for instance — and overnight were haunting our domain, pretending to help. Obstructionists all.

Of *Charley's Aunt*, which I directed, I recall only my daily exertions at the laundry tub. The girls wore white, the men were in white linen trousers. Each morning during the run I laundered the white dresses and trousers that had been on-stage the night before. I washed them by hand in a huge tin wash-tub outside the annex, hung them in the sun to dry, and later ironed them. "In poverty, hunger, and dirt," as the poet said. As for hunger, the fried food and everlasting cardboard-backed pie at the hotel dining-room were unpalatable, and a box of berries and a quart of milk consumed in the middle of a meadow became my rustic pleasure.

Worse to come. Toward the end of our ten weeks I opened one of the cartons of CRT costumes and found mildew, a calamity of which I had heard my mother speak but which I had never seen. But I knew mildew when I saw it. Out with all the CRT costumes and into the wash-tub they went; but the mildew stains remained, like the blood on Macbeth's hands.

Dolores Dawson, who came from New York City with her mother to play Billie Dawn, was a nice woman and most professional. She always carried a little notebook, and at note-giving time she wrote down in this book every piece of direction that I gave her, right up to the end of the dress rehearsal. Then she would go away and study the advice I had given her. Professional, but never inspired. I liked her, and her mother did not interfere in any way, although we let her watch the rehearsals; sitting at the back of the Red Barn, she broke during the week three theatre seats. Was the structure of the seats at fault, or the large structure of the lady? A little of both perhaps.

Norma Renault came for *Harvey* and *The Man Who Came to Dinner*, and the arrival of such a talented young actor was a tonic to me. Her sharp comedy and her remarkable face were not everyday commodities in the theatre. I proceeded to overload her with direction, like an amateur gardener watering a favourite plant, and I think Norma took that to mean I considered her hopeless. Far from it.

Actors had taken to coming late to rehearsal. I would arrive before ten and sometimes when the ten o'clock hour struck I would still be alone, except for English actor Timothy Moxon. He expressed to me amazement at the lack of discipline in Canadian theatre. I begged him not to judge Canadian theatre by the laissez-faire standards of the Red Barn. All I could have done was walk out, and I had not the heart nor the stupidity to do that.

So I would sit up in bed at night and read the Psalms to soothe my spirit. One night I made myself ridiculous by throwing my housecoat or a shawl over my nightgown and travelling down the hall to where a small but noisy party was getting under way, and I stood in the doorway and said in character for Queen Victoria, "You are preventing me from sleeping. Please be quiet." I enjoyed making that little scene, so starved was I myself for relaxation and entertainment.

My mother came over from Bracebridge for a few days during *Born Yesterday*. When you have known someone all your life, you can be too close to see them with clarity. It was Silvio who had first made me aware that my mother possessed unusually clear perception and good sense. He was fond of her and she of him. "What is the matter with you all? You are so strange." This she asked me quietly not long after she had settled in. Her presence added a warmth, but the ice remained.

When we have creative energy we are commanded by our nature to channel it into something. I don't think it always matters into what creative form. It may be in writing or painting or acting, or in making new slip-covers for the sitting-room, or in caring for someone who needs our love. All things can become grist for the mill. A creative person cannot just read, watch television, go to movies and parties, buy new clothes. There must of course be fallow periods when he or she rests and refills, but always what has been received must be given back in one form or another. Sometimes one kind of expression blots out all the others. At this time, a kind of desperation made me put all my energies into the theatre. It demanded so much physical energy, and if I deviated and gave energy elsewhere then the job would be poorly done, watered down by dissipation.

Silvio at this same time made a sudden revolt against the appalling demands of the theatre; he didn't deliberately choose this 1951 summer to revolt. It just happened. Nevertheless he worked like a Trojan, but not enjoying it. There is a time for all things, but unfortunately we cannot choose the time ourselves; we never know when the time for mourning, or for joy, or for loving, or for hating, or for revolting, is going to pounce. Life is change, and change does not await our convenience.

I think it was during *Harvey* that Silvio missed the half-hour call one evening, and we had to hold the curtain. I suppose he and I exchanged a few words. He shrugged: "What does it matter? We'll all be dead in twenty years!" Then I spat out with sudden passion: *"That's why it matters!"* I surprised myself, and him. In four words I had expressed a philosophy we once shared.

It is not easy to root into the heart of the past. I have tried unsuccessfully to sketch a part of mine here. I always live on a variety of levels and am aware, even if my heart is aching, of the humour in any situation that has grown out of my own and others' imbecilities, yearnings, and imperfections. It is only when we are in situations that we cannot control, acts of God and nature, or acts arising out of the cumulative and compounded evil of men, that we find nothing to laugh at. So one part of me could smile while at the Red Barn, and smiles again now in recollection. It is the hurting part that I cannot recreate, because I see it through a cloud of past and present self-deceptions.

I directed the final play, *The Man Who Came to Dinner*, but I refused to play my old role of the "Lizzie Borden" sister, brief though it is, because I felt ill. My refusal meant another salary. Once the play was on the boards I retired to a room in the main house of the hotel and was ill the whole week. I do not recall a doctor in attendance, yet the thought was vaguely present, "Am I going to die?" If I was, it would not be for the first time. Life is a succession of deaths.

When I came out of this purdah I learned that there would be no profits. Our $1,500 had flown. Even a seventeen-dollar pay envelope of mine had disappeared out of the office one Friday, vanishing by sleight of hand. The pop and candy concession had lost money. Incredible.

Meanwhile, back at the Mountain Playhouse in Montreal, the production of Coward's *Present Laughter*, in which I had been down to play the leading lady, had run for seven glorious weeks! The male lead had been in the capable hands of a newcomer from England called Barry Morse.

The mistake had not been in turning down the Mountain Playhouse. The mistake had been in biting off more than I could chew and going into management. I ought to have left that opportunity to others. I myself had had the opportunity to show what I could do at the CRT. But of course the CRT of 1950–51 was the Elysian fields in comparison with the limited set-up of the Red Barn.

CHAPTER 13

JOHAN AND NORA AND CHARLES

We made our various ways back to Ottawa from Jackson's Point in the late summer of 1951. Silvio had volunteered to drive the Red Barn truck back to Ottawa with all the gear, and the truck broke down near Tweed. Paul Charette and Bob and John Barclay had piled all their luggage into an ancient car driven by Dino Narizzano, and after three blow-outs and a night spent sleeping by the roadside, Dino went home by bus, leaving the other three to the car and two more blow-outs. I travelled back to Ottawa from Toronto by train, ready to prepare for our third season at the CRT.

Our heads were off the chopping block; the axe was not going to fall at LaSalle Academy after all, because Mr Southgate had got the bishop to relent. If Mr Southgate would give his promise that no more questionable plays would be presented, and if he would allow a censor to read the plays before they were decided upon for production, then the bishop would sanction that the CRT carry on in LaSalle Academy. Charles Southgate gave his promise, and the bishop chose as censor Father John A. MacDonald, head of the Catholic Family Services of Ottawa. A busy man.

Sam Payne, in Vancouver for the summer, was appalled that we now had a censor. He wrote: "I am going ahead with my plotting of *The Taming of the Shrew*, assuming that the immortal bard will escape the hammer blow of the Archbishop's boy. When one considers that Willie was a Protestant in a severely Protestant reign and times, it is likely to be taboo." Since Sam could not contain himself on the subject of Roman Catholicism, I was always to be the one who dealt with Father MacDonald, a cultured and charming man.

Had this arrangement with the bishop not been made I do not see that we could have carried on. David Haber and I had looked over the Glebe Theatre, which was reputed to be for sale for $25,000, an astronomical sum in our world. But we did not pine that we could not afford it, because while its foyer and its seating were comfortable, its lack of wing space, building and painting workshop space, dressing-room and storage space all made it impossible.

The nine permanent company members for the season were to be Sam Payne, Robert Barclay, Ted Follows, Gertrude Allen, Silvio Narizzano, Eric House (whose best friend from University of Toronto days was Ted Follows), Bea Lennard, Richard Easton (whom we knew from Brae Manor Playhouse, where he had cut his acting teeth), and myself. We were also to bring in for brief engagements Roy Irving of the Dublin Gate, Donald Davis of the famous Canadian acting family, Araby Lockhart, Lynne and George Gorman, Michael Sinelnikoff, and also Florence Fancott, Christina Drever, Beatrice Whitfield, John Gilmour, Eddie Nunn, Fred Carlofsky, and others out of that fine pool of talent at the ODL. Altogether eighty-eight people would appear that season on the CRT stage, of which eight would be children. There would be a further swelling of our ranks by two dogs, one rabbit, and a number of chickens. The Ottawa Ballet Company, under the direction of Yolande Leduc, would appear with us, five dancers strong, and we would use four musicians.

David Haber would take charge of lighting as well as being production manager. Michael Gardiner would be with us for a few weeks as stage manager; we would have a new ASM whom I had obtained from the Sterndale Bennett group in Toronto, Lew Davidson. Paul Charette of course would still be carpenter, and Charles Brennan would assist with lights. Laurette Neal of the ODL would now look after costumes, since Joan Hossick had been badly injured in a car accident. Later in the season to work backstage would come Geraldine MacIver, and later still a young Bermudian, Richard Butterfield.

As designer Martha Jamieson, from Kingston, joined us around October 2, in time to do the fourth and subsequent productions. She had been scenic designer the first year of the Peterborough Summer Theatre, and then went on a scholarship to work under Michel St Denis at the Old Vic. She was doing work with rep in England but wanted to come back to Canada. We were pleased to welcome her to the CRT, in place of our beloved Penny Geldart.

In the upstairs office, besides Bruce and Peter Sturgess, would be a newcomer listed as promotion assistant, Stanley Montgomery. Betty Leighton, Gerry Sarracini, and Derek Ralston had all gone off to work at Bermuda's Bermudiana Theatre, which was a Bruce Yorke–Michael Sadlier enterprise where so many Canadian actors were working. Chris Plummer, Kate Reid, Barbara Hamilton, John Atkinson, and so many others went there and worked in the sunshine.

Ron MacDonald did not return to theatre. He had served us well in our 1950–51 season. He was a tall, handsome, quiet man with a sense of humour, not versatile as an actor, not really an actor at all, and too intelligent to deceive himself on that score. Ron came to us from the business world because he liked theatre and enjoyed being with theatre people. It was a kind of holiday for him, I think, and he left us to return to that world. In 1956 he married the Canadian actress Sharon Acker.

We all approached the new season with high hopes. Bruce was able to announce to the press that seven evenings of the first four weeks had been sold to theatre parties. If that pace were to keep up, perhaps we might soon be able to double the length of our runs. This year we raised our seat prices, which now ranged from sixty cents to $1.50.

We opened with *The Taming of the Shrew* on September 18, 1951. Roy Irving was Petruchio, and Trudy Allen his Kate, and also in the cast were Ted Follows, Silvio, Sam, Richard Easton, Peter Sturgess, and Bea Lennard.

Roy Irving was a young man with a great deal of theatre experience. He was not able to do more than one play with us at the CRT because he had a university job for the winter. He had known Penny Geldart at the Liverpool Playhouse, had toured extensively during the war with the Dublin Gate in the Mediterranean, had been in the film *Odd Man Out*, and had worked extensively in the United States and in Canada, where he had founded the St Marys' Little Theatre near London, Ontario.

I found it quite touching to watch this experienced professional each evening after the performance walk around the stage and wings and Green Room, gathering together his costumes and his personal props and getting them in readiness for the next evening. A real old pro.

His Petruchio was not a swashbuckling sadist but a rather gentle fellow who was also a consummate actor and used his dramatic skill to transform Kate from Kate the choleric to Kate the kind.

We next presented Ted Follows in the lead role of Harry Segall's comedy, *Heaven Can Wait*. There were twenty-nine people in the cast, and everybody backstage was in it, plus Peter Sturgess from the office, and recruits such as Norah Hughes and Doris Stacey from our reinforcements abroad. Ted was able to show to advantage his amazing vitality. Lauretta Thistle said, "Mr. Follows must be using at least 5,000 calories per performance, for he's a diligent boxer-in-training, doing PT all over the stage ... Scarcely more than a bantam in physical size, Mr Follows is a heavyweight in mental studies of the subtleties of his role, and his Joe Pendleton is a real, living character."

Ted had been born in Ottawa but had travelled a great deal in his childhood and early youth, because his father was in the permanent Air Force. He had been to the University of Manitoba, had won a scholarship to the Banff School of Fine Arts, had been part of the Vancouver Everyman Players, and then had gone on to the University of Toronto, and had become one of Robert Gill's actors. He had appeared for several summers, as had Eric House, with the Davises' Straw Hat Players in Muskoka.

As Martha Jamieson had not yet joined us, *The Butter and Egg Man*, by George Kaufman, was designed by the master of all trades, David Haber, and executed by Robert Barclay and Paul Charette. The butter and egg man (a theatre term for the "angel" who backs the production of a play) was Richard Easton. Dickie had come to us from Montreal, where he was a veteran in radio, having been heard on "My Uncle Louie" and "The Way of the Spirit." He had appeared for the MRT, the NFB and Crawley Films, and had spent summers at Brae Manor Playhouse, under the Sadlers' instruction, since he was fourteen.

The Butter and Egg Man was a young, small-town boy up in the Big City with stardust in his eyes, just itching to sign away all his grandma's legacy of $20,000 if it will get him into showbiz. Dickie Easton was barely nineteen, yet he was going to play for us, superbly well, a range of roles that season from teenagers to old Captain Shotover in *Heartbreak House*. He would also play a number of middle-aged roles, which are more difficult, and he would succeed there as well. In his first entrance, as the gauche and hopeful Butter and Egg Man, he triggered laughter before he had opened his mouth. By his second appearance he had become one of the showbiz boys, attired like the producers Eric House and Ted Follows in one of those awful, navy-blue, heavily pin-striped suits that went with the twenties.

In the cast list for *The Butter and Egg Man* was an actor called Johan Fillinger, a Norwegian actor-director whom I had helped to bring out to Canada by offering him three months' employment. How had it come about that an actor in Norway had asked to come to the CRT?

Actually the CRT was rather well known in distant parts, because members of our embassies and legations read about us, in newspapers from home, or knew us from attending the CRT when they were in Ottawa. If they became friendly with actors in the countries where they were stationed, of course they spoke of us and our hard work. In Oslo, where Elsie Hall was stationed with the Canadian consulate in the late 1940s and early 1950s, actors had heard about the ODL and her friend Amelia Hall. That was why in late 1949 she had invited me to fly over on an RCAF plane from England to Oslo to meet Norwegian actors. Had I done so I would have met Johan Fillinger. But I was stupid, and did not go.

Then in 1951 I discovered that Johan had known Penny Geldart when both were at the Liverpool Playhouse. He had been in North America with Donald Wolfit and wanted to come back and work here. The generous, crazy Geldarts, most hospitable people in all the world, had promised that they would look after Johan's keep if the government would let him come. Of course it would facilitate matters if he had a job to come to! For my part, I had found it difficult to understand why anyone living in a country where there was a national theatre, state subsidies, year-round contracts, and vacations with pay would be so unappreciative as to give it all up and come to Canada.

Johan had studied first to be an architect. During the war he had been a prisoner of war, and, like Michael Langham and John Atkinson, he had directed his fellow prisoners in plays. After 1945 he had got a scholarship to RADA in London. Then came the Wolfit tour and the Liverpool rep. After that he went back home and became part of the Oslo Studio Theatre, introducing to Scandinavian audiences new English, American and French authors. The group was partially state-supported, as an experimental group, until commercial theatres and the National Theatre picked up the idea and easily outbid the 350-seat Studio for Norwegian rights. The Studio lost its raison d'être and its subsidy. It was taken over by a commercial group, and renamed the Det Nye Theatre, and Johan became producer there.

Johan said he was scared to death when he arrived at the CRT and found we had only one week of rehearsals. After two weeks he said to the press: "They accomplish so much and work so efficiently. There's so much discipline in rehearsal." As soon as he arrived, it was obvious that although he had acted in England and had studied at RADA he had a foreign accent to our ears; clearly his usefulness would be as a director.

I was intrigued and glad to see him come, but I had made this decision myself, against a noticeable lack of enthusiasm from Charles Southgate or Sam or Bruce.

I was too busy to get to know Johan when he arrived, all eagerness, and of an outgoing and loving disposition. He had told me in his letters that he would bring with him new Norwegian plays that might interest me. I never got to look at these. His first directing assignment would be Ibsen's *A Doll's House*; he wanted me to play Nora. When I was fourteen the older students at Mrs Baker's had said that one day I would play Nora. It was going to be a rare treat to get away from all those middle-aged and old ladies I had been playing all my acting life.

In the mean time we did three more comedies: *You Never Can Tell, George Washington Slept Here,* and *Two Blind Mice.*

When Bernard Shaw was told that he was incapable of writing a commercial farce, *You Never Can Tell* was his answer. There are some charming roles in this comedy about a "modern," liberated woman of 1897, who brings up her children to be free souls. Trudy Allen played this strong-minded woman who had walked out on a tyrannical husband. She celebrated her five hundredth performance on the CRT stage and received a gift from the company on-stage on the Wednesday night, and a party afterward. Trudy told the press that she was conscious most of all of the effect that various powders, tints, and dyes were having on her hair! Of course we did not have wigs. "Like other members of the Canadian Repertory Theatre, Miss Allen is not the stagy type. Like any good business woman, she works hard. About ten hours a day including a daily performance and rehearsal for the next play."

Dickie Easton played the young dentist with "a suavity and finesse that are remarkable for one week's rehearsal"; and, I must add, remarkable in one so young. Bea Lennard was teamed romantically with Dickie, as in the previous two plays. Eric House was delightful as the philosophical elderly waiter. Ted Follows and I played the precocious, inseparable, irrepressible twins, and I have seldom enjoyed a role or a playing partner more. It is such a pleasure to be happy and free, bubbling and buoyant on-stage, especially if off-stage you deal daily with problems, problems, problems!

There were three sets to this piece, which meant lots of work for Martha Jamieson and Paul Charette, and problems for our small crew shifting scenery in our limited backstage wing space. Apparently it was a long evening, but the second-act terrace set was much admired and "worth waiting for." Martha was always at her best with outdoor sets.

Richard Coates of the *Ottawa Journal* wrote an article on Paul Charette at the end of October 1951. Along with it went a large picture of Paul, holding a carpenter's ruler. It is a remarkable photograph, his face serious for once, and it reveals the dreamer and poet. Dick Coates went in search of Paul in the cellars of LaSalle Academy. Peter Sturgess gave him careful directions to where he would find a sign below announcing Paul's Perch:

> ... which led us past various flats, paint pots, cornices, fireplaces, chests of drawers and cobwebs, to the lair of Mr. Charette who sat brooding on the plans for *Clutterbuck* freshly come from the inventive mind of Miss Jamieson.
>
> Mr. Charette does not often brood. He hasn't time for it. But every Wednesday he has a moment of despair. His work in building is a temporary thing and must be torn down each Saturday night after the final show. Then when the furious work of creating another set is finished each Tuesday, the day following is one of searching question as to whether the whole thing is after all worth it.
>
> In due credit to this young man it may be said he recovers swiftly. But the thought that some day CRT may arrive at a two-week run spurs him on.

Mr Coates learned that Paul Charette was a carpenter who had once been a bridge builder, spending four years with the army hauling bridge parts for the Engineers. He got into the business of set-building with the Canadian Army Show in western Europe. His age was thirty-two, and he had been born in Ottawa.

The LaSalle Academy stage was not "plumb." If doors were built straight as they should be, they stuck when they were put on that stage. This was Paul's weekly cross. Doors and staircases had to be built not quite straight if they were to *look* straight and not lean awkwardly to one side. "While the continual putting up and pulling down of sets in no way alters the housing shortage, it does tend to make Mr. Charette a philosopher."

Martha Jamieson and Paul Charette would be challenged again in *George Washington Slept Here*, by Kaufman and Hart. The plot concerns a businessman (Eric House) who wants to get away from the rat race and return to nature. He buys a house of supposedly historical interest and sets about restoring it. His sceptical wife

(Trudy Allen) bears with him through sudden shocks and bitter disillusionments. Ted Follows appeared that week in his first character role for CRT, the phlegmatic local hired man and contractor. George Bloom played a Monster Child with relish and attack.

Martha and Paul produced a Pennsylvania farm-house interior in various stages of rustification and restoration. I have but one mental picture of this production: myself sitting in the balcony at the dress rehearsal, where I always sat, notebook in hand (or in the hand of a member of the crew, if one was free). The music fades, the house-lights go down, and the red velvet curtains part to reveal the decrepit interior of an old farm-house, holes in roof and walls, a threshing-machine centre stage, chickens running around. Then Eric and Trudy are there, Eric arguing with the old farm-hand, who is Ted in deep disguise. The chickens must have been controlled by David in some way or other ... probably cotton thread attached to one leg of each bird. David said that when the curtains parted the chickens all fell down.

While I was directing *George Washington* in the day-time I was playing in the evenings in *You Never Can Tell*. That didn't leave me much time to think about *A Doll's House*. As soon as *George Washington* had opened, I plunged into the learning of Nora's words, and I don't think I returned to the Kaufman and Hart play after seeing it through opening night.

I think we may have used a translation of the Ibsen play by R. Farquharson Sharp, and I regret to say that it did not come trippingly to the tongue. You cannot do anything with a part until you have the words. I knew I was ripe for Nora, that I could play the role with great range; like silk off a spool it would come, so long as the words did not impede me. So I learned the words dead on. Every evening of the rehearsal week I started at seven o'clock, lying on the floor of the living-room on my stomach. Wednesday evening I learned act I. Thursday evening I learned act II; Friday evening I learned act III. By then we had completed three day-times of rehearsal. Saturday morning we had about two hours' rehearsal and then two performances of *You Never Can Tell*. Sunday, Monday, and Tuesday I could live *A Doll's House* every waking minute.

The rehearsals with Johan were a revelation to me. He worked to get me out of the concentric attitudes that one uses when playing middle-age and age. He showed me how to be as free as a bird. My arms were to be always loose from the shoulder, whether hanging by my side or lifted up to heaven. In the first two acts, I always *leaned*, on tables, on the backs of couches or chairs, always seeking support, stretching and indolent as a kitten. In the third act, after Nora goes out to take off her fancy dress, there was no more leaning on furniture. Nora was self-contained and self-supporting.

Nora was a woman in the cage of the home, but in my playing of her I was released out of *my* cage, and under Johan's direction my body became an instrument that could express not only superficialities but also my deepest feelings. Perhaps he knew so much about Nora because he was a close friend of the elderly actress in Norway who was considered to be their greatest Nora.

I found the first act wonderfully relaxing. It was a holiday to be playing someone as carefree, as pleased with herself, as Nora is at the beginning of the play. I recall rocking in a low rocking chair, one arm above my head playing with the chair back, the other hanging indolently to the floor and swinging as I rocked, asking my unfortunate friend Mrs Linde to tell me about her life and then, before she has a chance, telling her about my *own*. It seemed to me that act one was the easy act, and so I was surprised when another actor phoned me when the production was finished and said that she had never seen the first act played so well, that the first act was the difficult one.

Every night that we played *A Doll's House* I would have a moment somewhere in act one (it varied every night) when a black blind seemed to come down in my mind and I would not know what words came next. The blind must have gone up again immediately, because I always carried on afterward with added enjoyment, relieved that the moment of fatigue had come and gone.

In one scene in the last act Torvald is caressing Nora, and she is longing to respond, yet she knows that this night she must run away and kill herself, so that Torvald will not have to take the blame for her crime of forgery. That is a scene in which you hold the whole of your life in your hands, the whole of your love. I used to feel at that moment a contact with the whole audience, a great inexpressible sharing. Bertha F. Davis wrote to me: "Nora — I shared last night all your inner turmoil and admired and almost wept at the covering of gaiety."

Such "sharing" by an audience is a most potent force. I am sure it must contribute much to the concentration of feeling that builds up inside the actor. Sometimes I have felt, "I did not know that I could contain so much." I felt full and complete all through this act, and when Torvald left to read his letters in his study and I put on my cloak to leave and stood there saying a silent good-bye to all that I loved, I did not need to *do* anything ... and I could have stayed there alone on-stage a very long time and never been emptied. Then Torvald rushes out with his accusations and his anger, and Nora bursts forth with all her pent-up love, "I have loved you more than anything in the world!" It is all-important to play the last scene remembering that the scales have only just dropped from Nora's eyes. She has not been planning for six months to leave Torvald.

Dick Coates in the *Journal*, opened his remarks by saying that the sensation produced by this play in 1880 was hardly valid today. I wish he had been at our Saturday matinée, for he would have got the surprise of his life, as I did. In the final scene, in which Nora and Torvald sit down and have that first real talk they have ever had in their married life, Nora tells him that never for a minute did she expect him to let her take the blame for the forgery she had committed; the wonderful thing would happen, and he would take the blame upon himself; that was why she was going to kill herself.

At this point Torvald explains to Nora that while he would suffer many things for her sake, "No man will sacrifice his honour for the one he loves." To this Nora replies, in a voice of complete maturity if the actress knows what she is doing, *"It is a thing hundreds of thousands of women have done!"* When I had said that line, at the matinée, there was a sudden intake of breath from the house, and then with alarming spontaneity all those women broke out into a fury of applause. I was stunned. I felt my neck and face turn red with embarrassment for all of us, for all women. "Don't! Don't!" I wanted to say. "Don't *tell!*" That was the most naked emotion I have ever felt openly expressed by an audience.

Playing that final scene was a challenge. It was obvious by dress rehearsal that Sam, as Torvald, did not know his words. I learned them. Even waiting in the wings, while I was taking off my fancy dress, I was looking at Torvald's words so that when necessary I could ask myself the questions and answer them. I am sorry it happened like that, because you can never make the great discoveries on-stage if you (or anybody else) do not know the words, so that they are, as it were, subconscious. Only then can you swim around in a role, and go deep underwater. But it did not spoil it for me. There were such wonderful ideas to express, and all the pain of the end, "Oh Torvald, I don't believe any more in wonderful things happening!"

Years after *A Doll's House* my proud mother told me that the Norwegian minister to Canada, Danile Steen, had told her that I was the finest Nora he had ever seen outside of "the" Nora they had back home in Norway. Johan said that, too, and during 1952 he did his best to make it possible for me to play Nora in New York. But of course it was impossible, because I was not known there. It is seldom, I suppose, that the right role comes to an actor at exactly the right time for *her*; that was how it was with me then. Something seemed to take possession of me, something in my innermost being, and Nora lived in *me*, blown into flame by Johan.

Johan had sent me a note for the opening night in which he had written; "Dearest Millie: the words are not in my vocabulary." That was a beautiful thing to say. I thank him still for a most fulfilling experience, and one not in any way a disappointment. That is a rare event for an actor in the theatre.

Silvio had been off for two shows, so that he might go to New York. He came back in time to see the Friday or Saturday performance. When the curtain came down on the final act, he came backstage at once. I was still on the stage, perhaps not wanting to go downstairs and get away from the play just yet. I shall not forget his face as he stood there, an expression on it I had not seen there for a long time. Then he came over and put his arms around me, and after a few seconds he said, "Sometimes we forget."

Silvio had decided to go into CBC television and would be leaving us at Christmas. His last play with us was *Three Men on a Horse*, by John Cecil Holm and George Abbott. This is the play that catapulted Hume Cronyn into stardom when he was a young actor in New York. Eric played this leading role—the little greeting-card poet who works out winners on the racing sheet as he commutes to work each day. He never places a bet and is only mildly surprised when his choices turn out invariably to be right. The sharpies who take him in hand were Silvio, Dickie, and Ted.

On the last night, of course, we had a farewell party for Silvio. He had presents for us all, and each gift was a second-hand book that he had bought in New York during his few days there. The choosing must have taken time, because each book title was a satirical comment on the recipient. My own name was a book by John Masefield, on how to produce Macbeth. On the flyleaf Silvio had written, "To Amelia Webster Hall, for bigger and better productions always." This was perhaps a reference to one or two newspaper stories during the Red Barn campaign, in which I had been compared to Margaret Webster; "but Miss Webster," remarked one columnist, "only produces Shakespeare." (But then we can't all be versatile, and I'm sure poor Miss Webster was doing her best.) I was not too pleased at this dig from Silvio: a Margaret Webster I was not, though lack of time and of money threatened to turn me into a Lilian Baylis! Amelia *Baylis* Hall hit closer to home. At the bottom of this flyleaf Silvio, in softer vein, wrote: "Sic Transit Gloria Mundi. It'll all be right on Monday. Time cures, heals, and makes better."

And so Silvio left us, in body if not in spirit, to be trained at the CBC as a bright young television producer, to go from there to England and be voted top television director of the year 1958, and then to direct films. Kicking and screaming, you might say, he had been dragged down the roadway to success.

My scrap-books show me what others were thinking about us; they do not tell me what I myself was thinking, and at that time I kept no diary. We who were putting the shows together had no time for dreaming or looking far ahead; actors and backstage folk, whenever they had time to stop *doing* and start dreaming, hoped for better plays, something you could get your teeth into week after week, and better directors, and two weeks in which to get the play ready.

What we wanted most of all was an audience that we could rely on to come to the theatre. I don't recall anyone ever complaining about having to learn a big role week after week. I don't recall actors complaining about their salaries or the hours that they worked. They were not the least concerned about Canadian plays; they were extremely critical of any play that they felt was not first class. Dickie Easton, going away for a few days of holiday, read *You Touched Me* before he left and scoffed at it. He came back to us in time to see our production and scoffed no more: he was then proud to be one of us!

Naturally you do not tell the press and the public your daily problems. Nothing succeeds like success, and the papers told a success story. It *was* a success story, too. What you could not let people know was that working so hard so many hours a day seven days a week makes one very tired. Did no one realize what a toll it takes on bone, muscle, and nerves to present a play a week, of high standard, thirty-five weeks of the year, with so small a staff? If I wanted to hire someone from Toronto I did not call a secretary; I wrote or typed the letter myself, usually after midnight, always at home. I had no office. I made my production notes at home. If I needed something from the library or from the National Gallery, or from a music shop, I went myself. I phoned people myself to hire them. And in between directing and acting and doing these extra necessary chores, we held emergency meetings in Bruce's office, and once in a while (thank the Lord for Charles Southgate, who called meetings only when absolutely necessary) we had a meeting of the board.

At the CRT there were no extra hands. We who were responsible for management and for getting the show onto the stage had no entourage of helpers. Often Charles Southgate would come back-stage after the day's rehearsal; perhaps he had come down from

Bruce's office upstairs, or he might have come down to the Green Room from the street, his face all rosy with the Ottawa cold, returning from a flying visit to a u.s. paper company. He would bring new energy into the atmosphere, a warmth that made the work a family affair; when he asked quietly, "Are you tired, Amelia?" I could answer, truthfully, "No, I'm not tired!"

Another responsibility that devolved upon me was the ever-present problem of getting the rights to perform a play (unless, of course, it was an old play or a classic, which would be in the public domain). I had to write to whatever royalty house in London, New York, or Toronto controlled each play and get from it permission and pay it the royalty. There were about a dozen such houses. The royalty was around $150 a week for a professional company, and $200 was considered very high. There were various reasons why the rights might not be released. If the play were still on in New York, or if there was a national tour contemplated or already on the road, it was impossible. It did not matter if the tour would never reach within hundreds of miles of Ottawa, or that it was not coming to Canada at all; if there was a tour, we could not get the rights. It made us very angry that as far as royalty houses were concerned Canada was a part of the United States.

In order to keep abreast of what was new in the British theatre, I subscribed to the magazine *Theatre World*, which I received every month. Every new play in London was discussed in its pages, and there were photographs by the great theatrical photographer MacBain. I would make my choices and send for the scripts to the royalty houses concerned.

Whenever I made a quick trip to Toronto, I would visit the Toronto branch of the royalty house of Samuel French, at 27 Grenville Street, and discuss plays with Mona Coxwell. The place was staffed with two or three older women. One of these would bring us tea, and Miss Coxwell, her Pekingese, and I would spend a pleasant hour, profitable for both her and me. In my Ottawa Drama League days, before I met Mona, I stood in awe of this fabled lady, over whose eyes one could never pull the wool. If you tried to sneak a quiet production of so much as a scene from one of French's plays without getting permission and paying up, she pounced. Had she eyes in the back of her head? My regard for her both as a superb business woman and as a kindly and most charming friend grew with the years.

By the fall of 1951 another friend, Elsie Hall, had returned to Ottawa after her tour of duty with the Department of External Affairs. Living now on Bolton Street, quite close to the CRT, Elsie began to serve me dinner every opening night. After the dress rehearsal I would walk over to the house, and after my main course Elsie would have me sleep for half an hour; then dessert and coffee and back to the theatre. These evenings at Bolton Street continued until Elsie was posted to New York City in January 1953. Elsie was one of the wonderful people who did all they could to make life easier for me.

I remember leaving the house one evening to find the streets and roads turned to solid ice: somehow I got up Bolton Street, clinging to the trunks of trees when possible. Arriving at the corner of Bolton and Sussex I navigated the corner on all fours. It was a treacherous journey to Guigues Street, and took me a long time, and all that time I was terrified that the cars that were slithering all over Sussex might skid on to the sidewalk and finish me. At LaSalle there was no sand on the steps, and I made immediate phone calls to have this remedied, lest we be faced with lawsuits from maimed customers. For we did have customers that night, in spite of the ice-fields.

There was also a Mme Blondin, of le Foyer de l'Art et de Livre, whose warmth and charm raised my spirits whenever on my journey home I stopped into her shop to chat. One year she gave me all my Christmas cards; I was free to take from her shelves the cards I preferred. At the back of this shop was a large room in which painters would meet after an exhibition, and they would drink wine and chat animatedly in French. If I saw the light on as I passed late at night I would join them, and over a glass of red wine, and understanding little of what was said, I would feel completely at home among family and friends, and tiredness would go from me.

Had my mother not been at home during the larger part of the CRT season I would never have lasted the course. It was because I did not have to give thought to housekeeping, shopping, cooking, laundry, and sewing that I was able to last longer than anyone else on the treadmill at the CRT. I think highly of the art of housekeeping, and have often enjoyed and even revelled in it, but like all arts it is demanding. I am never at ease in a house that has been given "a lick and a promise," and meals off the corner of the kitchen sink do not appeal to me. I bless my mother for providing an ordered household during five sometimes chaotic years. Furthermore, she endured, though not silently, the spectacle of her very best table (a "find" at an antique store on Bank Street) piled high with books and papers in hideous disarray, the polished, burled surface lost to view for weeks on end.

One aspect of the CRT days that I could never recapture whenever I returned to Ottawa was the *feel* of walking home at night from the theatre. It was lonely on Sussex Street and increasingly lonely as one left Confederation Square and went up Elgin Street, the way Toronto used to be lonely if you walked up Yonge Street on Saturday night, after a performance at the Royal Alex. One night, in 1950 or 1951, passing the Chateau Laurier and about to cross Confederation Square, Silvio and I had said, "Good evening, sir," to "Uncle Louis" St Laurent, walking home by himself from a late session in the Commons. No police around the prime minister then.

During this period of my life anything I experienced in living, any feelings awakened in me by painting or by music, I longed to put into some form on the stage. When I heard music that moved me deeply, or stirred me to excitement, I would want to find that feeling, that excitement, in a play, and express that piece of music as theatre. A painting might remind me of the mood or spirit of a certain play or playwright. I would feel that a particular play needed decor inspired by a particular painter. Sometimes I would, if I had the time, phone Jack Kash of the Ottawa Symphony, and I would tell him the *feel* of a certain play and ask him what composer would give that feeling, would be sympathetic. It is always a delight to talk to an expert on something one knows nothing about, provided that the expert is enthusiastic and amusing, as Jack Kash always was. Or I would go to see Kathleen Fenwick at the National Gallery and ask her what painter had such and such a *feel*. I did not take up too much of the time of these experts, because I had so little spare time myself. Talking to them was always a little holiday for me.

Meanwhile, the weekly grind went on. We all missed Silvio, and there were other changes as well. Dora Clarke joined us and took over props from Lew Davidson, who became assistant stage manager. Geraldine MacIver also came to us as stage manager, taking over from Michael Gardiner, who left to study in Chicago. David Haber was given the grand title of stage director — in other words, production manager.

The first play presented with this new team, in November 1951, was Priestley's *When We Are Married* — one of my favourites. Anybody who has ever been in it remembers many of the lines. My mother loved the play, and I would have her read it to me using as broad a Yorkshire accent as she could command so that I might get the full flavour of it. When I met Priestley some years later, he told me that he had always intended to write a sequel about the "three 'appy couples" but had never gotten around to it. Would that he had.

The three happy couples were Trudy and Sam, the latter as Alderman Joseph Helliwell; Miriam Wershof (Mrs Max Wershof) and Dickie Easton as Councillor Albert Parker and wife; Mae Holt and Eric House as Mr and Mrs Soppitt. Ted was the photographer (accent on the first syllable) 'Enry Ormonroyd, and Bea was the woman wi' dyed 'air, called Lottie. Lew Davidson, always anxious for a role, was Gerald Forbes, the organist of Lane End Chapel. Alderman Helliwell and Councillor Albert Parker were "big men at chapel," and Councillor Albert had expected the worst when this young organist was hired: "When I 'eard he come from t'South and 'is name was Gerald, *Lah-di-dah*, I said, that's what we'll get from 'im, *Lah-di-dah!*" What they in fact get from this young man is the information that they are not really married. The parson who had officiated had neglected to be ordained!

My favourite part is the early discussion of *The Messiah*. The young organist and choirmaster of Lane End Chapel of course produced this before Christmas, as did all the other church and chapel choirs in town. "When we got it, it were a good one," says Mr Soppitt. "Aye," replies Councillor Albert Parker, "but by that time, who cared? If you don't get in your Messiah before t'end of November you might as well take it and chuck it in t'canal!"

I played the cheeky housemaid, Ruby Birtle, as well as directing. At the Saturday matinée I was sitting in the front row of the balcony with Eric and some others of the cast when I suddenly realized that the front door-bell was going off-stage and that meant that in three seconds I was due on-stage to answer the door! A leap out of my seat and a dash down the side of the balcony and a plunge down the staircase that leads into the stage wings. Then I turned into Ruby Birtle and walked on stage.

This was one of the hazards of Saturday matinées: we always sat in the balcony at any time we were off-stage for a bit, and we'd get so wrapped up in the play we'd forget we were in it. Eric was the worst offender. You would hear a sudden, "JEEZ!" and there would be the clatter of frenzied feet along the side of the balcony, and he would take the stairs six at a time. The company was delighted when I joined the club by missing an entrance as Ruby. I can still see Bea giggling away for the rest of the afternoon.

Carl Weiselberger called the opening night one of the smoothest, fastest first nights of the season, and said Eric House's Mr Soppitt, meek, taciturn, and hen-pecked, was the subtlest figure.

Why was our next production, *Home of the Brave,* a disaster at the box-office? Bruce had put out a program sheet ahead of time especially to promote Arthur Laurents' first play as "an honest play by an honest playwright." He quoted the foreword by the drama critic of the *New York Journal-American*, Robert Garland: "Arthur Laurents, American, and now a G.I. out of uniform, walks right up and faces the predicament of a lad who is a soldier and a Jew, but above all is a human being, sensitive to the shock of prejudice ... It is more than a soldier's problem; it is the problem of people everywhere." The huge ads included a soldier, gun in hand, going in terror "over the top" and perhaps this kept people away. The reviews were good but revealed the theme of war and prejudice, and people did not want to see horrors on-stage after living through them for so long. Even word of mouth did not bring people in, though every evening, in the final curtain call, the entire tiny house would stand, something that I don't recall ever having happened at the CRT before.

The six men in this cast were Sam, Bruce, Eric, Ted, Dickie, and Bob Barclay. Bob played the lead, Coney. Ted, everyone said, played Mingo magnificently and took the honours of the evening; further honours went to the set, designed by Martha and painted and built by Paul.

I did not get to see this production till the third performance, on the Thursday night. I was aghast at the size of the house. I sat through the play without going out at intermissions, and I still sat there after we had all stood up in tribute at the end, during that immensely moving curtain call, with five of the men on one level, and Dickie Easton, the one who had been killed by the Japanese, appearing at the back like a "shade." It had been one of the most moving evenings I had ever had in a theatre in my life. What did it matter what the theme of a play was, so long as it broke down the hardness of our hearts as this production did? Why were people afraid of being touched?

Dickie Easton's parents came on the Saturday night, and we were all invited to their room at the Chateau Laurier for a drink afterward. His charming parents had had a shock that night. Dickie had invited them, and they had come in all innocence and seen him brutally killed on-stage. Since he was their youngest son, and the only one they had left after the war, the Eastons can't have enjoyed the play. Maybe that was how the public felt in general — they preferred to sit that one out.

As this play was closing, I met Mr Southgate in the lobby of the theatre. He smiled his wonderful smile, "Amelia, we've lost a thousand dollars this week. *But we can be jolly proud of ourselves!*" Only once did Charles Southgate ever question my choice of a play.

"What would you feel as an old soldier if I were to produce *Journey's End?*"

"If you want to do that play, Amelia, you do it. I wouldn't want to stop you. But I couldn't come to see it. I couldn't."

I wanted ardently to produce that play, the greatest to come out of the First World War. I thought that if I could tackle this play it would get something out of my system, give expression to the thing I had lived with all my life, the death of the men I had not known but could never forget — my father, my uncle Harry, my cousin Albert, and the millions of others. "Let those who come afterwards see that their names be not forgotten."

Nobody ever talked about it, but for me that was the reality buried deep. I longed to pull it out by the roots and examine it. I had gone into the Peace Tower with Stanley Mann and had listened in silence to this playwright who hated war but seemed to have no personal knowledge of the deprivation of war. He stood in the Peace Tower and jeered. I was silent. I had something to say, too, a need to speak on the cataclysm that had affected all my life — but C.S. said, "Do it if you must, but I cannot come to see it, Amelia." So I desisted and remained silent, just as all those men who got back from that bloody time have remained silent.

Our next production was certainly a contrast. There was a cast of seventeen in *The Barretts of Wimpole Street*, by Rudolph Besier. Florence Fancott, Bea Whitfield, Jack McGrath, Werdon Anglin, Roland Smith, Frank Biron, and Carl Lachnan joined us. I remember mostly the jolly games of cribbage around the big dining-room table in the Green Room, where we who were not on-stage had to try to keep our noise level down or David might descend from the wings, hurling Olympian thunderbolts. I was playing Miss Bella Hedley, with but two scenes, and Carl Lachnan was my "dear Hawwy!"

Ted was Robert Browning, Eric was the father, Mr Moulton-Barrett, and Bea was Elizabeth Barrett. This was Bea's first important leading role with us. She was Toronto-born and had attended the University of Toronto, where she worked for Robert Gill at Hart House. She had worked in Vancouver's Totem Theatre and Theatre under the Stars and with the Woodstock Players in the United States. In Toronto she had appeared also with the New Play Society and Spring Thaw.

Something splendid was given to the play by Bea. Stephen Franklin, for the *Ottawa Journal*, said: "From her invalid couch, through the first two acts of an unconscionably long play, she gave the production its centre, its inner glow, and its integrity. She put out to her audience last evening that inner radiance which marks the triumph of the courageous spirit over weak flesh, and this is a considerable achievement. She wore a grave beauty, a look of the times, a nice resolution and as well an anguish which was never wrung falsely from her."

Our December presentation, A.A. Milne's *The Dover Road*, we pulled out because people had written in and asked for it. Lauretta Thistle said Johan Fillinger had given it a smooth production, with touches of directorial genius. Fillinger's direction seemed particularly apt in the ceremonial serving of food and in the discreet use of comic pantomime throughout the play. The story concerns a Mr Latimer, who lives on the Dover Road and keeps himself busy persuading runaway couples that hasty first marriages are folly and hasty second marriages practically suicide. She found Sam "absolutely stunning — there's no other word for it — in a tartan dinner jacket. There's more than a dinner jacket to his charm, however; this is one of his best performances."

This play closed on December 22. Christmas day was Tuesday; so instead of opening that day, which would be *death*, we decided to open with a matinée of *Treasure Hunt* on Boxing day. The actors were given two days off to go to their families or friends, with instructions to come back for a dress rehearsal on the Tuesday. This meant that up to their going away they had rehearsed the play for only three days, plus a couple of hours on the Saturday morning. All hands had promised that they would work on their words while they were away.

When we came together for the dress rehearsal, the play was in a state of unpreparedness such as I had never seen before at the CRT. We had a hasty meeting to discuss whether we ought to cancel the Boxing day matinée — a major disaster to lose one performance out of Christmas week — but in the end we decided to carry on.

This was the North American première of *Treasure Hunt*, which in London had starred Dame Sybil Thorndike in the role of Aunt Anna Rose, which I played in our production. She is a lady of charming and amiable craziness somewhat like the Madwoman of Chaillot, who travels in her sedan chair, set in the middle of the drawing-room in her family home, Ballyroden, in Ireland. Travel leaflets in hand, and with her overnight bag, she takes off to look behind the Iron Curtain, or she boards the Blue Train (non-smoker) for Vienna, or flies to the Caribbean. Meanwhile the younger members of this penniless aristocratic family are turning the house into an inn. The reviewers found the first act took time to get going, and Richard Coates blamed the author! Mr Weiselberger, however, noticed "curiously enough, although this sedan chair of Amelia Hall does not move, her lines move faster and livelier than those of the rest of the cast." Amelia Hall had not been away for two days at Christmas!

Treasure Hunt was Johan Fillinger's last play for the CRT. He had been with us three months, the length of employment guaranteed for him to come to Canada. Of the five works that he had directed for us, two were very good plays — *A Doll's House* and *Home of the Brave* — and with these he had done a superb job. I knew the actors had been enormously pleased with his work; he had administered a shot of adrenalin. The remaining three plays were not as fine, yet *The Barretts* had been a good production. *The Dover Road* and *Treasure Hunt* were not up to our highest standard, but that was not Johan's fault.

By December the actors were aware that Johan was leaving. A shadow fell across the whole company. Why did we not keep him on? I recall no discussion on this subject. Had there been a demand from Mr Southgate, or from Sam and Bruce, then he would have remained. He was not useful to us as an actor, and I think that Mr Southgate's opinion was that we did not need and could not afford three directors.

Johan had arrived with enormous enthusiasm. I think he had made great plans for what we would do at the CRT. When he saw how hard we worked and the level of our attainment his enthusiasm soared. It must have been hard for him to see that I could *not* say to him: "Here we are — direct us. We like you, be one of us." Nor could I say to Charles Southgate, "If Johan goes, I go!" Such an ultimatum never entered my head.

The 1951–52 company at the CRT, especially up to Christmas, had been a very different flavour from that of 1950–51. I would call it bitter-sweet — at times manic-depressive! In 1950–51 we had been a company of friends, fairly close, but all private people. And no cliques. In late 1951 people tended to bring their private lives into the Green Room. Since I had done *The Glass Menagerie* in Montreal I had not enjoyed a play so much as I had enjoyed doing *A Doll's House*; certainly I had never worked with a better director. But I did not care for Johan's involvement in all our little personal affairs. I can work very closely with an actor and with a director without putting my heart and soul into his hands. I am ready to show all my heart and soul on-stage, no holding back, but I do not want off-stage to surrender my privacy; I do not want to live in anyone's pocket; I do not want the heart plucked out of my mystery. I must have space around me, and when you work in a small area, such as we had, you are like the English on their little island — you have to insist on your right to stand alone. My feeling of being a disappointment to Johan because I was aloof, plus my being weary of the sea of emotion in which we all might drown, made me not care any more who left, if only we could have *peace*.

I really think we were all a little insane. Our minds, as Joy Thomson would have put it, had *snapped*, and we lived in the visceral area. Since an actor has to know a great deal about these lower depths, that was not altogether a bad thing. It was just a pity that we suddenly were not doing any plays in which we could put these juices to good use — *Medea, Oedipus Rex, The Bacchae, The Trojan Women,* and Tennessee Williams's, and *Ghosts, The Duchess of Malfi, Macbeth* — not the seemingly endless line of comedies on which we were about to embark.

Would keeping Johan have made a difference? Today it would, perhaps. Today theatres have got an audience, and numerous subsidies. We had neither of these. We had Charles Southgate, and if we lost him we were out of business. I was not such a fool in 1951 as to dictate to the man who made it possible for the one fairly stable theatre in Canada to keep going.

I think I served the early 1950s well because I was ready and willing to work so hard, and because I *never* said, "There is only so much you can do in a week." Only an enthusiastic fool would have taken on such a job, and stayed with it, to run a theatre with so few people on its payroll. Hard-working and enthusiastic I was, but no politician, no tactician. Possibly that was why I liked working with Charles Southgate, because he had no motive except love of creating theatre. He did not hanker after social position. He was not frustrated and lacking self-expression, for he got up at six o'clock most mornings to paint in oils before going to work. In a sense, he and I were both babes in the primæval Canadian wood.

CHAPTER 14

GOOD FRIENDS, ABSENT FRIENDS

I thought that the line-up for the beginning of 1952 was hardly up to standard. The one fine play we had announced, *Come Back, Little Sheba*, was struck from our list. Five comedies opened the year, none of them great. However, we did them well. Looking back, I think the emphasis must have been on plays that were likely to attract theatre parties. If this was so, it defeated its own ends, because by the end of the 1951–52 season the theatre parties had made a profit for themselves of $12,000 and the CRT was in the red perhaps as deep as $5,000. This situation prompted the Bank of Nova Scotia to send us a piece of advice: "Be just before you are generous."

Two days before we opened *The Happy Family*, by Michael Clayton Hutton, Florence Fancott had to leave us because of illness, and Lynne Gorman took over the role of the mother, Mrs Lord, with the kind of professionalism one expected from Lynne. This was an up-to-the-minute English comedy about the Festival of Britain, based, I think, on a true story. The new roadway to the mammoth festival, by an error of design, would pass right through the little home of the Lord family, and to alter its course would cost the country nine million pounds! A new house is offered to the Lords elsewhere, but an Englishman's home is his castle, and they refuse to budge. They stand siege against the government.

We all had to speak Cockney. Eric as Mr Lord spent the entire play carrying in his arms a huge pet white rabbit called Winston. The first rabbit we received from the farm was quickly withdrawn and replaced by her husband twenty-four hours later; apparently even farmers can't tell the difference between sexes in the rabbit world, and the first Winston had been pregnant.

When food became scarce during the siege I, as the old maid, Aunt Ada, wanted to eat Winston and kept a beady eye on him whenever I was not taking a quiet nip from the bottle on the sideboard, or consulting my Ouija board: "Blue Feather, are you there?" I think it was in the final curtain that I was obliged to levitate. I managed this from behind the chesterfield, my head and shoulders appearing, while I managed somehow to raise an effigy of my lower limbs to the public view. Most exhausting and calling for a contortionist. According to the press, the comedy was an excellent choice for the New Year, and I remember we had a lot of fun with it ourselves.

We got Araby Lockhart to come in from Toronto as guest artist for the next two plays. We advertised her as "Star of *There Goes Yesterday*," which had been a Davis production. She played for us the leading role in an English comedy of 1934 called *Jane Steps Out*, the story of an ugly duckling who blossoms forth and gives her beautiful, sophisticated sister (Bea Lennard) a lesson or two in how to be a femme fatale. Dick Coates said: "Miss Lockhart, who hardly seems to need words to express her feelings ... moves from drawing room to bedroom without missing a laugh or an innuendo. From her eye-blinking first kiss to her mastery of an off-the-shoulder gown her change from plain Jane to plain wicked is accomplished with a shy ease which appears to be altogether natural."

I enjoyed directing *Chicken Every Sunday*, which followed. But Mr Weiselberger in the *Citizen* commented: "The CRT last night continued its almost unbroken line of light, popular entertainment without any literary import. *Chicken Every Sunday* will be served throughout the week at CRT. But domestic comedy every Tuesday becomes a little monotonous for the palate of CRT boarders. How about a change in the menu?"

By February we had something that you could sink your teeth into: Shaw's *Heartbreak House*. Three evenings had been reserved for this by theatre parties. In our previous production, *Years Ago*, Richard Easton had played near his own age, as the teen-aged suitor of Ruth Gordon. In *Heartbreak House* this most versatile young actor was going to play the elderly Captain Shotover. Sam directed this play, and played Boss Mangan.

Shaw wrote *Heartbreak House*, which represents all upper-class European society, during the First World War, but he did not want it to be produced until after the war. The first successful productions were in Paris in 1928, in London in 1936 and 1938, and in New York, with Orson Welles, in 1938. Richard Coates remarked that the play seemed even more suited to the fifties than to the twenties. Of Captain Shotover he said: "Mr. Easton makes him an interesting and formidable figure who gives substance and reality to Heartbreak House."

The reviewers were kind, especially about Sam's direction, "always competent and sometimes brilliant. This is in addition to acting the businessman Boss Mangan superbly, skilfully portraying the confusion of this not-too-bright and just-barely-couth magnate when harried by the jibes of the decadents who assemble at Heartbreak House." Lauretta Thistle said that the Shavian play had brought out abilities not always used. "Gertrude Allen is consistently good as the enigmatic, eternal charmer."

The play lasted till midnight! Thistle complained that one needed all one's wits about one for the third act, since the play is rambling even for Shaw; since the third act did not start till 11:30, "day-time" people were by then yearning for sleep. Pleasure at the two admirable sets was tempered by impatience at the time it took to change them.

However, it is impossible to start a play sharp at 8:30 if the lobby is full of patrons not in their seats. If at LaSalle Academy we shut the doors on a small lobby crammed with people, and started the play without them, their chatter and their outcry could be heard in the auditorium by the irate customers who had arrived in time! As for changing scenes, our wing space was minute, and our crew small. We did the best we could.

At this time Richard Butterfield joined us from Bermuda. He was "a treasure"! Geraldine MacIver had left us back in early January, and since then no one had been listed as stage manager. David was still listed as stage director but was stage manager as well. Richard came as scenic assistant, more or less our lowest, most menial position. We seem to have had no one in this niche for some time.

Richard, who had had little training or experience in carpentry, nevertheless went to work with unerring skill. When he was building or painting on the stage, we would gather round to watch him, because he had come to work in a good suit, had taken it off, and was now sawing or painting in spotless white overalls! We found it uncanny that anyone could get so much hard, messy work done and always look so clean. Martha did a cartoon of the arrival of Richard Butterfield, splendidly attired in fine overcoat and felt hat. Paul and Lew are examining the coat, and Dora Clarke and Bob Barclay (electrical cord dangling from his pockets) are watching, while Martha, saw in hand, is saying, "Hey, you! Ever see a saw?"

Heartbreak House had opened on February 5, 1952. After midnight Bruce phoned me. "The King is dead." It was a shock, and we were deeply grieved. The immediate business, however, as Bruce pointed out, was to decide if we were going to cancel any performances. Should we cancel the Wednesday night, or ought we to wait and cancel for the day of the funeral? We did not cancel at all. The funeral day, February 15, was booked for a theatre party of St Martin's Anglican Church, Woodroffe.

We always played the national anthem "God Save the King " at the end rather than at the beginning of a performance. The anthem would burst forth right after the last curtain call, and the actors would remain on-stage, hidden from the audience, but standing in line, till it was over. During this week of the King's lying-in-state, we stood in line every night facing the audience while "God Save the Queen" was played. It was a memorable occasion to hear for the first time this anthem played for a female monarch. For those who had been born in the last century, it was a return to their youth.

At a time of public mourning a theatrical performance takes on a deeper quality both for actors and for audience. When President John Kennedy was assassinated in 1963, William Hutt, Zoe Caldwell, Eric House, and I were in Halifax to present Noel Coward's *Private Lives*. We had to decide whether to close or to carry on, and after I had telephoned Actors' Equity Association in Toronto, and Bill had telephoned friends of his in New York who were friends of Kennedy, we decided to carry on. We had a large audience that night of November 22, and everyone who came brought so much feeling into the house that *Private Lives* took on a larger meaning, and the act one curtain line, "To absent friends," which ought to have been funny, stuck in the throat.

It was back to comedy for our next production, Noel Coward's *Hay Fever*. Sam directed, and I was astonished to find he knew every line of the play! We would not have needed a prompter at rehearsals. Sam relished all the lines of this modern classic. I played the actress Judith Bliss, "a rich acting plum that runs the dramatic gamut from flirtation to grandeur, from long-suffering self-sacrifice to downright bad temper," Eileen Turcotte said. Eric House played Judith's husband, whose reading to the family of his latest novel, *The Sinful Woman*, causes such a row in the final act. His debonair charm would be missed — for Eric was leaving us, having heard the siren call of the Bermudiana Theatre in the sun. Trudy and Ted played our children, and the guests were Robert Barclay as the prize fighter, Bea Lennard as that "self-conscious vampire" Myra Arundell, Richard Easton as the diplomat, and Jane Graham as young frightened Jackie. Alice Ammon played the famous Cockney maid Clara. I think it was a good production, though the furnishings were not inspired. Not cluttered enough.

Meanwhile, another theatrical venture in Ottawa was threatened with closure. In January I read in the *Citizen*:

Must the Children's Theatre End?

To save the Saturday Players, a letter writer asked on this page on Wednesday whether parents could pay a yearly membership fee. No doubt they could, and if enough of them did so, Ottawa's theatre for children would become a financial success. But how could this or any other plan be carried out? Who would take the project in hand? The Saturday Players seem to need a sponsor — a committee of citizens, an organization of parents and teachers, perhaps a business firm...

With Amelia Hall, now co-director of the Canadian Repertory Theatre in Ottawa, Mrs. Murphy and Mrs. Taylor founded their company as the Junior Theatre three years ago. Since then they have produced many fascinating plays — Jack the Giant Killer, Peter Pan, The Glass Slipper, Rumpelstiltskin, Alice in Wonderland, Toad of Toad Hall, Pinocchio, Rip van Winkle, The Land of Oz, Tom Sawyer, and The Bluebird, among others. Thousands of young people have been introduced to the pleasurable experience of 'live drama'.

It may not be too late to save the children's theatre. The high schools might make a concession on rent of their auditoriums, used this year instead of the inexpensive but flat-floored halls of other schools. Some interested groups might sell tickets or season subscriptions in advance. Trucking costs could be eliminated if all productions were in one building. But would Ottawa children travel from their own neighbourhoods? In Toronto they do, and their theatre in Eaton's College Street auditorium is flourishing.

I entered the fray:

> Are the school boards going to allow the children's theatre to die? Teachers are paid salaries to teach drama and literature; as a former teacher of drama and literature I know from experience that attendance at a play will do more for a youngster's appreciation of literature than dozens of sessions in the classroom. I know also what a hunger the young people of this country have to see a stage play presented in a professional manner. Most of them have never attended a play in their lives.
>
> Now, just after the publication of the Massey Report, is hardly the time for the citizens of Canada's Capital to let children's theatre die in Ottawa.
>
> Surely a committee of citizens can be formed to assure Mrs. Taylor and Mrs. Murphy adequate remuneration for their intensive efforts. The public must be made aware, obviously, of the high cost of presenting even the simplest form of theatre. When we started the Junior Theatre some people were of the opinion that we were making a lot of money. We worked an average of 15 hours a day. At the end of each month we found we had earned what most people who have small jobs earn in one week; and sometimes we hadn't earned that much. Obviously if a theatre is going to have 25-cent admissions a large audience must be assured through the efforts of the citizens, or it must be subsidized.

This publicity generated some activity. A meeting of concerned citizens, chaired by Michael Meiklejohn of the ODL, formed a committee to raise money, and the CRT announced free matinée tickets for patrons' baby-sitters.

Later that spring the Children's Theatre won the Senator Rupert Davies Trophy at the Eastern Ontario Drama Festival, with André Giradoux's *The Enchanted*. Pierre Lefebvre, the adjudicator, said that it gave "as good a performance as one would wish to see, anywhere, by any company, professional or amateur."

206

That February became a month of reflection — and travel. Although the CRT was becoming a feature of the Ottawa scene, with loyal patrons and a sympathetic press, we were also in the minds of others in the theatrical profession. Our activities were certainly in the mind of Silvio Narizzano, now that he had left us for work in Toronto. He wrote me that February:

> The developments at CRT have not pleased me because it seems impossible now that you will get opportunity for a rest till end of season. I wish often that I was back seeing 'the good fight' and perhaps if I had had a different personality I could have shouldered much more. I should have liked to.
>
> In retrospect — and with an objective eye from this distance — I feel that CRT and all of Canadian theatre is passing through a second stage of development. When a thing is pioneered people are ready and willing to sacrifice much for it. But when it is institutionalized and the personal element of contribution is gone, then the actor, director and crew look to their own gain. This I think is normal. Also it appears that there are no new actors being developed in the colleges and little theatres. Joy's contribution has stopped and Sil here in Toronto seems to be in the doldrums. But this will start again, and the graduates like Plummer and Colicos and myself will be coming back. So perhaps a renaissance will come next year, or the following year.
>
> I do not think you would be unwise to throw the problem in the open and state that Canadians are not producing enough standard material to fill one theatre rostrum. That certainly gives you the opportunity to seek it in the States ...

Sam went off for a few days to adjudicate the Inter-Varsity Drama Festival, held that year at Bishops' College, in Lennoxville, Quebec. Bruce was off to arrange the two-week tour that we were to play after the close of the regular season; he had already been to Toronto to find an actor to play Falstaff in *The Merry Wives of Windsor*, which we were contemplating as our Easter presentation, but he had failed to find one. In Toronto Bruce had met with Silvio and Donald Glenn, and with Christopher Plummer, who would soon be playing for Jupiter Theatre in Lister Sinclair's play *Socrates*. The new director at the Bermudiana Theatre, under whom Eric would be working, was Johan Fillinger. Bea Lennard and Ted Follows were also taking a two-week holiday in Toronto. The visit was repaid by an interview with Herbert Whittaker, which he reported in his "Show Business" column of February 27:

> So far this season the CRT has staged about 24 plays, with the Torontonians playing leading roles in most of them. Vivid, dark Miss Lennard scored her biggest hit as Elizabeth in *The Barretts of Wimpole Street*, but had most fun playing the small part of the physical instructress in *Years Ago*. This play also gave Mr. Follows, off-stage a perfect juvenile, one of his best roles as the seafaring father.
>
> They head back to a spring season of 14 more plays but they head back with anticipation, for the CRT combats the 'end-of-the-season blues' among the actors by throwing them a series of challenging productions, ending with *Hamlet*.
>
> Starting Tuesday, the professional company is staging a special production of Molière's *The Imaginary Invalid*, with Guy Beaulne of the CBC French network as guest producer. Beaulne, who has studied Molière in Paris, gets a leave of absence from the CBC to work with CRT. In addition to the company, the production will feature its first ballet. Yolande Leduc's Ottawa Ballet Company takes care of this innovation.
>
> The next two shows bring the company back to the modern American scene with Paul Osborn's *On Borrowed Time* and Tennessee Williams' little-known play *You Touched Me*, for which Williams collaborated on an adaptation of a story by D.H Lawrence. Both shows, through theatre-parties, are already more than two-thirds sold out.
>
> The month of March being International Theatre Month, sponsored by UNESCO, the Ottawa professionals are celebrating it with a production of André Obey's *Noah*, to run March 25 to 29. A well-known Ottawa musician has been commissioned to compose a special musical prologue for the performance and high governmental officials have been invited to attend ...

> The rest of the CRT season will consist of *Black Chiffon*, Noel Coward's *Tonight at 8:30*, *The Petrified Forest* and *The Play's the Thing*.

We now found ourselves without the help of Paul Charette. Why Paul left us at this time I do not know. He had been at the CRT from the beginning. I have no idea what his salary was; he had been hired for CRT by Mr Southgate. In the rare moments he was not assembling or taking down our sets, Paul found the time to write poetry. I regret I did not ask Paul for copies of his work. Too late now: he died of cancer, at the age of forty.

Guy Beaulne arrived to direct *The Imaginary Invalid*. I had known Guy since I arrived in Ottawa, when he wrote reviews for *Le Droit*. When we first met he had scarcely any English; as time went by he came to speak excellent English, and I still had progressed no further in French. He used to come to see our Sunday workshop presentations at the ODL, and once he had presented a scene in the original French from *The School for Wives* with his own actors, and we had done the same scene in English with ours. Like myself, Guy had been on-stage and had started to direct plays in his teens. He received scholarships to study abroad, and with these he studied for two years at the Conservatoire Dramatique National de Paris and under the personal tuition of Denis D'Ines, dean of the Comédie Française.

The Imaginary Invalid, Molière's last play, lampoons the doctors of his day, and their leeches, especially the "medicine days" of the court of Louis XIV. Consequently it was never presented at court. Molière himself played Argon in the first production in 1673, but after the fourth performance he was taken ill with convulsions and died.

Guy said that it was impossible to overact in this play. Attack and lively tempo were the essentials. He used the ballet of Egyptians dressed as Moors between the second and third acts, a prescription for good health that Argon's brother, Beraldo, says will do him more good than purges and potions. Deborah Dering did the choreography for this ballet, danced by Denyse Barrette, Judy Kuhns, Annette Desbrisay, Sheila Pierce, and Audrey Miscampbell, of the Ottawa Ballet Company. The ceremonial scene at the end, in which Argon is inducted into the company of doctors, chanting a mish-mash of Latin, pseudo-Latin, and English medical phrases, was used in its entirety.

The set was in green and violet, and the furniture was white. It was not a realistic set. Guy had wanted to use curtains, but we did not possess any. He compromised, for it was not a box set: the sides

209

were black "legs." The most prominent piece was the bed of Argon. Costumes and set won wide praise. The men had wigs! We must have got them from Malabar's.

The Tuesday opening, March 4, was our first trial of the Tuesday early, 7:30, opening, which was becoming popular in New York. Unfortunately an ice blizzard kept away many who had intended to be present, so it was not a fair test of early openings. Dick Coates said that in spite of the storm the curtain was able to rise only ten minutes late. We tried again next opening night, and were pleased to find that even at 7:30 we had a large house *on time*, without the benefit of a theatre party.

The theme of *You Touched Me*, by Tennessee Williams and Donald Windham, is fear and loneliness. A retired sea captain, a rum-soaked roisterer, has lost his direction in life; his unmarried, domineering sister hates all men and masquerades as a virtuous do-gooder. His daughter, completely dominated by her aunt, is a Laura-like, wraith-like creature, completely negative early in the play. Into this sunless household comes the sea captain's adopted son, the play's only "ordinary" character, and he sets about freeing the girl from the dream-world she has created and bringing her into the sunshine of love.

Williams's radiance of language makes them larger than life; we approached the play for depth of playing. Sam as the captain, Cornelius Rockley, Trudy as his sister, Emmie, Bea as Matilda, Ted as the adopted son Hadrian, Joyce Spencer as the addle-pated giggling maid, and Paul Blouin as "an ecclesiastical capon" (in the words of the captain) all created vivid, real people. I thought that Bea Lennard gave here her finest performance at the CRT in this extremely difficult role.

Because I loved this production, I may have gone to see it every night, and sitting in the audience one night I was deeply concerned in the scene between Hadrian and Matilda when for the first time he touched her. The play gets its title from this scene, of course. One or two stupid women in the audience giggled. I went backstage after-ward and found Bea very upset, as I knew she would be. I told her that there is nothing we can do about fools in the house, that the scene had been played beautifully, and not to be put off should it happen again. I have suffered from such idiots in the house often, and the knowledge that the rest of the audience is deeply absorbed does not help a bit, because the concentration of the actor, and of the audience, too, has been shaken. Of course there are places in dramas where the audience *has* to laugh for emotional release: there are many such spots in the most dramatic bits of *The Glass Menagerie*.

This year Canadians would take part for the first time in International Theatre Month, in which theatres presented plays emphasizing world peace or international understanding. The CRT and two other Canadian groups would take part; none, unfortunately, would be presenting a Canadian play. The CRT's choice was from France, André Obey's *Noah*, translated by Arthur Wilmurt. Donald Davis was arriving from England to play the role of Noah. Marjorie and Rex Le Lacheur had composed a special musical prologue which Rex Le Lacheur would sing, with his wife as accompanist. There would be a special Dance of the Animals arranged by David Haber, and the animals would be played by members of the Saturday Players and of the Ottawa Ballet Theatre.

In the play, Trudy Allen played Mama, who serves coffee when things get bad; Ted Follows was the dissenting son, Ham, and the co-operative sons were Robert Barclay and Richard Easton. Bea Lennard, Jacqueline Ellis, and I were the three village maidens; and Lew Davidson was A Man, primitive and superstitious, who tries to talk Noah out of building the Ark. Unfortunately, we could not afford a photographer, so there are no pictures of the Noah production, a pity since one reviewer said that we three village maidens were an extremely good-looking trio, and our dances "full of life and breezy charm"! Donald Davis used to send up my performance in these eurhythmic frenzies: "Oh, look at *me*! Oh, look at *me*! I'm stamping in the mud! I'm stamping in the mud!" Ted Follows likewise had this act in his repertoire.

Donald Davis gave a fine, authoritative performance as Noah, and Trudy gave a sensitive portrayal of the mother. George Bloom was a remarkably docile and feminine Cow, among the animals for which David Haber's Monkey was spokesman and guardian.

Bruce promoted our cause in the lavishly illustrated souvenir program:

> The aim of the CRT is to become so strong both artistically and financially that it will eventually be in a position to support and encourage Canadian playwrights, artists, directors and theatre people generally, in continuing their chosen profession *without asking for aid* — confident that the result of their endeavours will find a ready and appreciative audience among Canadian people.
>
> During the existence of our theatre to date, two hundred thousand tickets have been purchased by

the citizens of Ottawa, who are proving, day after day, that the living stage is not a dead medium of culture and entertainment.

Through its incentive, the CRT hopes that it will encourage other cities to follow Ottawa's example, until a National Theatre is truly and firmly Canada's heritage.

The italics are my own. We kept harping on this fact that we did not want subsidies, certainly not from government, though I often, in weariness and some despair, wished ardently that a rich brewery would take us up. This pleading for audience, this pleading the case for the living theatre, rouses my ire even now. What a homeland when the artistic children of the family have to go elsewhere to feel loved and wanted and capable.

In looking back on my life in the theatre in Canada, there is one question I have constantly asked myself: "What went on *inside*?" It is the business of the actor to ask that question of every character he plays; it is the business of *my* kind of actor, at any rate. It is also the business of the actor to hold out a loving hand, toward the characters he or she plays and toward the audience. To communicate. And it is the failure of communication *in life* that comes back to haunt me; I don't fail to communicate on stage. But did I communicate sufficiently with my fellow actors?

There was often a party on Saturday nights at the Geldarts' and often at the Gormans'. Sometimes I would be prevailed upon by Lynne, when she was with us, to go off to their house on Saturday night, a long distance from the centre of town, where I lived. Going to the Gormans' meant you got home at 5 a.m., if you were lucky. Lynne says I used to call their house on Oakdale Avenue "The Actors' Ruin."

I recall a bash I went to one Sunday afternoon that season. It was a champagne party given by the John Bannermans, of the Exhibition Commission. Yousuf and Solange Karsh were there, and when the party was breaking up they suggested I drive with them to their house, Little Wings, to see what a lovely place it was. I went, and had a fine relaxing time in stimulating company. Mme Karsh was one of the most stimulating conversationalists I have had the good fortune to know. She had great taste, and she was serious about serious matters but never about herself. I mentioned once or twice after 6 p.m that I must get to the theatre, where I was conducting a rehearsal at seven sharp; I must arrive ahead of time in order to be prepared. As we were driving to LaSalle Academy Mr Karsh smiled and said,

"After all, it will not matter if you are late, because you are the boss." He knew as well as I did, I am sure, that the reverse is true. When I finally arrived, late, everybody waiting for me, the whole company was smiling, delighted that I was late, delighted not out of malice, but out of, I think, affection. Bea said to me a few days later that it had been hilarious to see me being so dignified, trying to pretend that I was not the least bit under the influence of several glasses of unaccustomed champagne.

Many of the cast used to gather at the Connaught Restaurant for a snack after the show. Too seldom did I go with them: I had so many other responsibilities, so many plays to read, lines to learn, casting problems to worry about. But on the few occasions I was there, a Dr Stefan Orgel would always come to our tables. He was especially fond of Trudy. I am afraid we avoided him a little, because when you have been at your work all day and all evening you are not always aglow to discuss it at midnight! One of the strange things about actors is that although we do like to be adored, we shy away from too much display from the public. This devoted fan was not satisfied to see our plays once. He came two or three times a week. He would sit at the front always, and sometimes he would carefully roll up his overcoat, and place it on the far side of the apron of the stage, just by the proscenium arch, his hat on top. This annoyed me mightily. What if everyone did the same?, I would storm in my private mind. This was his way of establishing his ownership of his actors, perhaps.

Peter Sturgess sometimes attended the theatre with Dr Orgel, and he got to know him fairly well. Orgel was a Viennese, a doctor of science, and he worked in the civil service in Ottawa. His knowledge of theatre and opera was profound. His mind was extraordinarily alive and inquiring. And the reason he wore those funny, unfashionable, comic, low-hung baggy trousers was painfully physical: things had been done to him in the concentration camps. But I knew nothing then about his life under the Nazis. When I asked some years later what had happened to Stefan Orgel, I was told, "Oh, he died. He lived alone, and days passed before anyone knew that he had died. When they found him, they discovered the concentration camp numbers branded on his arm and the terrible evidence of his ordeal there." I had known nothing much of Stefan Orgel. I had only wondered why we seemed to mean so much to *him* when many people could take us or leave us.

I don't recall that Dr Orgel was ever invited to any parties that materialized around the CRT. Often on Saturday nights there were impromptu parties, small or large. I didn't attend very often, because a late night could play havoc with my energy for the rest of the week. Ted Kelly, another great CRT fan, didn't go to evening parties often either, but that was because of his health, not because he wasn't invited. Ted's Wednesday luncheons were such an institution that one could say he ran a salon. At his tiny apartment, people who needed to meet people met the kind of people they needed to meet.

Another constant member of the audience we were able to acknowledge publicly. During the run of *The Middle Watch*, which we had put on in January, June Davies attended her fifty-second consecutive performance. On the last night, after the show, Ted Follows, on behalf of the whole company, presented a bouquet to June on-stage. Aged thirteen, June was a student at Glebe Collegiate. She usually attended our theatre in company with her father, Frank Davies, superintendent, telecommunications establishment, Defence Research Board. Mr Davies went right on going to LaSalle Academy to see plays up till March 1955. The first play he had come to see at the CRT was *A Murder Has Been Arranged*, in late spring of 1950. He saw over one hundred plays, and June saw one hundred and twenty-four! She had no ambitions to be an actress herself.

In May 1970 Mr Davies wrote to me: "Memories of some Saturday evenings of those years when we travelled via streetcar and met lots of friends en route as well as during the intervals of the plays, are very pleasant. In retrospect I am amazed at how very good the exhausting series of weekly plays were in direction and acting. It was a strenuous time for many of you but 90% of my notes mark the play VG; only about four were marked 'Fair to Good!' "

A strenuous time it certainly was for all of us in that late winter of 1952. We had planned *Hamlet* for the week after Easter, and although we would be dark during Easter week — which would give us some extra rehearsal time — I was beginning to wonder if we weren't over-reaching ourselves.

Before *Hamlet* we were to present Shaw's lively comedy, *Arms and the Man*. I started out energetically on my production, but I was bone-weary before I got it before the public. I had directed this play before, in my amateur days with the ODL, but nevertheless I did a great deal of research. I studied the history of the Balkans and the customs of the people: they liked to be outdoors but were terrified of catching cold, always dressing warmly and eating onion and garlic to ward off colds. I asked Lew Davidson, who was playing Major Petkoff, if he would mind eating a raw onion on-stage. He declared that he was partial to raw onions. Thus it was that in act two, when the major eats breakfast in the garden, on returning home from the war, Lew ate, on-stage, with relish, a large, raw onion, to the amazement of the front rows, who were in tears, and to the discomfort of the rest of the cast, who tried to hold him at a distance for the remainder of the evening! I wanted the settings to suggest the meeting of East and West; so Martha and I decided that the sets ought to have the look of Matisse; Martha, her imagination fired by this concept, produced three excellent sets.

I have always thought the first act of *Arms and the Man* very difficult, because it opens a comedy and yet its theme is a soldier on the run, bullets whizzing around him, and he has not eaten or slept for three days and nights. This is not in itself very amusing. In any case, I cannot look at the first act objectively; it is too like the situation described in my own father's last letter from France.

Ted, as the down-to-earth Swiss mercenary Bluntschli, was very good, though not perhaps at his best in the first-act soliloquy, when he is falling asleep on Raina's bed and yet feels a half-awake compulsion to escape from the enemy. Raina was a splendid role for Lynne Gorman. Dickie Easton had trouble with Sergius, the Noble Warrior of legend who is the butt of Shaw's jokes. The whole production came out more farce than comedy, because I was too tired before the end to take a firm grip on it.

We started rehearsing *Hamlet* during the week's run of *Arms and the Man* and rehearsed all through Holy Week. Sam had thirteen days in which to rehearse the play. The production opened on April 14, Easter Monday. The press said that it was possibly the first professional Canadian *Hamlet*.

We raised our seat prices for *Hamlet* to seventy-five cents in the balcony and a top of two dollars in the orchestra. Fourteen hundred seats were sold ahead of time.

David went off to Montreal to choose and rent the costumes. Lieutenant-Colonel J.C.A. Campbell came in to do the fencing duel between Hamlet and Laertes. Sam used the text of the play edited by Charles Rittenhouse of Montreal for the high school version in which Richard Easton had first played Hamlet. The Fortinbras scene at the end was omitted, and the whole play kept within a fairly normal playing time. It was split into three acts, with seven, six, and five scenes respectively. The first night started fifteen minutes late and ended at ten minutes after midnight!

Bob Barclay was responsible for the lighting and the set. He made a simple combination of ramps and platforms serve as an acting area and changed the scenes with only the use of lights. No curtain was used between scenes. This allowed the play to move smoothly and rapidly, as it does on an apron stage. Bob placed turrets at either side of the stage. At the back a high block of parapet, a low centre platform, and a sweeping ramp were set against a blue curtain. He got permission to remove from the top of the proscenium arch the large CRT crest. Lew Davidson remembered: "Bob and I had devised an ingenious scene-changing device by which the raised dais, which was the throne area for Gertrude and Claudius, at the release of a rope would become Gertrude's bed. Unfortunately in one performance the rope released itself and a canopy came floating down from the flies like a huge bird and settled on top of Donald Davis and Gertrude Allen (Claudius and Gertrude)."

Authentic Elizabethan recorder music was played between scenes by Jean Low, Barrie Helmer, and Mary Hugessen. The recorder was a favourite instrument with us, since it did not come under the jurisdiction of the Musicians' Union!

At the dress rehearsal, when Claudius and the Queen were making a grand entry along the ramp at the back of the stage, Trudy fell off the ramp and disappeared between ramp and the deep blue curtains that formed the backcloth. There was much ado. Donald Davis recently reminded me, amid much laughter, that on this occasion I was so embarrassed that I apologized profusely in the wings and then said explosively, my face screwed tight with annoyance, "And furthermore, I have absolutely no right to be playing Ophelia! But I'm just too tired and haven't *time* to find anyone better!"

I see that the reviewers liked my mad scenes, found them touching, and I loved the songs. We used the traditional tunes. Herbert Whittaker said I managed only moments of lovely pathos, which is probably true. Frances Hyland is the only Ophelia I have ever seen who absolutely broke the heart.

With such a large cast, unused to Shakespeare, some had difficulty in handling and interpreting the Shakespearean phrase. That is a technique that must be learned, and it takes time. On the whole, though, the critics were kind. I liked the *Journal*'s heading for Richard Coates' review: "Tough-Trained CRT in Ring with Hamlet." Harold Whitehead of the *Montreal Gazette* said: "The Canadian Repertory Theatre in Ottawa has sprung many surprises this season. The company had done several classics with encouraging box-office returns, a fact that reverses the generally accepted theory that highbrow material does not go over with the mass of the public. Hamlet, though, even with past classical successes to go on, is still a serious undertaking. It is a pleasure, then, to report that the group has staged a wholly satisfactory production and one that has broken all existing attendance records at CRT's home."

What of the Prince, whose strong, thoughtful, and youthful visage could be seen on our posters all over town? This is the first time to my knowledge that we ever used a poster. It was a fine portrait of Dickie Easton; I shall quote Herbert Whittaker:

> On that final night, when this reviewer saw the show, the CRT Hamlet was running very smoothly. It had pace, and emotion, a fair quota of fine speech and plenty of excitement with a rip-snorting duel to finish. And, first of all, it has a fine young Hamlet in Richard Easton.
>
> Richard Easton, it would be safe to tell your New Canadian, is Canada's best Hamlet at the moment. If he can find enough opportunities to play the role, one will be able to repeat that statement without having to add that he is the only one.
>
> Mr. Easton, a tall young man with a schoolboy's head, graceful and sure where you expect him rather to be gangling, has already acquired amazing authority in the role. His Hamlet takes the famous soliloquies with a pace and clarity which is touched with brilliance. He has a surprising depth of feeling, and an understanding of the part which is compounded of both intuition as well as serious study. His Prince is markedly the student of Wittenberg, and must be one of the least introverted Hamlets since Freud cast his shadow into Elsinore.
>
> The performance is marred by some lack of continuity, principally brought about by Mr. Easton's occasional lapses into a cheerful schoolboy humour where irony is called for. There is no irony in this Hamlet's soul, although the antic humour of his farewell to the king ('Farewell, dear mother,') provides one of the best moments of the evening.
>
> Another flaw, perhaps, is the occasional reaching for theatrical tricks — such as an Olivier-like leap to the throne-dais and a finger-pointing to climax the Play Scene.
>
> But this Hamlet is definitely a Hamlet to be watched.

The trap-door in the stage of LaSalle opened right down into the actors' Green Room, about fifteen feet below. If the trap was in use on-stage, we had to turn out all lights in the Green Room and in the two dressing-rooms partitioned off the Green Room. When Ophelia was "buried," I was not lowered by ropes on the bier but taken bodily from the bier and handed down in a vertical position, feet first, into the grave, while below me, uplifted hands grasped me in a variety of places and got me down in one piece to the floor of the Green Room. These hands belonged to any of the actors who weren't on-stage at the time.

Earlier in the grave scene, when Second Gravedigger, in the person of Peter Sturgess, had to climb down into the grave and get on with his digging, a long ladder was held from the floor of the Green Room up to the lip of the grave. Peter would descend, feeling in the dark with his feet for a rung of the ladder, talking the while to First Gravedigger. Came a performance when Peter waved his feet around the inside of that grave and could find no rung to perch upon. While he explored with his leg in wild search of the ladder, a hand grabbed his ankle. Barely recovered from this change in the script, he was further alarmed when his foot was guided to a precarious foundation, that *slithered*. He was handed Yorick's skull from below; meanwhile he had sunk so low on his uncertain perch that he eventually disappeared from view altogether, to Hamlet's alarm.

Apologies and explanation followed. The ladder belonged to the LaSalle Academy Brothers. During the afternoon the brothers had borrowed it back, but had told no one, and had neglected to return it. The absence of the ladder had not been noticed until the scene was under way. Some one had neglected to "check your props." There had been a mad scramble in the dark Green Room, organized by David, to create a substitute. A table had been dragged into place underneath the trap, a chair put on the table, another chair mounted on the first, and cushions placed on the seat of the second chair to give the seat more height. It was the cushions that *slithered*. All hands below were holding the table and chairs securely in place. But how was Peter to know?

Lew Davidson recently reminded me of the story of the helmet worn by Hamlet's father's ghost: "It was taken from a suit of armour that stood in the lobby of a local movie house. The full suit of armour stood in the lobby of the cinema, and when I went to return the helmet the rest of the suit had disappeared; so the manager suggested that I take the helmet for myself. It has always had pride of place wherever we went afterward and is known as the 'Ghost of Hamlet's Father.'"

It may appear to the public that it is easier to do a one-act play than to do a three-act, especially *Hamlet*. It isn't. We took on a monumental task with three one-act plays from Noel Coward's *Tonight at 8:30*. Sam and Ted and I each directed one of these; all members of the company were involved in at least two, and some in all three. It meant three sets for Martha and Dickie Butterfield to design, build, and paint, with help from Charles Elmy; actors who came in from outside had to be fitted in to a tight and complicated rehearsal schedule. Outsiders were Fred Carlofsky, Bea Whitfield, Joy Spencer, Helen Lefebvre, and Jack Ammon, and even Charles Elmy of the crew got to play a part on-stage at last. Winnifred Canty came in to play the piano for the music hall numbers in *Red Peppers*. How David managed to organize the small wing space to hold the furniture and props as well as the scenery for three separate plays I cannot imagine.

Ted Follows must have had St Vitus's dance the week of *To-Night at 8:30*: he played a leading role in *Ways and Means*, directed *Still Life*, played the lead male role in *Red Peppers*, and he staged two dances.

I think that *Still Life* came off best. It was made into the fine movie *Brief Encounter*, with Celia Johnston and Trevor Howard. Trudy and Sam played these roles effectively, and Trudy especially received good reviews for the deep feeling she brought to her role.

I directed the comedy *Ways and Means*, which finds Dickie Easton and Bea Lennard taking breakfast in a large double bed and wondering for how much longer they can stay as guests in this household. They cannot leave because they are broke. Ted played the chauffeur-burglar, and Bob Barclay, a simple Cockney lad, in *Still Life*, was raised to the peerage. The decorative Bea and the languid Dickie Easton in that double bed would bring repercussions the next season.

My mind was shooting forward to *The Petrified Forest*, by Robert Sherwood, which I started to direct as soon as we got the Coward plays on the boards. The playscripts that arrived were old and had "been in the wars." My battered prompt copy had been covered in pencilled notes by another director. Why hadn't the royalty house re-typed a fresh copy? I had to ignore the pencilled-in blocking — not much room left to write in my own.

We were all much impressed by the set that Martha and Dickie Butterfield provided, and Bob Barclay was so carried away by lighting this lunch room that I had to call to him from the balcony, when he was setting light levels, "Light *my* actors, not *your* set!" I wanted to use music here and there, because of the play's poetic quality, so I phoned Jack Kash and had a long talk about the "feel" of the play. I used a haunting piece of music as a theme for Alan Squier the poet, (Leslie Howard in the film), and played for the CRT very movingly by Richard Easton, bearded and forty-ish. The music was heard quietly just before the audience first saw him, as he passed the windows of the Black Mesa Bar B-Q, and died out as he entered.

I used Dvorak's "New World" Symphony to open the play. I had a miserable time getting everything synchronized: the curtain was to part on a certain bar in the music; the lights were to start up on another musical cue and were to reach full power at a certain point; and the first actor to speak was to open his mouth just as the music gives a braying ass sound. I rehearsed this opening over and over. I think the first character on-stage to speak was a telegraph lineman, played by Stanley Montgomery from the office, who had no pretensions as an actor. I think that when I produced this piece I was subconsciously wanting to direct a film. If I had nine lives, in one of them I would be a film director, and I could edit out what I didn't like.

The old-timer, Gramp Maple, was played by Sam, while Ted had the role made famous by Bogart, Duke Mantee. Sam, pipe-smoking in his rocking chair, wove his spell of far-fetched reminiscences. Ted brought out the quixotic quality of the killer, who is tempted to fall under the influence of Alan Squier. Bob Barclay was Duke Mantee's henchman, Jackie, providing some comic relief. Bruce Raymond played the big businessman and Trudy his disillusioned wife.

My favourite scenes in this play, and the easiest to produce, were the ones between Gramp's granddaughter, Gabby, and Squier, played by Bea and Dickie. In two long scenes, about ten minutes each, I had them sit at a table, down centre, and just talk. You could hear the proverbial pin drop in the house during these scenes. After we had opened, I decided to look over my dog-eared prompt copy: as I had suspected, the previous director had blocked these quiet talk scenes always with one of the two actors on the move, fearful that the audience would be bored if there was no action. If one character sat down, then a second or two later the other would rise and start pacing. It made me grind my teeth to read such blocking! How many times I have sat through amateur and supposedly professional productions and watched this kind of direction in which the audience are made incapable of listening because there is always movement to distract the eye. As soon as you distract the eye the audience ceases to listen. Why else do the old actors say, "Don't you walk on my lines"? If two actors cannot sit down on a stage and speak for ten minutes the excellent dialogue that a good author has given them, then they are not actors at all. In such a scene the attention of the audience can be further concentrated on the actors by subtle use of lighting centred on the area where the actors sit. I once heard that the great Komisarjevsky used to say, "When people come into a room, normally they *sit down*. So why don't they sit down on stage?"

I was enormously pleased with the work of Bea and of Dickie in this play. It would be their last show for the CRT; and Ted's too, as things turned out. Bea and Dickie I would work with again the opening Stratford year of 1953.

Music and sound effects were not taped then. We used recordings, either our own or borrowed from CKOY radio station or from Myer's Music Shop. David Haber would mark the record with a piece of chalk so that he would know where the sound effect needed was located on the disc. Sometimes gunshots were used from records. It is hopeless to shoot off a blank if you want the shot to sound as if it is coming from a distance; a shot fired backstage makes such a noise that the audience jumps and then laughs.

So backstage that week, in the second of the two acts, during the gunfight near the end, David had been rather busy putting on a sound-effects record on a turn-table with one hand, pulling a light switch with the other hand, and using his foot to pull the master light switch (equipped with a loop of rope). Two feet away from him, blank cartridges were being fired from the window of the Black Mesa Bar B-Q and he was dodging in the ensuing smoke to avoid the blanks, and not to impede actors who were dashing on-stage and off. For some minutes it was a hot spot, that crowded Prompt Corner where the light-board stood. David also had a small role in the play!

The following week David would be overseeing the packing away of our equipment and the returning of borrowed props and furnishings, and he would be sending out letters to the people who had lent us things, private people whose names had not been on the program in the acknowledgments section; he would write thank you notes as well to the sixty-eight companies, businesses, and institutions acknowledged on the programs. His letter to my mother says: "It was indeed very kind of you to give us so much of your time with costumes and to loan us all the props that you did. I know that you enjoy it ..." The personal touch, and nobody asked him to undertake this task.

David was also the "cook" who supplied the food consumed on stage. Steaks were bread soaked in coloured water; bananas were used, plain or tinted, disguised as a variety of foods; eggs were peach halves served on rounds of white bread. All drinks were various concentrations of Jonas colouring in plain water, and the bill for Jonas at the CRT was large. How often I complained to David about these Jonas mixtures! They always tasted to me like banana extract. But David was adamant: Jonas colouring was cheap and fitted into his budget. It cost 59 cents a bottle. If tea had to be made on-stage, David had to supply the real thing, though it broke his Scrooge-like heart.

David would be leaving us at the end of this season. He had stage managed one hundred and one plays for the CRT and he had played in a number of them. Sometimes he had handled as many as four turn-tables in one show, plus an extra switchboard; often a show called for three light-cues per page; seldom had there been a chance to go down to the Green Room and sneak a quiet cigarette. And, beyond the call of duty, there were all those times he had pinned the ladies into bath-towels to give us middle-aged spreads.

But it was not the desire to escape the heavy workload that had lured David away from us. He was returning to his first love, ballet, and was joining Celia Franca and the newly formed National Ballet of Canada.

When Peter Sturgess left us at the end of this season he would, as it turned out, be gone for more than a year. Never one to sit around and wait for an acting job to fall into his lap, Peter had taken on a summer job, as he had the previous summer, at the Somerset Movie House, owned by Mr Berlin. This gentleman appreciated Peter's business-like qualities and prevailed upon him to stay on in the fall of 1952 as assistant manager. I don't think Peter would have accepted had we been able to offer him a full-time acting job. He was a popular actor, but we could not use him on-stage every week.

Many were the faces not to be seen at the CRT again. During the course of the summer Bruce was going to decide not to return. The blonde head of Martha would be seen no more in the cellarage, and I would not see her again until some years later, when we both were working at Stratford, she in props. During the summer I would be facing the problem of finding three key people: a business manager, a set designer, and a stage manager; they would not be easy to replace.

We had had wonderful coverage in the press all of the 1951–52 season. In addition to the reviews in all three Ottawa-area papers, the *Citizen*, the *Journal*, and *Le Droit*, we had had editorials and huge ads in the *Citizen*, the generous gift of Mr H.S. Southam.

Lauretta Thistle, at the end of the season, interviewed Bruce Raymond about the financial history of the season. The theatre had a deficit of $5,000. The program presented had been as broad as possible. Over thirty-four weeks the public had patronized classics as well as light comedies. The three Shaw plays and the Ibsen had shown a profit, but lively box-office business had not covered the costs of the other classics and near-classics. *Hamlet* had lost money in spite of an attendance of four thousand; so had *Noah* and *The Imaginary Invalid*. The post-Christmas slump was to be expected, but not its continuation into February. The whole entertainment industry, including the movie houses, had been in a slump. Light comedies, not so expensive to produce, were the fare we had offered, but they had not drawn the public; however, by the end of February the light comedy *Nothing but the Truth* had been a best-seller. Operating costs were going up, and, with television arriving in Toronto, salaries would have to go up if actors were to be enticed to come to Ottawa to work on-stage. There were now other stages, too: Totem in Vancouver, and the occasional Jupiter Theatre production in Toronto. We needed, said Bruce, some kind of guaranteed support, such as two thousand regular subscribers, instead of the four hundred.

I had committed myself to join Donald Davis and his Straw Hat Players for the summer. About this time I had a letter from Mavor Moore, chief producer at CBC television. He wrote: "Since our chat last week, I have wondered whether you might not be interested in discussing the possibility of your joining us here at CBC Television. We are most anxious to develop women directors and your experience strikes me as making you singularly eligible." I never gave this proposal any serious thought. I had to finish the job I was on at the CRT. I have never been one for looking far ahead.

CHAPTER 15

STRAW HAT PLAYERS

"Would you mind putting these in your car and taking them to Gravenhurst so that I can paint on them this summer?" Donald Davis looked at the ten or fifteen masonite boards, cut a variety of sizes, each of them painted with two coats of flat white. He sighed and gallantly put them into his car. Once again I had made this gesture toward painting, deluding myself about spare time after rehearsal to get out in the midst of Nature and paint.

Nineteen fifty-two saw the fifth summer season of the Straw Hat Players. In 1946 a new permanent director had been appointed to Hart House Theatre at the University of Toronto. He was an American, Robert Gill. A number of students at the university were becoming really serious about theatre — just as in Montreal. In the summer of 1947, Gill was taking with him a group of Hart House actors to the Woodstock (New York) Summer Theatre, where he was directing. Murray and Donald Davis were of this group. By the summer of 1948 the Davis brothers decided that it would be pleasant if they could act in Canada, and since they found no employment here, they decided to create a summer theatre themselves.

Now, five seasons later, with a larger company than their original eleven, the Straw Hat Players were firmly established, and plans were growing for a theatre in Toronto, to run fifty-two weeks of the year. The problem was to find a theatre in which to play.

We started to rehearse in Toronto on June 9. Donald wrote me in May to tell me that because of illness Robert Gill would not be directing; the management had obtained Peter Potter, director of the Glasgow Citizens' Theatre, and Russell Graves, of the University of

Florida. Because these directors did not know any of us and had not cast the plays themselves, "either director will be at liberty to alter any cast at his discretion." In the event, I don't think any alterations were made.

We were to stay in Toronto for just two weeks, to prepare the two shows that would open the season. The double-bill of Robertson Davies's *Overlaid* and Terence Rattigan's *The Browning Version* would open June 23 and play for one week at Gravenhurst; meanwhile *Clutterbuck*, by Ben Levy, would play a week at Port Carling. The following week we would switch. We would have two weeks to rehearse each of the ten plays being presented. Two plays would be in rehearsal at the same time, and we who were part of the company for the whole ten weeks would be in no more than five plays each.

I had the good fortune to start out in a show directed by Peter Potter. He was directing Donald and Ted Follows and myself in *Overlaid*, and Rattigan's *The Browning Version*. Peter said to us the first day of rehearsing the Rattigan play that we might think that he had not studied the play, because he had not planned the blocking. He let us more or less discover our own moves as we started work; the next day he would watch us through and afterward point out where we seemed uncomfortable and make suggestions. If he had no immediate solution, he would say, "I'll think about it." Next time he would have an answer. His method resulted in very simple blocking, with great clarity of intention, and concentration of energy. He was a relaxed director.

Peter is a huge man, six feet five. He is very English, Eton and Oxford, and the Grenadier Guards. He is warm and kind. When we started on *The Browning Version* he said that Millie Crocker-Harris was not going to be an easy role for me because "you are such a sympathetic person: you come across to an audience with such warmth." It isn't every day that I got a chance to play somebody that the audience is not supposed to like, though I quite enjoyed the experience. So in about ten days I had Peter convinced that he need not worry about my sympathetic quality: I could be very bitchy when I had to be. I enjoyed giving Peter this little surprise! He said he found that I could express passionate feeling with more ease than could English actresses. Less inhibited.

While we were rehearsing in Toronto I lived in a tiny room on Avenue Road, in a huge house that was used for club entertainments, wedding receptions, and the like. I was happy there. The area not long before had been a splendid residential section; now apartment buildings without character predominate. It was still rather grand in 1952, but in the seventies many of the big houses have gone.

I used to leave rehearsal, take dinner at some restaurant on Bloor Street in that area, and be in my bed studying my lines by 7:30 each night.

By the end of June we had gone up to our living quarters in Gravenhurst. We were all billeted in a converted army hut at the Gateway Hotel, on the fringes of Gravenhurst. The Gateway, once a tuberculosis sanatorium, later a prisoner-of-war camp, was right on the lake. Its army huts had thin walls, only one bathroom. Cosy and family style. Right away I went out the first Sunday on the rocks and painted the lake.

About twenty-six people were part of the company that summer. We all took our meals seated around a variety of tables in various rooms and on the porch at the home of Archdeacon J.B. Lindsell. It was relaxing not to have to sally forth three times a day to find restaurant meals, though we might enjoy a late-evening snack in the fine ice-cream parlour and restaurant of our friend Gordon Sloan, who had our pictures hanging on his walls.

On June 27, Herbert Whittaker's review of *The Browning Version* appeared in the *Globe and Mail*:

> Terence Rattigan's compact study of a frustrated school master brought The Straw Hat Players up the ladder of achievement by several rungs.
>
> Mr. Potter admittedly had some excellent material to work with. Donald Davis, since the founding of the company, has developed into one of its best players, specializing in elderly roles. The part of the dry, unhappy school master, Crocker-Harris, was one that he could be expected to play with understanding. Similarly, Amelia Hall, a recruit this season but long a distinguished member of the Canadian Repertory Theatre, has nearly always played women twice her age.
>
> For the third important role of the wife's lover, there was Ted Follows, who had gone from the original Straw Hat company to become a strong member of the Ottawa Repertory company. And another, Eric House, recently back from Bermuda's theatre, played the headmaster, bearer of bad tidings.

We were not so successful with Robertson Davies's fine little satire, *Overlaid*. Perhaps the play was not quite Peter's cup of tea, dealing as it does with Canadian foibles. Donald played Gramps, who wants to take the money that insurance man Ted has just delivered into his hands and go to New York to see the Metropolitan Opera; maybe he'll give some chorus girl fifty bucks for her brassière! Ethel, scandalized, finally admits that she wants the money to buy a family headstone, "With the name on the base cut deep." The play is a beautiful bit of Canadiana.

I had never before in the professional theatre been in a play in which all the costumes were designed by a real designer and made by people hired by the management. I was impressed to have my costumes made for me, with real padding, to give me the corseted look for Lady Bracknell in *The Importance of Being Earnest*. I had a wig, too, and splendid hats. The aquiline false nose I made myself, of putty. Peter Potter directed this piece. Donald was John Worthing; Ted, Algernon; Eric, Dr Chasuble; Barbara, Gwendolyn; Araby Lockhart, Miss Prism; and Honor Blackman, Cecily Cardew.

Before Honor Blackman donned mod leather clothing for the James Bond films and *The Avengers* she was our ingénue that summer, playing not only Cecily, but a fine Laura in *The Glass Menagerie*. She had come to Canada with her husband, who was ill and taking treatments over here.

In this happy production we had some rare fun. One night Donald, in the last act, hearing from Miss Prism that years ago she had lost a handbag with a baby in it, rushed upstairs to bring down the handbag in which he himself had been found in the cloakroom at Victoria Station when he was a babe in arms. After his exit there are supposed to be noises from above of suitcases and what-not being thrown about as he searches. Meanwhile there are a few remarks from those on-stage, such as Gwendolyn's "The suspense is unbearable. I hope it will last!" On this occasion, however, the suspense went on and on. We could hear Donald, throwing things about in the wings, though we were pretending that the sounds came from upstairs. Was Donald playing a joke? Finally, a somewhat dishevelled Donald arrived back on-stage and said to me, with dejection, "Lady Bracknell, I cannot find the handbag." Tableau! as they used to say in *Punch*. At this point Araby Lockhart saved the night by starting to describe *her* handbag to John Worthing: "Did it have a stain in the lining caused by the explosion of a temperance beverage?" etc. Thus she proved the handbags were one and the same !

On the last night of this show, we all knew that the handbag concealed a doll that looked exactly like a baby. This would of course make dear Araby break up. While Donald was off getting the handbag, "we in the know" all began to smirk a bit, and when he

227

came back and handed the handbag to Araby we were all ready to collapse; Araby, however, opened the handbag and did not bat an eye. Not a quiver, though the rest of us were shaking.

Araby gave a party on an island in the lake one Sunday afternoon. Everyone swam but me. It was a lively affair, and some sort of gin cocktail was served. Maybe they were martinis, a concoction unknown to me at that time. I had several and finished the afternoon like Desdemona, "Her hand on her bosom / Her head upon her knees. O willow, willow, willow, willow!" Gin seems to bring all the nameless horrors to the surface, instead of burning them out in the nether depths. My only experience as a curst and sad drunk.

Peter Potter's wife, Elspeth Cochrane, had joined us in Gravenhurst, to visit Peter. She was a stage director, and we would unexpectedly find ourselves working together next summer. Elspeth was a charming, quiet woman with one of those marvellous English complexions. She later became an actors' agent in London.

The problem with theatres that are not really theatres, such as the Opera House in Gravenhurst and the Memorial Hall in Port Carling, is that you cannot get a blackout at 8:30 of a summer evening. Peter Potter, in presenting *The Glass Menagerie*, could not open on a darkened stage and gradually bring up the lights as Tom addresses the audience from the apron. Curtains were on the windows, but they did not produce a blackout. Peter had to think out another way to open the play. He covered the furniture with dust sheets and had these removed by stage hands as the play was starting.

At the first run-through of the two acts I did not know that the rehearsal had started, with all this opening business of uncovering the pieces on the set. I walked out on-stage and called out, "Peter, we haven't got all the props here on the tea-tray." And the answer to that remark was *"Get Off the Stage!"* in the voice of the Grenadier Guards on parade. I got off the stage. What in the world was going on?

I listened to the voice of Tom, walked out on cue, and sat down with Laura at the table. As soon as my first speech came up, "You should *chew* your food," etc., I started, to my horror, to cry. I cried through the whole of the two acts.

It did me a lot of good to have a good cry. Later at luncheon, Peter stopped me for a chat as I passed where he was sitting, but he did not bring up the subject of shouting and weeping, thank God.

The other two presentations I took part in were directed by Russell Graves. I did not find him in the same class as Peter Potter. Probably the difference is that Peter was a working professional director, while Russell was a teacher.

John Atkinson, Eric House, Deborah Turnbull, and I were the cast of *The Late Edwina Black*, a thriller by William Dinner and William Morum. Russell had us first number each speech from 1 to 10, in descending order of importance. The production seemed to have no rhythm. It is the only time I have ever been in a play when nobody seemed to know the lines. Learning lines has a lot to do with rhythm. Before it opened I was so terrified of the ordeal before us that I wondered if I could run away!

We were saved, I think, by a catastrophe. On the opening night John Atkinson and I were jogging along in the first act. He was playing a schoolmaster whose wife had died in the room above. I was her companion, and he and I were in love. He was marking school papers. We were both supposed to be in a state of terrible tension because of Edwina's death by poison. How had it come about? Who was responsible? I had sat down at the table beside him to help with the marking, and we had turned to each other and had kissed. At that moment there was a rumbling sound above our heads, increasing in ominous volume — bombers flying overhead? Another war? Suddenly, with a roaring crash, the proscenium beam to the right of us fell crashing to the stage floor, bringing down with it curtain and plaster. The audience gasped. There was a long pause. I did not know what to do, and then I decided to carry on. I looked up to the ceiling, and said my next line, which happened to be, "I thought I heard a sound upstairs!" The audience collapsed in laughter.

Donald was furious about the falling of the proscenium beam. He examined it and found that the nails that held it were far too small for that purpose. Had it fallen a couple of minutes earlier I would have been under it. The prompter in the prompt corner had been buried in fallen plaster. Donald was none too pleased about our shaky lines, either.

The *Orillia Packet and Times* did not care for the play but pleased me with: "Amelia Hall was her usual expert self and is so good an actress that one inclines to take a good performance by her as a matter of course instead of the very fine piece of acting it really is. Eric House played the role of a Scotland Yard Inspector and resembles Miss Hall in that one is never surprised when he turns in a fine job of acting." It is very true that spectators can take an actor's work for granted. I don't think we actors ever take our own talent for granted. "What if it doesn't happen this time?"

French without Tears was the fifth and final play for me. They had turned the French professor from M. Maingot into Mme. Maingot, and guess who was it? I was, with *my* French pronunciation! I had all my lines written down and fastened to the flats near the entrance door so that I might study them before each entrance. When I breezed on, exuding confidence and Gallic charm, calling "Bonjour! Bonjour!" to my students, this first entrance was greeted with expectation and warmth by the audience. I think they even applauded. After that first exhausting effort I collapsed into inadequacy, and I could feel that the dear souls realized I was in deep waters, and would have liked to rescue me.

I was able to see a few times the company's production of T.S. Eliot's *The Cocktail Party*, which Peter Potter directed. I was standing at the back of the house one night watching it with the janitor. "Well," he said, "she's pretty deep, but I'll get to her by the end of the week!"

I have lots of pictures of the plays that season. Lots of pictures too, of all of us on the beach. David Haber is in one of them, up for a visit. We all look so *young*. Delectable company. I never got down to painting those masonite boards.

CHAPTER 16

OLGA AND THE EMBASSY

When on September 6, 1952, the press announced "Advance Box Office to Test Opening Date for Repertory," I was not yet back in Ottawa, and our office and our box office were not yet open. My mother telephoned me to report that so many phone calls were coming in, and so many letters with one and five dollar bills and cheques, that she had set up one corner of the living-room as her office. My mother was as excited as only she could be!

I had got a promise from Max Helpmann and Barbara Chilcott while I was in Muskoka, after Straw Hat, that they would come for the ten-week season before Christmas, after which they were returning to England. Max wanted to direct as well as act, and now that we had lost Bruce from the office and David from backstage, we *had* to have another director, so that I would be free to oversee the whole operation.

Visiting the Peterborough Summer Theatre in its fourth season, I was in time to see *O Mistress Mine,* by Terence Rattigan, with Betty Leighton and William Hutt. I thought Hutt quite marvellous and was delighted when he said he would join us, but had other commitments after January 1953. Betty had promised to come for six plays. At Peterborough I also hired young Ron Bailey, who would act and help in the office as well.

In Toronto, George McCowan committed himself for the first ten weeks of the season; after that he might pursue his MA in philosophy, because he still wasn't decided about theatre as a career.

At Hugh Webster's summer theatre at Oakville, I hired a young Dane called Leif Pedersen to replace Paul Charette and Dickie

Butterfield as carpenter and assistant to the designer. Never in my life have I met anyone as anxious, as headstrong, to be hired as this young man, who bedazzled me with his high-powered salesmanship, his readiness to climb the highest mountain or stand five hours on his head if it would make me say yes.

Leif Pedersen was in his late teens. He had come out from Denmark on his own, because he did not want to stay at home and become a shoemaker, like his father. In Toronto he had worked at night at Acme Screw and Gear Co., and in the evenings he had studied at Sterndale Bennett's Canadian Theatre School. He had given up the night job to join Hugh Webster's Oakville summer theatre, and his request to me for an interview had been written for him by a scribe, because as yet Leif was struggling with spoken English and could neither write it nor read it.

But there was no sign anywhere of an experienced stage manager to replace David Haber. At the CBC on Jarvis Street, I hawked my wares: "I have a job for a designer. Does anyone know an unemployed designer?" I gave my speech in the cafeteria (where they served that awful coffee Max Ferguson used to talk about on his *Rawhide* program), and I gave it in the corridors. To no avail. Television had devoured all the stage designers. Before leaving the building I pinned up on notice boards my urgent request to hear from a designer willing to work at the CRT, and I left my Ottawa telephone numbers.

During the summer John Atkinson, with the Straw Hat Players, had told me that he was longing to play the Gielgud role of Mendip in *The Lady's Not for Burning*. "In fact," he said, looking at me slyly, "if you'd do the play for me at CRT I'd be willing to take on the job of business manager!" This had been a totally unexpected offer. We decided that he would do.

Dora Clarke was going to be assistant to the business manager, Peter Sturgess having decided to stay in the movie-theatre management business for another year.

Where had all our people gone? Richard Butterfield, like David, had gone to the National Ballet. I do not know where Martha Jamieson had taken her talent. Of our actors, Ted Follows was off to join the Glasgow Citizen's Theatre, as was Donald Davis, under the direction of Peter Potter. Eric House and Bea Lennard were doing TV, both of them appearing in an adaptation of Stephen Leacock's *Sunshine Sketches of a Little Town*. Trudy Allen was teetering on the edge of falling into a lucrative career as a New York businesswoman and went off that fall to New York to be secretary to Maud Franchot, Franchot Tone's aunt. I would have asked Richard Easton back, and perhaps he would have returned, but Sam did not favour the idea, and so Dickie took off to Toronto and TV.

Once I was back in Ottawa, Dora Clarke and I opened the office, ordering tickets and getting our publicity campaign going. I was reading plays. The opening play was to be more or less the same production of *Private Lives* that Max Helpmann and Barbara Chilcott had headed that summer at the Straw Hat Players. Penny Geldart had consented to do the sets for this before she would go off to Toronto to design the set for Jupiter Theatre's production of *Anna Christie*. She had worked at the Niagara Falls Summer Theatre that season, but she could not come to the CRT for 1952–53 because she could not desert her family.

A vigorous telephone campaign for subscriptions had been started, headed by Doris Stacey, one of our occasional actors; the ballet teacher Gwen Osborne; Freda Carlofsky; and Bea Whitfield. We were out to get nine thousand members; London, Ontario, with a smaller population, had ten thousand members for its amateur productions at the Grand Theatre.

The Helpmanns and George McCowan were due to arrive at the end of the month. For *Private Lives* we would not need the full company — but the censor intervened. I had argued on the telephone with Father MacDonald: "*Private Lives* has already been seen at LaSalle Academy! The Stage Society presented it." Father MacDonald said he knew that but he could not pass the play; already last season he had had complaints about the Coward play *Ways and Means* because two of the actors, Bea Lennard and Richard Easton, had been *in bed* together. "There was a big breakfast table between them," I protested, "and they were playing a *married* couple!" But it was no use. On the rare occasions when I was to argue with Father MacDonald I would do so just for the exercise. I knew I never could win. I realized that divorce was the theme that was taboo. Eliot and Amanda had divorced, and each had remarried; then, each on their second honeymoon, fate had brought them together at the same hotel, and they had run away together from their new spouses.

Now I would have to find a new opener, direct it myself from scratch, and have all the company arrive at once to be in it. I chose as opener a play I had read about in *Theatre World* — *Captain Carvallo*, by Denis Cannan. On September 20 Max replied to this suggestion. He thanked me for the contract letters. (These must have been the first contract letters I ever sent out for the CRT.) He was unhappy that I wanted him to act in four of the ten plays. He would prefer to be in only the first and the last and to direct the rest of the time. In the

233

event, Max directed six of the ten, acted in the opening play and the closing one, and had two plays off, to prepare his work. He played a third role, in *The Cocktail Party*, which he also directed, but it was a role he had already played during the summer.

Max had suggested a comedy called *Castle in the Air*. It must have been the Sunday after I received that suggestion that I went off for a holiday — one half-day spent at the Seignory Club with Violet and Charles Southgate and my mother. I was a silent companion that day, for after the excellent luncheon I spent my time in the glorious sunshine reading *Castle in the Air*. I read it three times. The second reading I devoted to cutting out all of the divorce theme. The third reading was to discover if I still had a play! I had.

We were still without a stage manager. But Sam Payne came up with a suggestion. During his summer in Vancouver with Totem Theatre he had come across a fellow who had had experience of opera and ballet production in France. So we sent for him. I had hired Bill Glen as assistant stage manager, hoping he would learn how! Bill had been in my production of *The Stolen Prince* in late 1948, when I was starting the theatre for children with Julia and Marian. He was very tall, and very young.

Another assistant stage manager hired was Margaret (Nonnie) Griffin. Her father was nervous — she would have a long journey home at night. I was nervous about this, too. I never let her remain on Saturday nights to help with the striking of the set. Nonnie was very pretty, and very young, but she was completely at home in a costume piece; she could handle a costume and did not walk as if she were wearing tennis shorts. She was a splendid actress. I had met her at Hugh Webster's Oakville Theatre that summer. She had studied at the Conservatory in Toronto with Clara Baker and had been in several Hart House productions under the direction of Robert Gill.

By the end of September we were able to announce to the press that opening night would be October 7 and the play *Captain Carvallo*. Two days later Austin Cross headed his "Cross Town" column with "Amelia, Sam and Betty Are Coming back."

A long distance call received one day in the office had been a most blessed event. I answered it, to hear a slow, soft Scottish voice ask: "Is it true that you are looking for a designer?" "Indeed it is true," I replied, holding my breath, and giving Dora Clarke a look to indicate that this might be important. "Well," he went on shyly, "I'm a designer. I saw your note at the CBC. My name is Basil Armstrong." "When can you come?" was all I wanted to know. He arrived in time to design the opening play.

On September 25 John Atkinson arrived to take charge of business and promotion. For two weeks Dora Clarke and I had been ordering the printing of tickets, arranging program printing and advertising, corresponding with actors, hiring, writing for play rights, ordering scripts, promoting the theatre, arranging actors' accommodations. Throughout that season Dora authorized expenditures, and it was because of her carefulness, her sheer *meanness* about spending money, that we finished the 1952–53 season in the black. It was as if Dora, on being asked by Leif Pedersen for nails, put her hand into a paper bag and took out *six nails*, but wanted to know where each was being used before she handed them over!

While Dora and I had been going quietly mad in the office those first two weeks, we had had a visit from a Montreal actor. I had never worked with him, but I knew of his work in Montreal. After twenty minutes I asked him if he would mind returning in an hour, when I would be free to continue the interview. After he had left I looked at Dora.

"Well?"

She laughed.

I continued, "Since your impression is the same as mine, I'll take him for a walk when he comes back and set him straight."

He came back, and we walked along Sussex Street. I asked him, "Since you came to Ottawa for the purpose of asking me for a job, why did you behave in the office as if you had come to ask me for a date?"

"Bruce told me that was the way to get around you."

"Bruce must have been pulling your leg. It's not very flattering to me to suggest that I am so desperate for male attention that I have to pay a man a salary to receive it!"

He agreed.

"And furthermore, I don't care much what you and I feel about one another as a man and a woman, just so long as you do your work well. Now, I don't think you are a character actor, and since you'll probably play only young men, I won't be able to put you on stage every week. I can give you a job if you can do some work in the office when you aren't acting. Can you?"

He could. And that was how young William Shatner came to the CRT, as actor and promotion assistant.

The first publicity about the new season spotlighted Max Helpmann; he was the brother of Robert Helpmann, Sadler's Wells's great character dancer, and had the previous winter been with the Olivier company in New York when it presented *Antony and Cleopatra* and *Caesar and Cleopatra*. After his ten weeks at the CRT he would be going back to London to join the Old Vic. In a sense we were creating a new image through Max. To the general public any Canadian actor at the CRT was just a young person getting experience, hardly the equal of actors in countries where the theatre was established. It would help to change our image to have an actor and director come to us between engagements with the Oliviers and the Old Vic!

Max and Robert had started their careers in ballet, in Australia, but Max had turned to the stage after he was badly injured in an auto-racing crash. After Max received his discharge from the Royal Navy he went back into theatre and there met Barbara Chilcott when they had appeared in a West End comedy together, some four years back. They had been married in 1952, before the Straw Hat Players' recent season. Before the war, Max had directed the Dundee Repertory Theatre in Scotland, so he was experienced in weekly rep. In fact he had once worked in one of those English companies that present not one, but *two*, plays a week.

William Hutt, who was to play the name role in *Captain Carvallo*, had gained most of his experience at Hart House, under Gill. This was after he came back from the war, where he had seen service in Italy and been decorated. For the last three summers he had appeared at the Niagara Falls Summer Theatre, playing with the stars that it was that theatre's policy to employ — Sarah Churchill, Franchot Tone, Edward Everett Horton, and Fay Bainter.

The second day of rehearsals of *Captain Carvallo*, Bill Hutt was on-stage holding his script. I steeled myself to say, "Bill, at CRT we do not hold our books after the first day of rehearsal." He looked startled and a little embarrassed. I was embarrassed too. He explained politely that he had not understood this. I think the strength of the CRT came from this pressure to learn the lines at once and from our rehearsing from the second day with the real props or "mock-ups."

Meanwhile a ghastly discovery was made by our interim stage manager, Bill Glen, and Leif. They did not know how to work our makeshift lighting system! David Haber and Bob Barclay had departed with the secret locked in their heads. "Apparently it was all done with mirrors," Sam remarked in awed tones. So Bob returned and saved our first three shows by lighting them. Leif Pedersen soon mastered the light board.

People really took notice of our opening night that season, probably because we almost hadn't had one. The Ottawa Little Theatre Workshop and the management and board of directors of the Ottawa Little Theatre trumpeted our opening with telegrams, as did Trudie Allen and Betty Leighton, and also Dickie Butterfield and David Haber from the National Ballet. David said, "If you find my heart roaming around backstage please send it back. Wish I could be with you tonight. Best wishes for a wonderful season."

236

We seemed to be off to a good start. An ordered quiet seemed to have settled upon the Green Room, where for some reason there was a sudden dearth of furnishings; we had to send out requests for donations. We had voted to take only half an hour for lunch, and we all brought our own sandwiches. The dinners down the street at Bruce's boarding-house were no more. This acting company seemed older and wiser; the crew was younger and sillier! In previous years, actors and crew had been on a more equal level of experience and theatre know-how.

A strong stage manager is essential to the smooth running of a theatrical company. He or she makes the prompt book during rehearsals, runs the show, and can take over in the absence of the director and the crew. We had Bill Glen, who came from the Saturday Players, a fine group, though to my mind short on theatre discipline. But was it not part of our scheme to train young people, even at the expense of my sanity? In any case, I liked him.

The batman in *Captain Carvallo* had been played by a newcomer, Russ Waller. I had interviewed him in a restaurant in Toronto, and I had been impressed by his earnestness to give up his work in an office and plunge into the uncertainties of life in the theatre. He stayed with us quite a long time and worked hard, both as actor and eventually as stage manager. Later he went west, took his university degree, and was ready to teach theatre when the colleges started to give theatre arts courses.

Lynn Wilson I had brought in to do props. She came from St Marys, near Stratford. Lynn was about eighteen, fresh-faced, bright-eyed, animated, beautiful, with a fine figure, an even temper, and great joie de vivre. Just the person to cajole furniture and props from middle-aged shopkeepers. She was a breath of fresh air in that world below the LaSalle Academy stage.

Leif, Bill, Nonnie, and Lynn were my Katzenjammer Kids. I do not recall ever railing at Leif; but I was stern with him. The reason for the sternness was his relationship with Basil Armstrong, our new designer. Basil was Leif's boss, and Basil was not always available when wanted; Leif always was. Rows were not infrequent when these two were working together, and when Basil absented himself much of the work was done by Leif. I did not realize at that time Leif's talent as a designer. Basil was really a painter, especially murals.

Bill Glen and Leif got on well together. The first stage set these two put up was for *Captain Carvallo*, and this Laurel-and-Hardy pair managed to put it together upside down! In between work there were "ballet breaks" in which huge Bill was attempting to teach Leif the rudiments of dance. Though we could not "fly" sets at LaSalle, there being no fly gallery, naturally we had light beams hanging from the stage ceiling and teasers that hid these lights from the audience. The one step-ladder we owned was of the household size and was not high enough for use in reaching these light beams.

The Brothers owned an ordinary straight high ladder, and Bill and Leif contrived a method for using this ladder to manipulate the spotlights that hung from the beams: they would lean the high ladder flat against the back brick wall of the stage; Bill would hold it while Leif would climb it, his face to the brick wall. As Leif clung to the ladder they would tilt it backward till it rested with its lower end against the wall and its upper rungs leaned against a rope that they had attached between two iron poles that stood permanently, one on either side of the stage. The ladder now leaning at an angle, Leif would climb round the ladder so that he now faced the auditorium, and he would climb higher and higher and get at the lights, praying that the rope would hold the ladder in place!

Leif often prompted. He held the book, pretending that he could read English, and relied on his memory of the script.

Early in the season Leif got a nail right through his foot while he was taking down or putting up a set. Sam rushed off to the hospital with him. At the hospital it was taken for granted that Leif was Sam's son, and Sam had a good time playing the role of anguished father! Leif was told to stay off his feet for two weeks. He was back at the theatre next day, hobbling painfully and with a great grin on his face, enjoying carrying on in spite of everything.

On October 14 we opened *The Happiest Days of Your Life,* by John Dighton. Max directed it, and I played the role Margaret Rutherford played in the movie of the headmistress of a girls' school, which by the mistake of someone in the Ministry of Education is billeted for the duration of the war in a school for boys. Sam played the Alistair Sim role of the headmaster, Godfrey Pond. Joyce Spencer returned to us to play Miss Gossage, the hearty, hockey-playing games mistress — Joyce Grenfell's role — and she took the honours, I think, for best performance. She took a serious approach to her role, always essential in comedy, especially in farce. Lauretta Thistle wrote that we were playing this farce "with a polish that our calendar tells us must have been acquired in a week, but which bespeaks much longer rehearsal."

On the final night, in the last scene, when there is general mayhem on-stage, in the midst of all the shouting and scrambling, Sam suddenly cried out, "*Send for Charlotte Whitton!!!*" This reference to Ottawa's colourful mayor made the audience fall about. *I* was quite aghast!

Basil Armstrong began painting for us some magnificent backdrops. These appeared behind windows or doors to suggest the countryside, or the urban setting of a play. Many of them were painted on the back wall of the stage, only to be painted over the following week. Those that were on canvas I would have liked to keep, had I lived in a large house. They always gave enormous depth to the stage. Basil had done a great deal of mural painting for bars and hotels and private houses, especially in the Bahamas; for a Montreal department store he had created a 38-foot by 8-foot panorama of the history of fashion. He had created the Memphis palace scene for the film *Caesar and Cleopatra*, the stairway scene in *Stairway to Heaven*, and had worked on *Brief Encounter*, *Great Expectations*, and Olivier's *Henry V*. He was a veteran of the British army and had studied theatre design at the St Martin's School of Art in London and at the Chelsea Art School.

Basil looked like an artist. He was big, had tousled curly brown hair, and a somewhat crumpled appearance, in his corduroy jacket, paint-stained trousers, open shirt, and casually knotted tie. He was immensely shy. He was not always around when you needed him on a Monday night, when the set was being finished and the lighting arranged, and it would distress me to have his assistant, Leif, confide, "I know where he is. I can go and get him." I knew that Basil liked his wee drop, but I regretted that it should be pointed up to me by his assistant. Basil was a loner and a wanderer, and you had to go along with it.

Bill Hutt, Barbara Chilcott, and George McCowan had the leading roles in Aldous Huxley's *The Giaconda Smile*, which Max directed. In the recollections of the CRT that I received from Lynn Wilson in 1971, she recalls: "You phoned to see how the opening night of *Giaconda Smile* had gone off — it was about 11:30 p.m. — imagine your dismay when you were told we hadn't started the third act yet — seems Leif Pedersen had run out of stage braces, and had *nailed* the second act set to the floor!"

I remember well. I was in my bed when I phoned. No, they had not yet started the third act. I could not believe it was really happening. Next day the *Journal* was not hard on us. Richard Coates admired both the play and the performances. "It suffered, however, from technical mishaps of lighting and set changing with the former causing some bizarre and sudden changes of mood and the latter being responsible for an overly long interval following the second act." The *Citizen*'s heading ran, "Suggest Early Opening at CRT." We had dropped the Tuesday 7:30 openings, and Lauretta Thistle thought we ought to bring them back! "Since the 8:30 (or 8:45) opening prevails, since Huxley has been extremely verbose, and since the backstage staff was having difficulties with scene changes, the smiles of even the most loyal CRT supporters were rather fixed and stiff by closing time." (She ought to have seen *my* face, back on Cooper Street!) Mrs Thistle also found Huxley's play to have enough talk for two plays and enough suspense for half a play.

Lynn Wilson recalls a further disaster that evening: "During the climax when George McCowan (playing the doctor) was attempting to wring a confession from Barbara Chilcott — the ploy being the clock, set an hour ahead of the actual execution of an innocent man — he did this most forcefully, and all eyes were directed to that most important prop when he said, 'It is now twelve o'clock.' There was just a flicker of pain on his face when George realized that the clock hadn't been set! I'd neglected to set it properly."

The day after we opened my abridged, no-divorce edition of *Castle in the Air*, there was an article about the CRT in *Variety*. Paul Gardiner was its Ottawa representative. *Variety* reported three plays "nixed": *Private Lives*, F. Hugh Herbert's *For Love or Money*, and *Portrait in Black*, because of a last-act suicide. There was more, about our subscription scheme, and about the Helpmanns. *Variety* never seemed to tire of our censor situation. Through its pages we became known to the New York actors, who mailed in their pictures and their résumés, asking for work.

Sam directed *Castle in the Air*, which is about an impoverished Scottish lord ready to rent his castle for a pittance to anyone who will keep it in repair. It was one of many English comedies about post-war England. Reported Lauretta Thistle: "The backstage staff as well as the acting company, seemed to have all their problems well in hand this week". (When the curtains closed on the first act the set started to fall down! Our comedy team, Glen and Pedersen, rushed out and pushed the set back into place, the audience applauding them throughout their endeavour). "William Shatner, a newcomer, is making an excellent impression as an individualistic Scots man-of-all-work — incidentally, the only actor who adopts an accent and sticks to it. Lynne Gorman, in her first big role this year, looks extremely handsome, and is properly aggressive as the wealthy American. Barbara Chilcott's portrayal of cool efficiency as the secretary makes for good contrast. ... William Hutt's flair for both comedy and charm is well exploited in this role ... Basil Armstrong ... once again has provided a glimpse of countryside that suggests an excellent artist as well as a practical set designer."

The program announced the following week's play as *The Cocktail Party*, by T.S. Eliot: four members of our company had been in Peter Potter's production at the Straw Hat Players last summer, and we would be using Peter's notes. This play was reported to be the third best attended in our history, superseded only by *Hamlet* and *Harvey*. Two hundred people were turned away on the Saturday night.

It was our first production to carry on its program the proud announcement, "Under the Distinguished Patronage of the Right Honourable Vincent Massey, C.H., Governor General of Canada." It was also the first program to print under the title of the play: "Plays produced under the management of Amelia Hall and Sam Payne."

John Atkinson left the business office to take on the role of Sir Henry Harcourt-Reilly — "one-eyed Reilly." That one-eyedness intrigued me as did the fact that the Julia I was playing, the silly old woman who is not silly really, wears glasses in which *one* side has a lens. "Eliot must mean they have the Cyclopean Eye in the middle of the forehead, where the pineal gland is located!" Thus actors and audience alike look for meanings in such a play. William Goldman, an American novelist and screenwriter, in his entertaining book *The Season*, calls *The Cocktail Party* the first of "the snob hits" and claims that the two requisites of such plays is that they be British, and unintelligible!

I have seldom been as nervous as I was on this opening night. As Julia, one of the three Guardians of the other characters, I had the opening speech, a long and complicated piece of verse. I was shaking so much that I was surprised to get to the end without spilling my cocktail down my silk dress. Just before we started to rehearse I had been greatly inconvenienced one day by a smarting pain in both eyes. An eye specialist explained to me that the pain was caused by fatigue. The remedy was to rest, wear dark glasses, and under no circumstances to read! That was a fine how-do-you-do! I certainly could not lie down and rest, and I had to learn all those involved speeches. "You'll just have to read them to me till I know them," I said to my mother. "Read them to me over and over."

Every day, whenever I could, I lay on the couch and mother sat on a chair facing me and reading the lines. She read with great expression! "No, no, that's not the way to read that line," I would say, greatly irritated. She would try again. My mother, like most good actors, was not a superb reader. As an actress on the silent screen, I believe she could have given Lillian Gish competition, for she had a most volatile face, one that reflects readily the complexities of a character endowed with intelligence, humour, perception, and feeling. Now she was giving a performance as Julia. "Look, mother, just read the words to me, *flat,* and as fast as you can. I'll decide later on how I'm going to say them!" This was hard on my mother, to whom it came naturally to bring drama into life.

We were said to have added cubits to the stature of the CRT by this excellent production of a difficult play. I enjoyed Austin Cross's approach to this "snob" hit. Gratifying, he called it. "As far as I can see, this is not a profound play, it is just a lot of entertaining talk. When you go to a strip tease, you do not look for any message, you just want to be entertained. I have come to the conclusion that every so often a talkative play — a real downright gabby play — is good for you. That the play gets nowhere and has no meaning is of no significance whatever. If I had to pick a star it would be Max Helpmann who was a real smoothie, as suave as could be. And the man can wear clothes."

Irene Worth created the role of Celia in *The Cocktail Party,* and when I was staying with her at Stratford during her summer there in 1959 we discussed the play. She was surprised that I had never played Celia. Celia had won my heart because of one single speech, my favourite in that play. In this speech she says to Harcourt-Reilly, to whom she has gone for help,

> But even if I find my way out of the forest
> I shall be left with the inconsolable memory
> Of the treasure I went into the forest to find
> And never found, and which was not there,
> And perhaps is not anywhere? But if not anywhere,
> Why do I feel guilty at not having found it?

That to me was the heart of the matter: the expectation of a revelation that does not take place.

We now plunged into our second Molière, *The Miser,* which we were presenting with Bill Hutt. We decided to have the costumes made on the premises instead of renting them at considerable expense from Malabar's. Our costume mistress, Mrs Laurette Neal, took on this chore single-handed. Laurette was a light-hearted, energetic, slightly built lady who had become a friend of my mother when they laboured for love together in the dungeon depths of the Little Theatre on King Edward Street; those Ottawa Drama League costume rooms had a smell of damp and decay that only a little theatre devotée could love.

Whatever Laurette attacked she was *quick,* and she was the fastest talker I ever have known, even faster than our beloved Jane

Mallett in a state of high excitement! Laurette never changed her hair-style, which was tight back with a bun; she used little make-up, was neat as a pin. I think we paid her twenty dollars a week. In former years, when costumes had to be hired, the hiring had been David's department; he might make a trip to Montreal to choose. It was Laurette's job to make rented costumes fit, or to mend the holes in them, for we were often outraged by the condition in which costumes arrived. Every week she was needed to organize even a modern production, often making do with whatever was in our costume room (smelly and windowless, just like at the ODL) where hung all the clothing, ancient and modern, that had been donated to us.

For *The Miser* Laurette designed and constructed eleven costumes, at a cost of four dollars! This, she explained to Richard Coates who interviewed her, was spent on thread, stockings for the men, odd lengths of ribbon, and pins to hold buckles in place. A rental bill for the costumes would have been at least $300. George McCowan's fine costume as a dandy was made out of an old velvet drape and bits of lace and ribbon; delicate gowns for ladies were produced from old lace curtains. Because this show had depleted the costume boxes of old drapes and lengths of ribbon and lace, Laurette put forth a request for further donations from the public.

Carl Weiselberger remarked in his review that the king of France had advised Molière, "Smile. Use if you must the blackest stuffs of life. But smile. Write comedy." And, Carl said, the large opening night audience had smiled. He found that Hutt had not played Harpagon in the shadow of tragedy: "Mr. Hutt was particularly successful in portraying this foolish side of Harpagon. He played the miser as a haggard, yellow-faced, old decrepit fool, who tripped across the stage with the comical, dangling movement of a commedia dell'arte marionette. If, for a moment, he fell out of his character and his assumed, high-pitched voice, he managed skillfully to snatch them back. At the discovery of the theft of his precious treasure-box, he rose to a strong, expressive climax."

Nothing daunted, we next plunged into an even greater challenge, *The Three Sisters*. Nine months they took in some countries to rehearse Chekhov. But how could we ever do Chekhov if we waited till we had weeks and weeks in which to rehearse? I was ready to take a gamble, so was Sam, and so was Max, who said he would direct it. I was ecstatic about our doing *The Three Sisters*, and I do not regret the decision.

Max chose me as Olga, Betty Leighton as Masha, and Nonnie Griffin as Irena. (I might have played Irena a few years before, if

243

anyone had ever asked me to; when she was in her late teens she discovered, as I had, that she had to do things she didn't want to do, such as teach.) Olga was the sister I least wanted to play, simply because she was so held-in, and got headaches. Yet hers is a wonderful part, and her opening and closing speeches are magnificent.

Olga closes the play: "The band is playing so gaily, so bravely, I feel I really want to live! Dear God! The years will pass, and we will all be gone for good and quite forgotten; they will forget our faces, our voices, and even how many there were of us. But our sufferings will turn into joy for those who come after; happiness and peace will reign on earth, and people will remember us with kindness and bless us who are living now. Come, my sisters, let us live! The music is so gay, so joyful, it seems that in a little while we shall know *why* we live, *why* we suffer. If we only knew, if we only knew!"

I find this speech one of the most heart-rending in dramatic literature.

The purpose of all the hustle and bustle, the physical sweat, the sleepless nights, of an operation like the CRT, is the sharing with the audience of these great questions, these universal hopes and disappointments — this human condition.

The Three Sisters was in four acts, with ten-minute intervals between, and with three sets to be constructed. Basil compromised by using a few flats and screens, wisely compensating for lack of grandeur with facility of scene change. We made do with costumes from our costume cupboard.

Lynn had an overwhelming amount of furniture and prop hunting to do. Backstage was a shambles, as it was later on at the Crest in Toronto when this play was presented in 1955. Probably Lynn never watched a rehearsal and hardly read the play.

We had sent invitations to the Russian embassy for opening night, and these were accepted. I think that the return invitation for us to be entertained at the embassy must have been for Sunday, December 14, because some of our members had already left, or were taking a brief holiday. I recall most vividly walking into the main entrance of the embassy on Charlotte Street and seeing before me the picture of Stalin. This was my first experience in coming face to face with something I had seen only at the movies and read about in the papers. Suddenly Stalin really existed in my world! Only the warm hospitality in the reception rooms restored me to a feeling of well-being.

We were taken to a filming room and shown some fine films, some of them on ballet. At the buffet afterward we drank, I think, Caucasian wine, and the conversation was animated. I recall one of the wives wondered when next we would present an Oscar Wilde, and I gathered that he was very popular among the Russians, at any rate among those present. I felt that, polite as they decidedly were, they had not found our *Three Sisters* to be the definitive production! Yet they only made one overt criticism: "You know, the uniforms that the soldiers were wearing were all quite wrong."

"I realize that. They were old uniforms borrowed from the Ottawa Police Department." The Russians were speechless; so I continued: "Don't you agree that it is better to present Chekhov with the soldiers wearing incorrect uniforms than not to present Chekhov at all?"

I think they must still have been puzzled, because the next question was, "Who gets the profits from your plays?"

"There are no profits. Last year we ended in debt. Just now we are about breaking even. We are a non-profit organization, and if we make profits they will be ploughed back into the company. In the mean time the generosity of two patrons has kept us going. We all receive very small salaries, and of course the patrons receive nothing but our thanks."

After that I was often asked to the embassy, and when I was introduced to the next ambassador at a reception it was obvious that he knew all about me, and he said that anything he and his staff could do any time to help our theatre would delight them.

The USSR cultural attaché greeted me again in Toronto in 1955 when I played Olga, at the Crest this time. He came with the ambassador, a few days before the Russians marched into Hungary. The roses they had sent me were still in my living-room when that dire news arrived. In 1957 this same attaché visited my apartment in Toronto, having phoned first, and he came by taxi, two hours late, and had apparently evaded the RCMP. He brought a gift from his own library, a lovely book on productions of Chekhov in all the main Russian theatres from their first productions, when Chekhov's ink was scarce dry. One can see the same actors appearing again and again, and getting older. A lovely present. In later years Christmas cards came from Moscow, with un-Christmas-like pictures, such as a view of Red Square.

After *The Three Sisters*, we — and our audience — were ready for some lighter fare. It was my custom to send to Father MacDonald about half a dozen plays at one time. When I had included in one batch the French comedy *Nina*, by André Roussin, I had been in a facetious mood. On the day when I called at his offices, which I think were on Rideau Street, to hear his views on this collection, I was expecting the worst. Even the tone of his voice when he said, "Sit down, Miss Hall," suggested that we were in for a long session, and I thought, "Here it comes!" He drew from the group of plays the typed copy of *Nina* which had come from the agents. "Now this play, *Nina*. ..." He paused. I already regretted my impudence in wasting a busy man's time, giving him a play to read that he could not conceivably approve! But Father MacDonald started to chuckle! He leafed through the script. "It is a very funny play," he said. "It will, of course, have to be very well acted!" And that was that.

Nina is a play that concerns a wealthy young idler, Gerard Dupuis, involved with so many married women that at the opening of the first act he is desperate to escape from them all, especially from Nina. He decides that suicide is the only escape. At this point Nina's husband, a methodical civil servant, arrives, intent on shooting his wife's lover. The husband delays when he finds Gerard so ready and willing for death, and the two are becoming fast friends when Nina arrives. The next twenty-four hours are spent in Gerard's apartment, the husband in bed with a fever, and Nina consistently outwitting the men.

"Naughty Play Featured by Repertory Theatre" was the splendid heading for the *Citizen* review. "Mr. Helpmann's somewhat sketchy improvised portrayal is very amusing and full of fine, intelligent shades and nuances. His listening is often as telling as his talking. (And last night, if he did not talk, it sometimes happened because of passive resistance on the part of his lines.)"

Lynn had done it again! Max had devised little cards with his lines written on them and had deployed these about the stage in strategic positions on opening night. Lynn had come along after his exit from the set, and in checking her props she had removed many of these, as she thought, quite unnecessary little cards!

So ended the first ten weeks of the 1952–53 season. Our subscription list had now reached the grand total of 1,087. The Prompt Sheet, printed this season on the back of the program, instead of as a separate sheet, told the public that this season so far attendance had made it possible for us to pay our way, largely because of rigorous economy on our part. Just before Christmas *Variety* reported: "Canadian Repertory in Black on 10-Week Fall Season; Volunteer Selling Aids."

It had been a hard slog, from an uncertain start in September. But we had had fun, and we all had our own special memories of those weeks. Mine were mostly concerned with the responsibilities of management. Others were more light-hearted. Years later, Lynn

Wilson shared some of her memories of that time with me:

I remember Bill Hutt rounding up us supers (ASMS), those making $35 and under and when the huddle was complete (we still didn't know why he'd summoned us), he looked at us sternly and said: 'If you can't dress well, dress fantastically.' We thought he was putting us on, but he wasn't. He explained that the public expects actors to look like actors. 'Your gloves don't have to match,' and 'Don't tuck your scarf inside — let it flow.' All this so we could make a grand entrance at the Connaught Restaurant! I always felt, and still feel, that we were the first of the hippies ...

I always got a cosy feeling on Saturday morning when the Brothers presented their weekly movies for the school children — somehow, walking through the theatre to the Green Room, in the dark, must have reminded me of the not-so-long-ago Saturdays when I too went to the movies! We saw Ottawa late at night — so still — as if they'd left the lights on just for us. Sometimes the only place open was Boles lunch, behind the station, and there we'd be, dressed so fantastically that you couldn't tell which of us were actors and which were rubby-dubs.

Usually we ate supper at one of the Honey Dews. I used to eavesdrop on civilians, and I'd hear them making plans for the evening. I wondered what it would be like to have a whole evening free.

I don't think Mrs. Glen (Bill's mother) ever really accepted our weird hours. We'd be in the middle of rehearsal, Bill up to his ears in lighting plots and dimmers, and the 'phone would ring: it was his mother, telling him his chicken dumplings would be ruined if he didn't hurry home ...

I could go on and on. The essence of those years, I think, is the closeness — the only thing comparable might be group therapy — and yet there were loner moments too, when, after so much closeness, we each had to get away for a while — alone.

CHAPTER 17

FIRE AND AIR

When we closed *Nina* on December 13, 1952, we regretfully said goodbye to Max and Barbara, wishing them well in England. The remainder of the company dispersed for a five-day holiday, to return for rehearsals at 10 a.m. on Friday, December 19. We would have a full seven days and nights in which to rehearse for our next production, *The Lady's Not for Burning*, which would open December 26 and play till January 3. If the public wished it, we would carry it over for another week.

Those five days that the company was on holiday were among the busiest I had ever experienced. During that time I set up all the production end for *The Lady's Not for Burning*. I had been down to Montreal and had chosen the costumes from Malabar's. I had studied the pictures of the set from the London production, and from these and from my memory of the play as I had seen it there in 1949 I drew for Basil the ground plan of the set, with all its levels, steps, windows, doors, and winding staircase. Then I set forth to find the levels in order to save us the dreadful cost of lumber with which to build them. I found what I wanted at the Technical High School. Thomas Mendip would thus be able to enter at the centre window onto a platform running the length of the set, and the mayor, Hebble Tyson, could have his high desk on this level, and there would be steps the entire length of this platform for the servant Richard to scrub, leading down to the main stage level.

I sought out recordings of appropriate early music, and sound effects, and worked out the elaborate lighting effects that I wanted.

In the mean time, Bill Glen, who had to translate these lighting plans into actualities, had gone off I knew not where. I wanted him back before rehearsals started.

Arriving home for my dinner one night during that week I found among my Christmas mail a card from David Haber. "Millie, darling: Hear you're overworking but doing a marvellous job ... Naturally. Hope to see you for *The Lady* at least. Best wishes, dearest, and all my love. You're wonderful. David." At that point I threw myself on the couch, buried my head in a cushion, and bawled my eyes out! "It isn't fair," I sobbed, "it isn't fair that when Gielgud produces *The Lady* he has weeks and weeks of time, and hands to help, and loads of money. Why am I expected to do it by myself?" This was a very low point caused by fatigue, for I was extremely excited to be directing again and to have my fingers in every pie connected with this play. Before the rehearsals began every detail of production would be settled — if only Bill Glen would return in time for us to discuss the lighting!

William Shatner was going to return to play the role that had made Richard Burton famous — the role of the orphan servant, Richard. A new actor was coming from New York, hired sight unseen except for his photograph, and he was to play Nicholas, the light-hearted son of Dame Margaret, the role I was playing myself. George McCowan was playing the dark, devious son Humphrey, and Nonnie Griffin would be young Alison Eliot. Ron Bailey was to be the little violin-playing chaplain; Bill Hutt the justice, Edward Tappercoom; Sam Payne the drunken tinker, Mathew Skips; and Lew Davidson the mayor, Hebble Tyson. The leading role of Thomas Mendip was to be played by John Atkinson, who had come as business manager on my promise that he play this role, and the Lady was to be an English actress I had seen at Peterborough, Patricia Moore. She had attended a drama school in Bradford for two years run by that fine actress and co-worker with Tyrone Guthrie at the Old Vic, Esmé Church.

The first rehearsal of any play is important, and the first rehearsal of a play you are excited about is especially important. On December 19 we had all met before ten o'clock, and had removed our outer garments and had heard from those who had been away their news from abroad, and all was good cheer. The company had settled in the front seats of the theatre, and we were ready to start on the dot. I had just got rolling in my opening remarks when the door to the auditorium opened again and a smiling newcomer walked down the aisle. This was our new actor from New York. The words leapt from my mouth without intent to wound but as an expression of deep annoyance: "Here we do not arrive at ten o'clock. We *start work* at ten o'clock." He looked dismayed, and sat down. I carried on, nettled.

When you are looking forward to an act of creation for which you have planned carefully, there is no need to apologize if you are angered by the tardiness of the ill-organized. There is a chapter in Stanislavsky in which the director dismisses the whole company because one actor arrives late. "You have destroyed the atmosphere in which it is possible to create. We will start tomorrow."

The production was rehearsed mostly in a classroom while the levels were being arranged on the stage and the set built around them. We were all pleased with our man from New York, who could not have been more charming as Nicholas. Indeed, everyone seemed to me to be quite perfect!

I think it must have been the Monday after rehearsals started that Bill Glen put his nose inside LaSalle Academy again.

"Where have *you* been?" I roared.

"I went off to Montreal. I needed a holiday." Or some such rotten excuse.

"I wanted to discuss the lighting with you before I had my hands full of rehearsals!"

"Good grief," cheeked back this impossible youngster, "I've read the play. It won't be any problem to light *that*!"

"Indeed. And who is directing this production, you or I?"

"You are."

"Well, for your information, my production of this play has more than eighty light cues!"

The lad blanched. During the next week Bill Glen became, from the stage-lighting stand-point, a man.

I do not recall at what point in this voyage Basil Armstrong did his disappearing act, but Leif says I was in tears, imploring him to reveal the whereabouts of Basil, which Leif had been sworn not to disclose. "You *must* tell me! I must find him," I sobbed, like a deserted spouse. You could always find Leif. He lived at the theatre from Fridays till Tuesdays any week of the season. Basil was devoted to a few other interests, and I had no idea where he lived. I never asked him a question about himself, and I could never have brought myself to speak reprovingly to him. I kept my "Where have *you* been?" attacks for Bill Glen, who was as yet untouched by the buffetings of life, and could stand being smacked about a bit. With the Basils of this world women are tender.

When we got onto the completed stage and rehearsed for the first time with the lights as Bill had set them, I found that I had to reblock most of the play, because though Bill had done such a good job with our poor lighting equipment, it was not possible to light just any area one wanted, and I had to fit people and groups into what lighted areas we could command. No problem there. We had light changes to reflect not only the time of day but also the condition of the weather outside as reflected in the lines of the play. We showed by lighting the clouds, the rain, and the sunshine afterward. We had candle-light moving across the stage in the evening scenes. The Malabar costumes against this lighting looked very beautiful. I could have gone into raptures over the production had I been deaf! It was a constant visual delight.

The glory of the set was the wondrous backdrop that Basil had done for the countryside, as seen from the large central Gothic window.

Because of the levels there was no great expanse of stage from the apron to the beginning of the steps leading up to the platform that ran the length of the room. Where could we place the fire which is supposed to sit in the middle of this fourteenth-century room? I decided to place it on the narrow apron in front of the red velvet stage curtain. As members of the audience entered the theatre they would see this firelight racing up the velvet curtain, and it would be a symbol of the play. This worked very well and left us the space we needed on the stage floor.

At the end of the eight evening performances and the three matinées we had played to 3,900 people and had taken in at the box-office $3,540 — making this the most successful production we had ever done. We decided to keep it on for another week

That second week ended on January 10, and that night, after the third-act curtain, once again a few of us stood on the stage and pondered whether or not we would say to the crew, "Tear it down," or whether we would risk yet another week. John Atkinson and I decided on a third week, keeping our fingers crossed that by taking this sporting chance we would not lose the profits we had made.

We need not have worried. The third week went well. Governor General Massey attended one night and came backstage afterward. Pictures were taken of him chatting with our two leading actors and with Sam and me. This gave us a big boost in the public eye.

Mayor Charlotte Whitton had also brought a party to see *The Lady* and had come backstage to review our troops. I recall her telling Nonnie Griffin and Bill Shatner how well she had thought they had played their love scenes, and then she had added, "I speak from *hearsay*, unsullied by experience!"

The crowning delight, our cup running over with beaded bubbles winking at the brim, had come with the invitation to attend at Rideau Hall on Friday, January 16, the day before our final glorious performance! Leif Pedersen recalls that when the invitation came only a few of the company were originally invited and that I said, "We are *all* going, or nobody goes!" Certainly I would not have gone unless we all had gone. I do not hold with an élite in a theatre company. There were eleven of us in *The Lady's Not for Burning*, and there were seven people working backstage or in the office. You can't have a group of eighteen people and weed out some of them as goats! A team is a team. As Leif recalls those days, "We were a football team going in to win!"

"Basil was bombed in the men's room at Government House!" recalls Leif. Fond and all as I was of Basil, he was bombed all right. I saw him in the entrance hall as I left, and he was slumped in a big chair, a happy smile on his sweet face, his body limp like a rag doll's, and arrangements were being made to convey him. Yes, a good time was had by all.

I remember getting back to the theatre from Government House, just in time to get our "slap" on to do the Friday-night performance, wondering if the liquor would damage our work, severely disapproving any contact with the bottle before a performance, and being so blissful I didn't give a hoot; standing in the Green Room, Bill Shatner and I giggled as I had not giggled since I was eight. The performance went off beautifully. Or so it seemed to *us*. We were all fire and air. Our other elements we gave to baser life!

I remember the funereal, unnatural quiet backstage during the matinée performance on New Year's day, when actors who had been up most of the night tried their best to hold themselves together and not let the audience down. I could not have dared address a word offstage that afternoon to George McCowan; no, not for a thousand pounds!

One night Bill Shatner was in a plight after the performance. He had asked two girls out on the same night! There were two exits from the Green Room, each leading into the auditorium, one at each side of the stage. At both exits waited a girl! Bill was a tiny bit plump then, but Lynn Wilson and others managed to push him to freedom out of the Green Room lavatory window.

I think that the final night of *The Lady's Not for Burning* David Haber must have been present. If he was not there, then I was thinking about him as I took as a souvenir a little twig from the tree that had stood outside the Gothic window in front of that Brueghellike backdrop. David and I had always hated to see the pulling down of the set of a play that we had loved. I still cherish that tiny twig.

I was entering, that winter of 1953, a period of terrible fatigue and disappointments. My spirits were high up to mid-February, when we were presenting *The Indifferent Shepherd*. From then on a black cloud of problems seemed to hang permanently over my head. For the season's last four plays (to be presented for two weeks each instead of one), we had chosen superior work: *Nightmare Abbey*, *Venus Observed*, *His Excellency*, and *Victoria Regina*. Charles Southgate had an obsession that season that as a salute to the coronation in June we close with a production of Housman's *Victoria Regina*. Sam was adamant that it was too big a show for us. I was willing to take charge of the production details and felt I could call upon enough outsiders to swell the cast. I could not direct it, because I was to be Victoria.

If Sam was to play a large role in *His Excellency* (and we certainly needed him to do so), he could not direct the play as well. Because I would have my hands full of the production details for *Victoria Regina* and the preparation of myself to play the Queen, I could not direct *His Excellency*. Who was to direct it?

I was aware also that while our present very small company of permanent actors was good, it was not large enough or brilliant enough for what we were attempting. It was not up to the strength we had maintained in the past. At the end of 1951 we had let Johan Fillinger go because we did not need three directors, and fourteen months later we were desperate for a third director. If we were going to present *His Excellency* and *Victoria Regina* we would *have* to have a third director. Where was Johan? Doing very well for himself in Bermuda, according to the last letter I had received, and according to a long epistle from Ronnie Bailey.

In the mean time, *Nightmare Abbey* was living up to its name. Although this play was to run for two weeks, it was to receive only one week of rehearsal. This was asking for trouble, and I cannot think why we were so foolish. Perhaps I thought that all the preparation that I had made for the production would sufficiently oil the wheels.

The day after *Nightmare Abbey* opened I brought the cast back for further rehearsal, to cut some scenes, and to try to inject life into the piece. Never before had we needed to bring the actors back after the opening night; fortunately, the next play, *Venus Observed*, would not open till three weeks hence.

I remember that Basil was not to be found at the time I was doing the lighting for *Nightmare Abbey*, on the Monday night. I remember at the dress rehearsal knowing that I could improve and shorten the production by cutting out the tedious scene with the butler, Reggie Malcolm; but it was Reggie's only scene and I couldn't face the surgery, not unless I gave Reggie an anaesthetic. (That summer I saw that Guthrie could be wisely ruthless when it came to making cuts just before the opening.) After we opened I went to the theatre every night to plead with Irving Lerner to go on that stage and "lift the scene," instead of doing the strange, introverted performance he thought was "The Method" and which changed from day to day. I might as well have saved my breath.

Weiselberger and Coates appreciated the play. Weiselberger was kind, although he had to admit that "the frolic was a little slow and heavy last night"; Dick Coates said that "most of the considerable wit and humour of *Nightmare Abbey* is lost. Chiefly, I think, because director Amelia Hall has treated it with too much deference and restraint. There are whole scenes which do nothing for the play and in fact serve only to make it tedious and discursive." True, oh, too true!

Suddenly I wasn't laughing any more. The rest of my time that season I was tired and unhappy, except for the evenings on-stage when I was playing Victoria. The seven weeks before *Victoria Regina* opened I was hanging to the edge of the cliff.

I was still casting around for another director to take over for *His Excellency* and *Victoria Regina*. I had been in touch with Elspeth Potter, the wife of Peter Potter, the splendid director I had worked with the previous summer at the Straw Hat Players. Elspeth did not have much experience, but Peter was always urging her to produce, and after sitting for seven years at his elbow, she felt she was ready to give it a try. She was free and in Toronto; I decided to take a chance and ask her. Elspeth was interested in the idea, but eventually the whole thing fell through. I'm afraid, in the precarious state of our finances at the CRT, we couldn't find an extra fifty dollars a week for her salary.

It must have been sometime during those last weeks that I was introduced to Raphael Kelly. He was originally from South Africa, I fancy, and had had some directing experience in England. He was a friend of Betty Craik, the artist who had over the years arranged our exhibits of local artists in the LaSalle Academy lobby. In desperation I appealed to Raphael to help us out, and he produced the last two plays of the 1952–53 season.

Victoria Regina taxed our strength in every way. The Housman play consisted of eleven different scenes, spanning Victoria's life from her accession to the throne in 1837 to the Diamond Jubilee in

1897, and it demanded a cast of thirty. The costumes for such an elaborate production were clearly beyond our limited resources and had to be hired from Malabar's.

Betty Craik had the inspired idea of commissioning portraits of some of the queens of England and Scotland from eight local artists. She herself contributed an excellent drawing of myself as the young Victoria, and our own Penny Geldart painted a dramatic Mary, Queen of Scots.

The play itself was rather less than dramatic. Raphael Kelly, unused to our ways, seemed unable to get the play moving; his perfectionist approach did not achieve the taut pace that such a fragmented play needed. On the first night it ran for over four hours; the audience endured lengthy scene changes and did not leave the theatre till gone midnight. Something had to be done. The following day, summoning up some belated ruthlessness, we made cuts. One whole scene was dropped, and hefty excisions were made in others; nearly an hour was trimmed. In spite of some adverse reviews, the public came in large numbers, and we were able to hold the play over for an extra week, closing the season on May 23.

Playing Victoria for three weeks drained what little energy I had, and by the end of the season I was exhausted. Yet even at my lowest ebb, there was one bright hope on the horizon — the promise of an exciting new enterprise that summer.

I do not recall when I first heard rumours of a Shakespearean Festival to be started by a man named Tom Patterson in a little western Ontario town called, appropriately enough, Stratford. When I read the brief newspaper report, I thought, "Probably some nut with money" and visualized a little man with a white beard.

I put it out of mind until another newspaper story indicated that Mr Patterson and his Stratford backers had succeeded in interesting the great Tyrone Guthrie in the project. Furthermore, Dr Guthrie was coming to Canada to meet with these wild-eyed idealists.

On July 16 of the previous year, while we were into the second week of *The Importance of Being Earnest* at the Straw Hat Players, the Toronto *Telegram* reported a press gathering to hear Guthrie on the contemplated Stratford venture. The newspaper described Guthrie as a "tall, ramrod of a man, fifty-two," and added, "he sounds like a realist as well as an artist."

It must have been some time in November 1952 that the phone rang down in the CRT's Green Room and a youngish voice announced that he was Tom Patterson and could he and Dr Guthrie come to see us? I said we would be most gratified, and I would acquaint the actors with the facts and make a list of those who wanted to be interviewed. Tom Patterson sounded quite jolly. Where was my rich old gentleman with the long white beard?

They came while we were presenting *The Three Sisters*. I heard that they saw some of the production. Too bad that the physical presentation for *The Three Sisters* fell so far short of the standard for which we had become justifiably famous.

I met Tyrone Guthrie in the schoolroom that we had arranged for his use. He came toward me grinning and saying, "You don't look at all as you did when I saw you in Muskoka." That had been when I was playing Lady Bracknell, and we had not known he was there. He, Tom Patterson, and I chatted, and I saw the model of the stage that Tanya Moiseiwitsch had designed for Stratford. The meeting was most happy, informal, and invigorating. The two plays they had decided to present were *Richard III* and *All's Well That Ends Well*. They were planning to recruit Canadian actors as far as possible for the supporting roles and hoped to secure the services of Alec Guinness and Irene Worth as the two leading actors.

Not all of our actors went to see Guthrie. Bill Hutt did, and George McCowan, and I don't recall who else. George, I believe, was later made an offer but did not accept. Bill and I were the only two who were interviewed on the CRT premises who went that first year. But of our old CRT actors, Eric House was in the company that first Stratford season.

A letter was sent to me on December 22, 1952, from Tom Patterson, signed by Mary Jolliffe:

Dear Miss Hall:

Thank you for coming to see Dr. Guthrie. He asked me to say what a pleasure it was to meet you.

You are one of a very small group of actors whose cooperation at Stratford we should particularly value; and whom we regard as potential leading players in our Festival Company.

At the same time, until our program is finally fixed, and until Mr. Cecil Clarke (Dr. Guthrie's Assistant Director) arrives, we cannot finally decide the casting.

Knowing, however, that your professional services are in considerable demand, we do not want to lose you because we cannot make an immediate offer.

> Would it be too much to ask you not to accept
> engagements for the ten-week period beginning June
> 7 without first letting us know?

Years later Dora Mavor Moore told me that Guthrie came back from Ottawa to tell her: "I have found just the actress to play opposite Alec!"

Cecil Clarke put in an appearance in Ottawa in March 1953. Lynn Wilson, our property mistress, recalled the event: "One cold grey morning in 1953 I'd come to the theatre, just by chance, extra early, to find a sorry little man (blue with cold) tugging at every locked door of LaSalle Academy. I felt a bit like a St. Bernard, so grateful he was to be rescued. I always believed that's why I was asked to go to Stratford; that cold little man was Cecil Clarke." Cecil Clarke had arrived in Canada to organize the physical side of the productions and to hire the artists. He came to my house and offered me the role of Lady Anne in *Richard III*. Before he left, standing in the hallway, he asked if I would be willing to stand by to play Helena in *All's Well*, if Irene Worth decided not to come. I agreed, and Mr. Clarke asked me to keep the offer confidential. I did not tell even my mother.

When he got back to Toronto, Cecil Clarke sent me a letter, written on paper with a real letterhead, "Stratford Shakespearean Festival of Canada Foundation."

> I would like to confirm with you that we wish you to
> play the part of Lady Anne in *Richard III*. *All's Well
> That Ends Well* has provided us with a problem, now
> that Irene Worth is definitely coming out to play
> Helena. Would you be prepared to play the Widow
> in this play? It is not a bad little part and I think that
> you will find that you will be able to do quite a bit
> with it ... Rehearsals will start the first of June at
> Stratford, and the season opens July 13 with *Richard
> III*. As soon as I know whether you agree to play the
> parts suggested, I will get Mr. Tom Patterson to get in
> touch with you with regard to terms.

Of course, I replied that I would be delighted to play any role they suggested. In his next letter, Cecil Clarke wrote: "I am delighted to have your letter and to know that you will be with us. I will arrange costume fittings in Toronto on your way through to Stratford. You have a beautiful costume as Lady Anne."

And thus it was that, after *Victoria Regina* closed on May 23, within a week I was plunged into rehearsals for one of the most exciting and momentous events in the Canadian theatre. The rest, as they say, is history.

But let us remember that history correctly. Some thirteen years after that first Stratford season I was flying back from the west and happened to leaf through the Air Canada magazine *En Route*. In it was an article on the National Ballet of Canada, and there I read that when Celia Franca came to Canada to try to form a national ballet company, the Stratford Festival had not yet been born, there were "no opera or professional theatre companies, ... and no Canada Council to supply government financial support." All of that is true, except the four words "no professional theatre companies."

In a Toronto newspaper I read recently, "There was no television, no Canadian Opera Company, no permanent drama companies across the country. There was, indeed, virtually no professional theatre except in summer stock terms." That is just not true! The Canadian Repertory Theatre had been in existence for two years by the time the National Ballet was founded in 1951, and the Stage Society for one year before that. The CRT was playing a thirty-five-week season each year and paying a living wage to everybody concerned. This does not make the fantastic achievements of these other artistic groups any less admirable. But let us at least get the record straight.

INDEX

Numbers shown in **boldface** indicate illustrations. Theatres are listed together under theatres.

262